Eternal Egypt

Eternal Egypt

Ancient Rituals for the Modern World

RICHARD J. REIDY

iUniverse, Inc.
New York   Bloomington

Inquiries and suggestions should be addressed to the author at 239 1/2 Collingwood Street, San Francisco, CA 94114-2419.

iUniverse books may be ordered through booksellers or by contacting:

iUniverse
1663 Liberty Drive
Bloomington, IN 47403
www.iuniverse.com
1-800-Authors (1-800-288-4677)

Because of the dynamic nature of the Internet, any Web addresses or links contained in this book may have changed since publication and may no longer be valid. The views expressed in this work are solely those of the author and do not necessarily reflect the views of the publisher, and the publisher hereby disclaims any responsibility for them.

ISBN: 978-1-4401-9246-3 (sc)
ISBN: 978-1-4401-9247-0 (ebook)
ISBN: 978-1-4401-9248-7 (hc)

Printed in the United States of America

iUniverse rev. date: 12/29/2009

Library of Congress Cataloging-in-Publication Data
Reidy, Richard J.
Eternal Egypt: Ancient Rituals for the Modern World 1. Rites and ceremonies–Egypt. 2. Egyptian Reconstructionist–religion. 3. Ancient Egypt–Spirituality 4. Magic–Egypt. 5. Neopaganism–Egyptian. I. Reidy, Richard James). II. Title. Includes bibliographical references.

TABLE OF CONTENTS

Acknowledgments

This project began in 1998 with the founding of the Temple of Ra in San Francisco. Our fellowship was and continues to be dedicated to researching and restoring the authentic rituals of the ancient Egyptian priesthood. The encouragement, enthusiasm and firm resolve of the membership have been invaluable.

In particular I wish to thank Allan Phillips, a founding member of the Temple of Ra, together with Katherine Michael and HiC Luttmers from the Kemetic Temple of San Jose, CA, for their patience, advice, assistance, and important technical support with the "birthing" of this book.

**This book is dedicated to the memory of my parents,
Paul Reidy and Zora Broydich Reidy
who nurtured in me a love of spiritual realities.**

"An offering-which-the-King-gives to Ausir [Osiris], Lord of Eternity, the again-born, heir of Geb, may he grant to travel in the divine barque in the train of the great god, for the Ka of Paul, true-of-voice, and for the Ka of Zora, true-of-voice."

"An offering-which-the-King-gives to Ptah-Sokar and to Anpu [Anubis] upon his mountain, that they may grant to go forth on earth to see the sun in the heavens every day, for the Ka of Paul, true-of-voice, and for the Ka of Zora, true-of-voice."

"An offering-which-the-King-gives to Amun-Ra and Atum, lord of what exists, remaining in everything, that they may give offerings of all things good and pure to the Ka of Paul, true-of-voice, and to the Ka of Zora, true-of-voice."

Author's Note:

The three invocations appearing on the previous page are closely modelled on ones used throughout Egyptian history on behalf of the blessed dead. They are reported in *The Tomb of Amenemhet*, by Nina De Garis Davies and Alan H. Gardiner (London: The Theban Tomb Series, 1915), 42-43.

From the time of the Twelfth Dynasty the formula *htp di niswt* [pronounced *hotep dee neesoot*] "an offering which the king gives" was widely used within both temple ritual as well as funerary rite. The king, as the link between the divine and human worlds, theoretically presented *all* offerings in *every* temple. In practice, of course, the priests stood in as his representatives. In royal funeral rites it was the reigning king who made offerings for the benefit of his dead predecessor, whether he was in fact related to him or not. From a theological viewpoint he was pre-eminently the type of Horus who as a pious son performed funeral rites for his dead father Osiris.

With the use of the *htp di niswt* formula we enter into both the historical current of the ancient pharaohs as well as the eternal current of the gods. And so, although we no longer live in the time of the pharaohs, we remember their central role, and, more importantly, we enter into the mythic and eternal reality of the great gods Horus and Osiris.

PART ONE:

Temple Rituals For Today

PREFACE

A BOOK OF THE EMANATIONS OF RA

Chapters One to Four

The second half of the twentieth century has witnessed a widespread growth of interest in ancient spiritualities and religions of the distant past. Modern day adherents who embrace those ancient faiths frequently have scant primary sources from which to reconstruct the authentic rites and rituals of their spiritual forebears. Whether the ancient religion is that of Greece or Rome, Celtic Britain or Scandinavia, all too often the written records are extremely sparse or are found only in very fragmentary form scattered throughout such unfriendly sources as the writings of early Christian polemicists who had been aiming to discredit their pagan rivals.

The words of those ancient rites, the specific ritual actions, their sequence within the entire rite–most all these elements of worship have vanished. Only the barest of hints of what took place sometimes survive in the carvings that decorate ancient sarcophagi or adorn various monuments of empire. Even contemporary accounts by classical writers only provide incomplete sketches of ancient rituals. We look in vain for any detailed writings of those pagan priests or mystics, for they were systematically hunted down and destroyed together with ritual texts, sacred images and any ritual items used in pagan worship.

The Christian sect, once it became recognized as the religion of the empire by the Emperor Constantine, worked assiduously and systematically to forbid pagan processions, close pagan temples, and dissolve the pagan academies. In the process, whole libraries of pagan writings were consigned to the flames. Indeed, the Dark Ages had descended on the entire extent of what was then the Roman Empire. For a detailed history of the persecution of pagans, the reader is referred to Ramsay MacMullen's scholarly and highly readable account in *Christianity and Paganism in the Fourth to Eighth Centuries* (New Haven: Yale University Press, 1997).

3

The single exception to this state of affairs is the religion of ancient Egypt. Although the native Christian Coptic Church worked hand in hand with the Christian Byzantine Empire to ruthlessly suppress the pagan spirit in Egypt, accidents of climate and geography preserved sufficiently detailed records of ritual texts so that today we can reconstruct a small but important group of sacred rites and begin the process of recovering the spiritual vision that had created such rites.

In Egypt, an arid climate made possible the preservation of texts on papyrus. Buried in tombs long ago covered by desert sands, these ancient documents contain the texts of sacred rites for the ancestral dead. In addition, on the walls of temples hieroglyphs preserve the words for rituals that had ceased being performed nearly sixteen hundred years ago. As populations relocated from one locale to another, some temples eventually were covered by the shifting sands, not to be rediscovered until the nineteenth or twentieth centuries. Other temples were converted into Christian houses of worship with images and hieroglyphs concealed under layers of whitewash. In both instances, though, sacred inscriptions were preserved for posterity.

On the walls of the temples each inscribed text accompanies a colorful sculptural relief (referred to in some scholarly literature as a "vignette" if used to describe an illustration on papyrus) graphically illustrating a specific cultic act, for example, offering incense, pouring a libation, anointing the god's image, or presenting one or another food offering. For the ancient Egyptians these representations were far more than beautiful and inspiring images. Once consecrated and "enlivened" through sacred rites (specifically, the rite known as "Opening the Mouth"), these depictions became tangible, material vehicles for the eternal and magical re-enactment of those sacred acts of worship. Referred to as "houses of millions of years," the temples were designed to guarantee the perpetual worship of the gods and goddesses as well as deified humans. Built of stone, with hieroglyphic inscriptions carved several inches deep into that stone, the temples of Egypt have survived until the present as mighty witnesses to the powerful spiritual vision that had endured for well over three thousand years. This last fact alone should recommend to us the value to be derived from a careful study of these religious texts, for as the Dutch scholar W. Brede Kristensen stated,

> A faith which has shown itself capable of supporting the life of a people for hundreds, sometimes for thousands of years has already demonstrated its value. Our approval it does not need ... Our task [is] to understand [those] religious values precisely as the faithful conceived and understood them.[1]

Typically the inscribed ritual texts would be preceded by the rubrical instruction *djed medu*, "words to be spoken [aloud]." Thousands of such beautiful scenes, accompanied by the recitational texts, bear silent witness to the rites and ritual actions that had once been performed within the sacred walls of the temples. Today we are able to correlate specific gestures, body postures, and liturgical actions illustrated in those scenes on temple walls with their corresponding cultic recitations. Due in no small measure to the tedious work of meticulously transcribing and translating the hieroglyphic texts–work undertaken by generations of dedicated Egyptologists–we have available an ever-growing body of ritual texts for use in the neopagan and Kemetic (i.e., after *Kemet*, the name the ancient Egyptians gave their land) Reconstructionist communities.

Finally, the sacred words can again be spoken aloud. Once again the great gods and goddesses of ancient Egypt can be invoked in prayer and praise, in petition and thanksgiving, using the same formulae intoned by the priests and priestesses of old. And just as in ancient times these gods were honored, not solely on Egyptian soil, but throughout the far-flung lands of the Roman Empire, so, too, today the gods are being worshipped across the globe.

Having said all this, we inevitably come to the pivotal question: Why should men and women of this present era go through the effort of recovering and re-enacting these ancient rites? Why not simply create new rituals for a new age? The answer is multifarious. First, rituals that have been enacted for over three millennia in the temples of ancient Egypt contain a certain inherent power built up with over thirty centuries of usage. By repeating those rites, by reciting those sacred words of power, we tap into an ancient grid of psychic and spiritual energy capable of enriching and strengthening us in our own religious development. In addition, these sacred rituals enable us to cross an expanse of time that takes us back not simply to ancient Egypt, but to what the Egyptians called *Zep Tepi*, the First Time, the time before time, the mythic "in the beginning," when humans and gods shared a common spiritual landscape, that is, when deities and human beings communed in a harmonious peace. By employing the ancient words and images, we reconnect to that mythic universe of ancient Egypt. Setting aside our preoccupations with everyday life, we break through to an ageless spiritual dimension that is at once both mythic and real, invisible and yet genuinely manifest to those who take the time to look.

A further reason for recovering and using the ancient rites is for the great spiritual lessons these rites may teach us. As citizens of a contemporary Western culture, we breathe, as it were, an atmosphere permeated with secular, materialistic assumptions. We live in a society preoccupied with changing styles and mutable values. But the rituals of ancient Egypt take us into a dimension where values are eternal and mythic truths unchanging. The sacred texts–profoundly symbolic and steeped in the ancient myths–call us to ever deeper levels of spiritual comprehension. They invite us to lay aside the cares of the moment and enter into that mythic time of gods and goddesses whose acts had, and still have, cosmic significance. Every action, then, becomes charged with divine energy. At this point two examples will have to suffice. First, with the most simple ritual act of striking a fire and lighting the lamp or candle, the priest recites, "Come, come in peace, O glorious Eye of Heru [Horus]," thereby transforming a mundane act into a spiritual reality having cosmic implications.

As the striking of a fire pushes back the darkness, so the living deity manifesting as the solar Eye of Heru dispels and defeats the enemies of life and light. Next to sunlight itself a fire ignited by a human being is the universal emblem of light dispelling the dangers of the dark. In ancient Egyptian ritual we see that this simple action–and *every* ritual action without exception–repeat anew on the earthly plane divine acts that occur again and again on the spiritual and mythic planes. The gulf between the mundane and the celestial is crossed. Earth unites with heaven. Human actions become divine acts. Or as the Hermetic text, the Emerald Tablet, observes,

> Ascend from earth to heaven
> and descend again from heaven to earth,
> and unite together the power
> of things superior and inferior.[2]

We need to be very clear about this: ritual actions on the earthly plane do not merely mimic or even emulate divine acts–in a mystical sense they *become* those divine actions. The newly lit candle or lamp is not *like* the radiant light; it *is* that light. For example, scenes or vignettes that show Djehuty (Thoth) and Heru (Horus) holding vessels filled with water and pouring that water over pharaoh point to an underlying truth. The scene shows streams of *ankh* hieroglyphs pouring forth from the vessels. Water brings life [*ankh* in Egyptian], and not solely physical life. When used in sacred rites, it brings divine life on the celestial plane. Such temple scenes, coupled with the accompanying inscriptions, graphically lift the veil between the realms of flesh and spirit. When viewed in that light, these rituals radiate a moving, even an awe-inspiring luminescence revealing to view the hidden spiritual dimensions of the various ritual actions. Every such action, therefore, is revealed as a heavenly action, with cosmic significance. Every item used in worship is seen as an object filled with life and the power of renewal and transformation.

Our second example, one that we shall encounter again and again, is the Eye of Heru [Horus], the *Wedjat* or sound/healthy eye. In two types of liturgies–the funereal and the daily temple cult–the priest announces "I bring to you the Eye of Heru . . ." as he presents various offerings, food, drink, incense, ointment, and the like. As W. Brede Kristensen explains:

This was not artificial priestly language, but an exact formulation of the idea which forms the basis for every act of offering. That is, the life of both god and the dead [is] ritually brought about or renewed by the offering of symbols of divine life. In this offering the divine energy is present, which guarantees the sacramental making of the sacrifice. "I bring you the Eye of Horus" therefore means: I bring you the divine life, which is present in the products (fruits) of the earth and that is your own life.[3]

The Eye of Heru is that victorious life restored after its injury is healed, just as the god Heru's Eye is healed and made sound or whole again after having been injured in cosmic battle. Once blinded, it is now restored to wholeness. The Eye of Heru possesses the power of renewal, the creative power of the god. Both gods and humans are restored and renewed by offerings once those offerings are transformed through the power of naming into the Eye of Heru. The priest "names" the offering as the Eye of Heru and through this magically potent act of speech the offering is revealed as containing divine life itself, a divine life emanating from the products of the earth–food and drink, incense, flowers, precious oils–the list is lengthy but not arbitrary. Every item used in offering has a mystical meaning and dimension. As water is seen to bring life, offerings identified with the Eye of Heru are seen to *renew* life. This vocabulary of mystical correspondences acts as a continuous revelation: divinity pushes through, as it were, the veil of material creation. It does not destroy the veil, but it casts a penetrating light that breaks through the denseness of the veil of materiality.

Every ritual of ancient Egypt exhibits this transforming power. Great transcendent archetypes hidden within the human psyche are played out, enacted, and made visible within these rites. (For an exploration of the Jungian archetype in one typical text, the *Amduat,* inscribed in numerous royal tombs, the reader is referred to *Knowledge for the Afterlife: The Egyptian Amduat–A Quest for Immortality* by famed Jungian analyst Theodor Abt and the well-known Egyptologist Erik Hornung [Zurich: Living Human Heritage Publications, 2003]).

These archetypes, however, are not simply noetic constructs or mental projections limited to the material or this-worldly sphere. They are profound spiritual realities whose full significance cannot be conveyed by words alone. They must be experienced. And experience comes through the enactment of the rites. You, dear reader, can experience this divine dimension once you prepare yourself through study and reflection–and then through the celebration of the sacred rites. By careful, thoughtful repetition of these rituals you will find the veil more and more transparent. Your efforts will be rewarded, for by emulating divine acts and pronouncing the sacred texts you will be entering a spiritual realm where gods and goddesses and the blessed dead have a true and priceless communion with those who invoke their blessing and aid. Be patient. Be persistent. The gods are not to be outdone in generosity. It was the vision of the ancient Egyptian priesthood that humans in this world of the living can effect such a mystical communion with the sacred beings of the spirit realm, with both gods and the blessed dead. It is hoped that this collection of ritual texts will help individuals achieve this lofty goal.

This book is especially intended to make available for the Kemetic Reconstructionist community a few of the central rituals performed in ancient Egyptian worship. Although these texts originally were published privately over the course of three years in separate booklets for members of the Kemetic Temple of Ra in San Francisco, taken together they comprise a basic core of rituals widely used in ancient Egypt. Chapter One presents the prototype for a morning rite while Chapter Two offers a nighttime ritual. Chapter Three contains two rituals for the transfigured dead, with one intended for annual celebration and the other for more frequent performance. The fourth and concluding chapter in Part One has three apotropaic rites aimed at the cosmic foe Apep. Taken together, these seven rituals lay a foundation of authentic texts for Kemetic priests and priestesses as well as for the individual worshipper. Each ritual is accompanied by a commentary that, while not exhaustive in scope, is intended at least to introduce the reader to important background information and major themes within the rite. Our present Common Era is currently witnessing a rebirth of interest in ancient Egypt, its gods and sacred teachings. It is my hope that this volume will assist in some way in that rebirth.

May Djehuty, lord of divine words [*neb medu Netjer*], inspire and guide your efforts and those of all who seek to recover the great spiritual treasures of ancient Egypt.

San Francisco, 6 August 2009
Feast of Wep Renpet, the Opening of the Year
(day 1 in the month of *Tekhy*, in the season of *Akhet*)
RICHARD J. REIDY

Pharaoh, as great high priest representing all Egypt, and by implication all humankind, offers Ma'at, the perfect offering, to the creator Netjer (god), Amun-Ra. Ma'at is more than an intellectual construct. She is the living divine hypostasis of goodness, truth, beauty, balance, and perfection. This central ritual action illustrates the ancient insight that humans and gods collaborate together in the daily renewal and maintenance of the cosmos—a cosmos of balance and harmony. (For the ritual recitation accompanying the presentation of Ma'at, refer to the Fourteenth Ceremony in the Morning Ritual.) Similar reliefs of pharaoh offering Ma'at are to be found in scores of scenes throughout all the temples of Egypt.

CHAPTER ONE

The Morning Ritual
in the
Temple of Amun-Ra

Introduction

Eternal Egypt: Ancient Rituals for the Modern World bears the additional and important subtitle *A Book of the Emanations of Ra*, or, as the ancient Egyptians themselves would have said, the *"Bau-Ra."* I have adopted the translation "Emanations of Ra" in keeping with the preferred phrasing of several eminent scholars–Blackman, Fairman, and Gardiner.[4] Two other Egyptologists of note, in trying to approximate the meaning of the expression, translate it as "manifestations of Ra's power"[5] and "the all-powerful effectiveness of Ra's power."[6] The Egyptians were referring to the collections of hymns and ritual texts used in worshipping the gods and maintaining the order of the cosmos in the face of the forces of chaos threatening to destroy it.

The words and rituals were themselves endowed with immense power, the very power of the creator god Ra. Significantly, their composition was ascribed to the god Djehuty (Thoth), who was himself the "Tongue of Ra" and "Lord of the Divine Words." In these sacred texts, collectively referred to as the *"Bau-Ra,"* the priests "could lay their hands on the elemental force the god Ra had set in motion to create the universe."[7] The rites and rituals and the spoken and written words accompanying those rites were a cosmic force, not simply lovely or emotionally moving religious services for the edification of onlookers and participants or even for pleasing the gods.

With the foregoing in mind, I venture to offer you a labor of love from the rich legacy that the ancient Egyptian priesthood has left us. It seems appropriate to begin with a rendition of that central ritual act that marked the beginning of each day in every temple throughout the entire land of ancient Egypt. Other rites and rituals were intended for special occasions (e.g., coronations, royal anniversaries, crises, death) or for calendar events (lunar, seasonal, or festal commemorations). This one rite, the daily temple liturgy, was *the* central act of service to the god or goddess.

It also seems appropriate to present the daily rite as it was celebrated on behalf of the chief god of the Egyptian pantheon, Amun-Ra, whose main temple was at Iunu (Heliopolis). It was this city that "exercised in early times a very far-reaching religious and political influence."[8] In the words of Aylward Blackman:

> Heliopolitan influence on Egyptian worship is to be recognized not only in the uniform cult of all divinities, but also in numerous cult-accessories and in the very constitution of the priesthood; furthermore, in the temple structures themselves and the views which the Egyptians entertained about them.[9]

As you read through the following ritual you are likely to derive the most benefit by approaching it as you would any great work of art, be it literature, painting, music, or dance–a work from another era and another culture. The deep beauty and the even deeper meaning will not reveal themselves to the casual observer. It is not only that the tonal quality of the ancient texts is so strange to our modern ear, but the mindset, the worldview revealed in the texts, is even now, after well over a century of archaeological discovery and analysis, only partially understood. As you read through the various Utterances which accompany specific ritual actions questions are bound to arise. You can use these questions as a springboard to discover more fully the rich meaning of the divine mythic world of ancient Egypt, a world that inspired and shaped that civilization for over three thousand years. The Notes and Bibliography may assist in locating scholarly texts of interest. Those books in turn can guide you to still other works that will help you in reclaiming the spiritual treasures of Egypt.

In this ritual and the ones following it the names of the gods and goddesses are transliterated from the ancient Egyptian language. Since many readers will only be familiar with the spellings of divine names as given by Greek and Roman writers, those classical names will appear in brackets after the ancient Egyptian transliteration; for example, Heru [Horus] and Djehuty [Thoth]. Other words, such as names of cities, will also appear in both forms. The original land we call Egypt was referred to by its people as Kemet, that is, the Black Land because of its fertile black soil. Those of us who practice this ancient faith usually refer to ourselves as Kemetic pagans or Kemetic Reconstructionists.

At some point one or another Utterance or action may touch your heart in a personal way. Adopt it. Make it your own. Use the words and ritual actions as your own special means to connect with the god or goddess you are drawn to. You can call upon Djehuty, the Lord of Divine Words, to help you in crafting the words so they honor that god or goddess in a manner faithful to the original intent of the ancient priesthood. Your hard work will pay off. The *Netjeru* [gods] are not to be outdone in generosity. The "Emanations of Ra" reach across the ages, calling once again to a revived pagan spirit to pronounce the words of power, the power of this great god himself, a power that can restore the Balance and reconcile the Polarities of existence, a power that daily can defeat the hostile forces of chaos. We have a role to play in this great divine/human drama. The ancient rites show us the way.

San Francisco, 4 August 2002
Rising of Sopdet (Sirius), Festival of the Opening of the Year
RICHARD J. REIDY

Commentary
on the Morning Ritual
in the Temple of Amun-Ra

The following daily ritual honoring Amun-Ra is based on a number of liturgical texts–inscriptions found on the walls of the temple built by Seti I at Abydos, as well as in an important papyrus from Thebes, known as the *Berlin Papyrus* (no. 3055). The modern language translations used as the basis for the present rendition are the French text in *Le Rituel du Culte Divin Journalier* by Alexandre Moret. For purposes of comparison the reader also may wish to consult an English text in *The Book of Opening the Mouth* by E. A. Wallis Budge. [Budge's work includes a translation entitled "The Ritual of the Divine Cult," which presents the ritual texts for the daily rite in the temple of Amun-Ra in Thebes.] Moret's translation is the more reliable.

Two more texts that have been used frequently in compiling the present work are *Religious Ritual at Abydos* by A. Rosalie David, which deals with the extensive temple inscriptions at Abydos, and, second, *Hieratic Papyri in the British Museum* edited by Alan H. Gardiner. This last work includes a translation and commentary of "The Ritual of Amenophis I," which presents the daily cult ritual of offerings performed in the temple of Amun-Ra at Karnak. Whereas the *Berlin Papyrus* is concerned primarily with the opening of the shrine and the preparatory toilette of the god, the Amenophis ritual focuses mainly but not exclusively–on the food offerings, the divine banquet as it were, with its attendant ceremonies (i.e., purifications, libations, censings, etc.). The present effort, then, tries to reflect all key points of ritual from the Karnak Liturgy, the Abydos Liturgy, and the Theban Liturgy, based on the available texts.

In undertaking the present work, I have attempted to retain as much of the original ritual as possible. With very few exceptions I have been able to compile the series of ritual formulae reflecting each essential liturgical action performed by the priests of ancient Egypt in the daily morning service to Amun-Ra. My intention is to offer a rite that actually can be adopted for use by contemporary adherents of this ancient religious tradition, enabling them to worship this important deity in a manner and spirit completely consistent with authentic ancient Egyptian practice. This has, however, resulted in several ritual actions being omitted due to a variety of reasons. For example, the original text calls for ritually assembling a brazier, lighting it, and then grilling select meats on it. For practical reasons including time constraints I have omitted this portion of the ritual. The recitations accompanying these actions do not add anything of significance to the overall rite; instead, they simply repeat ideas that are expressed elsewhere in the ritual. In addition, we know that offerings of cooked meat were also offered *without* the actual grilling taking place before the deity. Textual analysis indicates that the critical element was and is the actual offering and not its preparation.

A second example of the need to edit a given text occurs when the ritual papyrus presents more than one Utterance or Spell for the same ceremonial act. Some of these clearly were intended for special feast days; others appear to be alternative recitations. Very often they are presented in the papyrus with no explanatory remarks as to when they were to be used. (No doubt the Egyptian priests themselves would have known exactly when to use one or the other text.) They might be titled simply "Another Chapter" or "Another Hymn." But their content indicates that they were intended as alternate texts to the specific rite immediately preceding them. In constructing the following ritual I occasionally have taken the liberty of combining portions from several of such closely related "Chapters." In doing so I attempted to exercise a thoughtful and very conservative editorial discretion, seeking to be faithful to the original thoughts, mindset, and wording of the ancient liturgists and preserving all the most significant elements of each Utterance, but always with an eye to how any Utterance actually contributed to the overall movement of the entire rite being enacted.

My intent was to strike a balance between blindly copying a text word for word and, on the other hand, molding a more "user-friendly" redaction that persons of a modern Western mindset could more readily embrace. For example, the ancient Egyptians had a very wide array of mythical events to which they could make reference. Modern man no longer possesses the intimate, detailed knowledge of those myths. Hence, our comprehension of them is frequently quite limited, not unlike watching a movie in black and white from the silent era of films. We lack, as it were, the color and the sound that could make them vital and compelling to the modern mind. It was my considered decision to offer to the reader a rendition of texts that captures the essential mythic referents that had been normative from the time of the Old Kingdom Pyramid Texts down through the great Ramesside era. In practice this meant that occasionally interesting but redundant items as well as presently incomprehensible references would be sacrificed for the sake of brevity and clarity–brevity because contemporary Kemetic worshippers do not possess unlimited time for dauntingly lengthy rituals, and clarity because we want to avoid the pitfall of "not seeing the forest for the trees." The ancient liturgical composers luxuriated in florid and profuse verbal "bouquets" in their sacred utterances. Nothing was to be spared when it came to praising the gods. Terms like "opulent" or "lavish" come to mind.

Contemporary Western minds are often ill-prepared for such a rich diet of allusions, honorific titles, and genuinely mystical pronouncements. But that does not mean we should adopt a cavalier attitude when editing a text, chopping or cutting at random just to boil it down to some colorless, tasteless broth that might be palatable to contemporary taste. The present rendition of the divine rites is a first attempt, a tentative offering. Hopefully it will be improved upon over the years as more and more is learned about the rich spiritual legacy of ancient Egypt.

Nevertheless, I believe an ancient Egyptian priest would both recognize and be comfortable with each element in the version presented here. No attempt has been made to include sentiments or concepts from any other religious or spiritual tradition, ancient or modern. This project has *not* been in any way an exercise in eclectic syncretism. On the contrary, I have striven to make certain that the words, although in English, reflect in each and every instance an authentically Kemetic theological and liturgical vision as well as being firmly based upon the actual ancient ritual texts.

May Amun-Ra be pleased with this offering to his *Ka*!

The Morning Ritual

UTTERANCE BEFORE THE CLOSED DOORS
OF THE TEMPLE

The priest or priestess addresses the assembled deities of the Temple and asserts his/her innocence. As will occur repeatedly in the rite, the ritualist identifies him/herself with one or another Netjer. This is a strategy found throughout Egyptian ritual and magic. The ritualist's claim to be a specific Netjer (god) or Netjeret (goddess) puts him/her within a divine context, an otherworldly milieu that enables him/her to interact with deity on an equal footing. At the same time the priest/ess remains human, asserting his/her ritual and moral purity. There is no contradiction between being fully human and fully divine. This insight is central to the Kemetic religious vision.

At the first sign of dawn, or as close as possible to the dawn's first light, the priest/ess and all assistants proceed in silence to their assigned places before the closed doors of the Temple Chamber. All bow, touching the palms of their hands to their knees.

The priest/ess raises his/her hands in adoration (the *dua* or praise position), with arms held out to about shoulder height, with palms of the hands facing outward. The following shall be said:

"**O you** Netjeru [gods] **of this temple, you guardians of the great portal, great** Netjeru **of mysterious abode, who sanctify the god in his shrine, who consecrate his oblation, who receive the offerings in his presence in the Hall of the Ennead: I have made my way and I enter into your presence. I am one of you. I am Shu, the eldest son of his father, the senior** wab [pure] **priest of Amun-Ra. Do not repulse me on the god's path. My feet are not impeded. I am not turned back from the court of the great portal so that I may conduct the divine service, that I may present offerings to him that made them, that I may give bread to Amun-Ra. I have come on the way of the god. I have not shown partiality in judgement. I have not consorted with the strong. I have not reproached the lowly. I have not stolen things. I have not diminished the constituents of the Eye of Ra. I have not disturbed the balance. I have not tampered with the** requirements of the Sacred Eye. O Council of the Great Netjer [god] in this temple, behold, I have come to you to offer Ma'at to the Lord of Ma'at, to content the Sound Eye for its lord. I am Shu; I flood his offering table. I present his offerings, Sekhmet consorting with me, that I may adore Amun-Ra at his festivals, that I may kiss the earth so great is his majesty, that I may endow his image with life. I am pure. I am purified."[10]

THE FIRST CEREMONY
The Chapter of Striking a Fire

Standing before the closed doors, the priest lights the candle or oil lamp. As he does so the following shall be said:

"Come, come in peace, O glorious Eye of Heru [Horus]. Be strong and renew your youth in peace. It shines like Ra in the double horizon, and the power of the enemy of Ra hides itself straightaway before the Eye of Heru, which seizes it and brings it and sets it before the seat of Heru. The word of Heru is Ma'at by reason of his Eye. The Eye of Heru destroys the enemies of Amun-Ra, the Lord of the Throne of the Two Lands, in all their places. I am pure."[11]

The priest hands the lighted taper /oil lamp to an assistant who holds it in readiness until the moment when all will enter into the Temple Chamber.

THE SECOND CEREMONY
The Chapter of Taking the Censer in the Hand

In this and in the following Ceremony the priest addresses an inanimate object as if it were able to hear and respond. This is not an example of an animistic mindset, but rather indicates the Egyptian insight that all creation possesses a certain innate and unique intelligence due to its being an emanation of deity— created and sustained by a Divine Intelligence that gives form to all creation.

As the priest takes up the censer in his hand the following shall be said:

"Homage to you, O censer of the Netjeru who are in the following of Djehuty [Thoth]. My arms are upon you like those of Heru, my hands are upon you like those of Djehuty, my fingers are around you like those of Anpu [Anubis] who is at the head of the divine hall. I am the living servant of Ra. I am the wab [pure] priest. I am pure. My purifications are the purifications of the Netjeru. I am pure."[12]

THE THIRD CEREMONY
The Chapter of Placing the Incense Cup on the Censer

The censer shall include a separate cup for the charcoal. The priest affixes the cup onto the censer and the following shall be said:

"Homage to you, O incense cup. I am purified with the Eye of Heru so that I may perform ceremonies with you. Amun-Ra and his company of the Netjeru are pure. I am pure."[13]

THE FOURTH CEREMONY
The Chapter of Incense

The priest places grains of frankincense on the charcoal in the censer. As it begins to burn, the priest slowly and repeatedly raises and lowers the smoking censer before the closed doors of the Temple Chamber. As he does so, the following shall be said:

"The incense comes; the odor of the Netjer comes. The odor thereof comes to you, Amun-Ra, Lord of the Throne of the Two Lands. The odor of the Eye of Heru is for you, the odor of the Netjeret [goddess] Nekhbet is for you. It washes you. It ornaments you. It takes its place upon your two hands. O Amun-Ra, I have presented to you the Eye of Heru; the odor comes to you. The odor of the Eye of Heru is for you."[14]

THE INVOCATION HYMN

*According to Jan Assmann in his Egyptian Solar Religion in the New Kingdom
(15) this is the only such text whose liturgical origin is certain. Its use is attested
in three liturgical sources.*

The priest/ess holds his/her hands in the invocation/*nis** position,
with the arms stretched out and held at about shoulder level and
the hands held vertically with the thumbs seen on top.

The following shall be said:

**"May you awake in beauty!
Hail to you, Amun-Ra Harakhty, Atum, Khepri, Heru who
crosses the sky,
Great Falcon, adorned of breast,
Beautiful of face with the great double feather.
May you awake in beauty at dawn
At what the assembled Ennead says to you.
Joy resounds for you at evening,
Kenmut** (one of the first of the 36 decan or star-deities) **praises you
Who spends the night being carried in pregnancy.
The earth becomes bright at your birth.
Your mother protects you every day.
May Ra live and the enemy die!
While you endure, your enemy falls.
You cross the sky in life and in health.
You adorn the sky in the** Mandjet (morning) **boat.
You spend the day in your boat with pleasant heart.
Ma'at has appeared on your forehead.
Rise, Ra.
Shine as Akhty** (he of the horizon),
**Dark One with radiant face.
The crew of Ra is jubilant.
The sky and earth are joyful.
The Great Ennead pay homage to you,
Amun-Ra Harakhty has gone forth in triumph!"**[15] *(4 times)*

AN ALTERNATE INVOCATION HYMN

Adapted from an inscription at the Temple of Hibis which "comprised part of the beginning of the daily cult ritual of the temple." (Lorton, 159)

All present shall recite the REFRAIN. The priest shall recite the versicle.

REFRAIN: "May you awaken, may you be in peace, may you awaken in peace. Awaken, Oh Amun-Ra, in life and in peace! Awaken in peace!

"Oh Falcon of the Nome-gods, who lights the Two Lands, Bull of the Outpouring-of-Nun, who lives forever in his name of Ra, every day,

REFRAIN: "May you awaken, may you be in peace, may you awaken in peace. Awaken, Oh Amun-Ra, in life and in peace! Awaken in peace!

"Oh Living-of-Births in his left Eye, whom everyone loves, in his name of Moon, the god of minds and hearts,

REFRAIN: "May you awaken, may you be in peace, may you awaken in peace. Awaken, Oh Amun-Ra, in life and in peace! Awaken in peace!

"Oh He-exhales-the-winds, making throats to breathe, in his name of Amun, enduring in all things, the Ba of Shu for all the Netjeru,

REFRAIN: "May you awaken, may you be in peace, may you awaken in peace. Awaken, Oh Amun-Ra, in life and in peace! Awaken in peace!

"Oh Flesh-of-life who creates the plant of life, Nepery, who floods the Two Lands, without whom there is no life within the Two Lands, in his name of Nun the great,

REFRAIN: **"May you awaken, may you be in peace, may you awaken in peace. Awaken, Oh Amun-Ra, in life and in peace! Awaken in peace!"**[16]

THE FIFTH CEREMONY
The Chapter of Advancing to the Holy Place

The priest opens the doors leading into the Temple. Together with his assistants he enters in, and proceeds to stand before the closed *Kar*-shrine. The following shall be said:

"O you Bas [souls] **of Iunu** [i.e., Heliopolis], **if you are strong, I am strong; if I am strong, you are strong. If your** Kas [life force] **are strong, my** Ka **is strong at the head of the living; as they are living, so shall I live. . . . Sekhmet, the great** Netjeret, **the beloved of Ptah, has given to me life, stability, and serenity round about my members, which Djehuty has gathered together for life. I am Heru in the height of heaven, the beautiful one of terror, the Lord of victory, the mighty one of terror, the exalted one of the two plumes, the great one in Abydos. I am pure."**[17]

THE SIXTH CEREMONY
The Chapter of Opening the Doors of the *Kar*-Shrine [Naos]

Even the most simple ritual action such as opening the doors of the shrine becomes an act replete with cosmic meaning due to the priestly "words of power" that fill the mundane act with an otherworldly content. The priest/ess verbally acknowledges that the temple is the dwelling place of divinity. The temple doors, or the doors of the god's shrine house (Egyptian "Kar," Greek "Naos"), are seen as a cosmic gateway to divinity.

For the rite of "Seeing the god," the priest unbolts the doors of the *Kar*-shrine and slowly opens them. The following shall be said:

"The doors of the sky are opened, the doors of the earth are unlocked. Geb makes obeisance to the Netjeru who are seated upon their thrones, saying, 'The double doors of heaven open, the Company of the Netjeru send forth light. Amun-Ra is exalted upon his Great Seat, the Great Company of the Netjeru are exalted upon their Seat.'"[18]

THE SEVENTH CEREMONY
The Chapter of Looking Upon the God

Bowing before the sacred image which now is visible, the following shall be said:

"My face keeps guard over the Netjeru, and the Netjer keeps guard over my face. The Netjeru have made a way for me, and I walk thereon. Behold, I am sent to look upon the Netjer."[19]

THE EIGHTH & NINTH CEREMONIES
The Chapter of "Smelling the Earth"
The Chapter of Placing Oneself on Ones Belly

The priest performs a full prostration by first kneeling and then lowering himself completely onto the ground, with arms stretched forward and his entire body lying flat on the ground. In this position the following shall be said:

"I prostrate myself on the earth. I embrace Geb. I sing the praises of Amun-Ra. I am pure to him . . . . Homage to you, Amun-Ra, who are established upon your Great Seat. I have placed myself on my belly through fear of you. I am afraid of your terror. I embrace Geb and Hwt-Hrw [Hathor] that they may make me great, and that I may not fall down at the slaughterings of this day."[20]

THE TENTH CEREMONY
The Chapter of the *Henu* Rite

The Fourfold Salute is depicted in scenes showing the Ba-souls of Pe and Nekhen. These two groups of divine ancestors are from Pe (Buto) in Lower Egypt and Nekhen (Hierakonpolis) in Upper Egypt. When the Fourfold Salute is performed, it represents a reaching back into archaic times and, therefore, the gesture is a sign and token of a temporal "oneness" and continuity of praise, worship, and rejoicing.

The priest raises himself to a kneeling position. He then performs the *Henu* rite. He begins with the gesture of "Embracing the Earth." Then, remaining in a kneeling position on the floor, he brings his left leg up so that the foot is flat on the ground with the left knee pointing up. (The right knee remains touching the floor.) The priest salutes the god by raising his right arm behind his head, bent at the elbow, and with fist clinched. With his left fist, he gently taps his chest above the right breast. He then raises both hands in the adoration/*dua* position. This is done four times in succession, followed by the gesture of "Embracing the Earth." Having completed this series of gestures, the priest bows profoundly, and the following shall be said:

"Homage to you, Amun-Ra! . . . . I prostrate myself through fear of you. I have watched to do your will. I have not been overthrown by your enemies on this day. Your enemies whom you hate you have overthrown. He who adores his lord feels no weakness."[21]

THE ELEVENTH CEREMONY
The Chapter of Entering into the Temple

Rising to his feet, the priest raises his hands in adoration (*dua* position), arms held out in front and palms facing outward. The following shall be said:

"O God, Exalted One among the Company of the *Netjeru*, Mighty One of fear among his sailors, Great One of terror among the *Netjeru*. Behold, he is 'Ra' to what he has made; he is 'Tem' to what he has created. Come to me, O Amun-Ra, in that embrace wherein you came forth on the day when you rose as king, when you rose in the heavens. Do you yourself hasten to me as you hastened to your holy uraeus to deliver yourself from Apep [in Greek "Apophis," the chaos serpent].

"I have come to you, O Amun-Ra. I am Djehuty, who journeyed at the two seasons to seek for the Eye of its Lord. I have come. I have found the Eye. I have reckoned it up for its Lord.

"Come to me, O Amun-Ra. Guide me in the path whereon you travel. Make me to enter in in the form of a *Ba* bird. Make me to come forth in the form of a Lion. Make me to travel in the form of Wepwawet. And let me not be repulsed or turned back on the roads on this day, on this night, in this month, in this year. Behold, come to me, O Amun-Ra, and open for me the two doors of the sky, and unclose for me the two doors of the earth, and throw open before me the sacred space of your divine house.

"I have looked upon the *Netjer*. I have come to him, and his two uraei have enclosed me. I have entered in with the statue of Ma'at in order that Amun-Ra may create peace with his beautiful Ma'at on this day."[22]

THE TWELFTH CEREMONY
The Chapter of Offering the Heart (*Ib*) to the *Netjer*

"... The heart stands ... above all for will, consciousness, and memory.... The Ib (i.e., heart) ... designates the emotional and cognitive inner life of a person, his 'inner being.'" Jan Assmann, Death and Salvation in Ancient Egypt, 29. Offering the heart to the god, then, effectively enables the Netjer to once again have a vital presence in the sacred image. Divinity is brought into the human sphere by this action.

The Ib is fabricated of clay or wood and has the shape of the hieroglyph for "heart."

The priest picks up in his right hand the *Ib*. Cupping the *Ib* in his hand, he extends his arm and offers the *Ib* to the god. The following shall be said:

"Homage be to you, Amun-Ra! I have brought to you your heart, to set it upon its seat, even as Aset [Isis] **brought the heart of her son Heru to set it upon its seat, and as Heru brought the heart of Aset his mother to set it upon its seat, and as Djehuty brought the heart to *Nesret*** [the "Flaming or Fiery One," that is, Sekhmet], **and as this *Netjeret* was appeased by Djehuty."**[23]

THE THIRTEENTH CEREMONY
The Chapter of Incense

The offering of incense is both purificatory and restorative. Incense is identified with the sweat or exudation of the Netjer, and consequently both purifies and rejuvenates the recipient. It is both exudation of the Netjer as well as being the Eye of Heru. This doubling or even tripling of identifications is a frequent method of asserting the multi-aspected reality of divinity.

The priest places more grains of frankincense on the burner. As the smoke rises the priest slowly raises and lowers the censer before the god. The following shall be said:

"The incense comes. The incense comes. The odor of the *Netjer* comes. The breath of the *Netjer* comes. The grains of incense come. The moisture which drops from the *Netjer* comes, and the smell thereof is upon you, O Amun-Ra. The Eye of Heru hides you in the tears thereof, and the odor thereof comes to you, O Amun-Ra, and it exalts itself for you among the *Netjeru*.
. . .
"Peace be to you, O Amun-Ra. Let your heart expand, for I have brought to you the Eye of Heru, so that you may be great through that which your heart has received, and through that which your nostrils inhale at this censing. . . . I have bound up for you the Eye of Heru. The fragrance thereof comes to you; the fragrance of the Eye of Heru is to you, O Amun-Ra, lover of incense."[24]

THE FOURTEENTH CEREMONY
The Chapter of Presenting Ma'at

The offering of Ma'at is at the heart of the entire service. It is the central act because it reveals, confirms, and renews the divine-human collaboration in establishing and maintaining the cosmos. The priest identifies himself with Djehuty, the Tongue of Ra, and presents Ma'at to the creator. He speaks as the divine Djehuty but he never ceases being human. Notice how, throughout the entire ritual, the priest from time to time affirms his own purity but then asserts his divine status as one or another god. Here we have one of the most profound insights in the theology of ancient Egypt. Humans and gods cooperate and assist one another in the ongoing act of creation. Humans and gods both come forth from the creator-god, and hence, share a common origin and a common destiny.

The priest removes the statue of Amun-Ra from the *Kar*-shrine ["Naos" in Greek] and places it on clean white linen or freshly scattered sand atop the altar. Then the priest takes the censer and, by moving it to and fro so that the smoke enters into the *Kar*-shrine proper, cleanses the interior of the *Kar*-shrine. Having finished this purification, he puts down the censer and proceeds to pick up the Ma'at symbol. As he holds it in the palms of his hands, the following shall be said:

"I have come to you. I am Djehuty, and my two hands are joined under Ma'at. Homage to you, Amun-Ra, holy god, Lord of everlastingness! You join yourself to the upper sky, rising in the Disk each morning . . . .

"Ma'at has come that she may be with you. Ma'at is in every place of yours so that you may rest upon her. You are provided with Ma'at, Creator of things which are, Maker of things which shall be. You are the Beneficent God, Beloved One. You go onward in Ma'at. You live in Ma'at. You unite your members to Ma'at; you cause Ma'at to rest upon your head, and she makes her seat upon your brow. You renew your youth when you see your daughter Ma'at, and you live by her fragrance. Ma'at places herself as an amulet on your neck, and she rests upon your breast. The *Netjeru* serve you, and they offer gifts to you in

Ma'at, for they know her worth. Truly the *Netjeru* and *Netjerut* who are in you possess Ma'at, and they know that you live in her. Your right eye is in Ma'at; your left eye is in Ma'at; your flesh and your members are in Ma'at. The breath of your body and your heart are of Ma'at. You have peace and you flourish through Ma'at. Ma'at bears you up, her two hands being before your face, and your heart is filled with joy through her.

"Djehuty presents Ma'at to you, and his two hands are upon her beauty before your face. Your *Ka* is to you when Ma'at praises you, and when your members unite with Ma'at. You rejoice, you become young at the sight of her. The heart of Amun-Ra lives when Ma'at rises before him. You exist, for Ma'at exists. Ma'at exists, and you exist. Ma'at has made her way into your head, and she exists before you forever."

The priest places the image of Ma'at inside the shrine or upon the altar table.

"An offering of Ma'at has been made to you to give satisfaction to your heart, and your heart shall live in her, and your *Ba* [soul] shall live, O Amun-Ra. You are at peace and you flourish through her. Ma'at has taken up her position within your shrine. Djehuty, the great one of words of power, makes protection for you, and he has overthrown for you the enemies. Ma'at is established throughout the Two Lands, truly twice established. She is yours for ever and ever, O divine one, creator of joy, Beneficent God, whose word is law, beloved, Amun-Ra!"[25]

THE FIFTEENTH CEREMONY
The Chapter of the Festal Perfume in the Form of Honey

On special feast days dedicated to Amun-Ra, at this point in the rite the priest is to offer honey and the following shall be said:

"Hail, Amun-Ra. I present to you honey, the Eye of Heru, the sweet one, the exudation of the Eye of Ra, the lord of offerings. You are flooded therewith, for it is sweet to your heart, and it shall never depart from you. It is sweet to the heart of Amun-Ra, and beautiful on the day wherein he rests his heart upon it. I give to you the Eye of Heru; it is sweet to your heart. Let your face be gracious and good to me."[26]

THE SIXTEENTH CEREMONY
The Chapter of Laying the Hands on the God

This ritual embrace is a vehicle for transferring life force (Ka) into the sacred image. The priest or priestess is the conduit for the life renewing and life creating energy of three Netjeru—Heru, Djehuty, and Anpu—who each play major roles in the ritual animation of deceased persons.

The priest with reverence extends his right hand and touches the left shoulder of the statue of Amun-Ra. With his left hand he touches the god's right wrist. At this point of contact with the divine, the following shall be said:

"Homage to you, Amun-Ra. Truly, Djehuty has come to see you with the *nemes* bandlet around his neck and his *matu* bandlet behind him. Awake when you hear his words. My two arms are upon you like those of Heru; my two hands are upon you like those of Djehuty; my fingers are upon you like those of Anpu. I am a living servant of Ra. I am a *wab* priest, for I am pure, and my purifications are those of the *Netjeru*. I am pure."[27]

THE SEVENTEENTH CEREMONY
Spell for Taking Off the God's Apparel

As the priest removes the cloak and all articles of adornment which clothe the god, the following shall be said:

"Your beauty belongs to you. Your *m'r* cloth is around you, Amun-Ra, who resides in *Hut aat* ["Great Shrine," the name of the sun temple at Heliopolis]. I have seized for you this Eye of Heru. Adorn yourself with it. You possess your beauty; you possess your raiment. You are a *Netjer*, O Amun-Ra."[28]

THE EIGHTEENTH CEREMONY
Purifications Made with the 4 *Nemset* Vases of Water

The text below is based on a similar one from the Ritual of Amenophis (82).

The priest circumambulates the image of the god and sprinkles water from one of the white *Nemset* vases. As he repeats this four times–each time using water from a new vase–the following shall be said:

"Pure, pure is Amun-Ra. I have brought to you that which came forth from Nun, the waters of the beginning which came forth from Atum in this its name of *Nemset* bowl. O Amun-Ra, take to yourself your head, join to yourself your bones, fasten to yourself your eyes in their place."[29]

That which was fragmented and broken is restored whole and brimming with divine life—accomplished through contact with the life-giving, primordial waters of the First Time. Four bowls are used to represent the totality of the created order, as in the four directions. First, four white bowls and then four red bowls of water representing the Two Lands, Upper and Lower Egypt.

THE NINETEENTH CEREMONY
Purifications made with the 4 *Teshert* Vases of Water

The priest circumambulates the image of the god and sprinkles water from one of the red *Teshert* vases. As he repeats this four times, the following shall be said:

"Pure, pure is Amun-Ra. I have presented to you the water in the vases, the Red Eye of Heru. Your eye is offered to you, your head is offered to you, your bones are offered to you. Your head is established for you on your bones before Geb. Djehuty has purified it. Djehuty gives the Eye of Heru to you. Pure, pure is Amun-Ra."[30]

THE TWENTIETH CEREMONY
Making the Purifications with Natron*

The priest holds up a bowl of natron, presenting it to Amun-Ra. The following shall be said:

"Pure, pure is Amun-Ra, bull of his mother, chief of the Great Seat. I have presented to you the Eye of Heru so that its odor may come to you. The odor of the Eye of Heru is to you. Pure, pure is Amun-Ra."[31]

The priest washes and dries the image with a clean white cloth. He then holds four colored cloths/ribbons in his hands, presenting them to Amun-Ra. The following shall be said:

"Take the fabric in a state of absolute purity. I envelop your effigy in this fabric."[32]

* *Natron is a naturally occurring substance comprised of sodium bicarbonate (baking soda) and sodium chloride (salt). It is found in the dried river beds of the Wadi el Natrun in Egypt. It can be duplicated by combining equal parts of baking soda and sea salt with one and a half times as much water. Dissolve this mixture and heat to a boil, stirring frequently until it thickens up like oatmeal. Spread this on a cookie sheet and let dry for several days, or place in an oven on low heat. When completely dry, break it up into small pieces.*

THE TWENTY-FIRST CEREMONY
The Chapter of the White Bandlet (Head cloth)

Setting down the colored cloths/ribbons, the priest picks up the white linen head cloth, and before placing it on or touching it to the head of the god, the following shall be said:

"Hail, Amun-Ra. You have received this, your shining headcloth. You have received this, your apparel, this headcloth of beauty. You have received this Eye of Heru, the White One which comes forth from Nekheb. You rise in it, you are perfect in it in its name of '*Menkhet.*' The *Netjeru* strengthen you; the

Netjeru **strengthen it, even as they are strong through the Eye of Heru."**[33]

THE TWENTY-SECOND CEREMONY
The Chapter of Putting on the White Bandlet

The priest vests the god with the white cloth/ribbon. The following shall be said:

"Amun-Ra has arrayed himself in his apparel. Hail, Amun-Ra. I present to you the Eye of Heru so that you are satisfied in the Great Mansion of the Prince which is in Iunu [Heliopolis]. Your *Ka* is satisfied in spite of your adversaries."[34]

THE TWENTY-THIRD CEREMONY
The Chapter of Putting on the Green Bandlet

The priest vests the god with the green cloth/ribbon. The following shall be said:

"Wadjet rises, the Perfect One, who cannot be repulsed in heaven or on earth. The green bandlet refreshes Amun-Ra; it makes perfect and it renews youth, even as Ra renewed his youth. O Amun-Ra, I have presented to you the Eye of Heru, and you are strong by what is in it."[35]

THE TWENTY-FOURTH CEREMONY
The Chapter of Putting on the Red Bandlet

The priest vests the god with the red cloth/ribbon. The following shall be said:

"The Eye of Ra rises. Her majesty makes the word to go forth; the Creatress of the Company of the *Netjeru*. She protects Amun-Ra; she guards him; she causes the fear of him to exist. She makes him to be mighty of terror, and greater in his power than the *Netjeru*. O Amun-Ra, live, and renew yourself, and

become young like Ra every day. Songs of praise are offered to you because of your beauties. Your arm cannot be resisted throughout all the earth. I have presented to you the Eye of Heru, and you see by means of it."[36]

THE TWENTY-FIFTH CEREMONY
The Chapter of Putting on the Great Cloth
(the *Atma* Bandlet)

The priest cloaks the god with the white linen mantle. The following shall be said:

"Amun-Ra has received his Great Cloth [i.e., cloak] on the two arms of the goddess Tait for his flesh. *Netjer* unites himself to *Netjer,* and *Netjer* arrays himself with *Netjer* in his name of *idmi.* The *Netjer* who washed away his outflowing is Hapi, and the light of the bandlet illuminates his head. Aset [Isis] has woven it, and Nebet Het [Nephthys] has spun it, and they make the bandlet shine for Amun-Ra. The word of Amun-Ra is law against his enemies."[37]

THE TWENTY-SIXTH CEREMONY
The Chapter of Presenting Unguent

The priest anoints the image of the god with precious oil using the little finger of his hand. (Two fingers–the little finger and the index finger–are extended. The remaining fingers are folded inward toward the palm.)The following shall be said:

"Hail, Amun-Ra! I have filled you with the Eye of Heru, with the *Madjet** oil. It renews your strength [literally, "makes you green"], and it adorns you in its name of Wadjet. Its odor pleases you in its name of 'Sweet Odor.' The Eye of Heru, which is Sekhmet, burns up your enemies for you. Geb has given you his inheritance. Your word is law against your enemies. Wepwawet has opened the roads for you against your enemies."[38]

* A recipe for this sacred unguent appears on the walls of the temple of Heru at Edfu. It was used in the daily cult ritual in temples throughout Egypt. It is red in color and has a strong, long lasting fragrance including cinnamon, pine resin, juniper berries, and other ingredients. For the full recipe the interested reader is referred to Lise Manniche's Sacred Luxuries: Fragrance, Aromatherapy, and Cosmetics in Ancient Egypt (Cornell University Press, 1999), 43-45. During the pharaonic era myrrh oil had been the original Madjet oil.

THE TWENTY-SEVENTH CEREMONY
Spell for Placing Myrrh on the Fire

The priest places myrrh onto the lighted censer. Lifting the censer toward the god's image, the following shall be said:

"O Amun-Ra, come to this your bread. Come to this your bread which I give to you. All life is with you, all stability is with you, all health is with you, all joy is with you."[39]

THE TWENTY-EIGHTH CEREMONY
Spell for Bringing the God to His Meal
[From three Utterances in the Ritual of Amenophis I.]

Slowly elevating and then lowering the food offerings four times in succession, including the wine or beer offering, the priest says the following:

"Come, O Amun-Ra. Come to your body. Come at this invitation of you. Come to me, your servant. Bring your *Ba*, your *heka* [magic power], and your honor to these offerings of food. Enter into this your sanctuary, to this your food offering. I have filled for you your dwelling with all good things. Djehuty propitiates you with the Eye of Heru, the White One with which your face is illuminated, offerings of things good and pure. I am Djehuty who propitiates the *Netjeru*, and who puts things in their proper places.[40]

"Come to this your banquet in this sanctuary. Come to this city even as you came to Iunu [Heliopolis], even to this sanctuary for it is truly your sanctuary. Take these offerings which I give to you, and give to me all life with you, all stability with you,

all wealth with you, all joy with you, all health with you. Grant me many years that I may partake of you, of your *Ba*, and of your *sekhem* [power], in the name of Atum who is at the head of his Ennead. I give these offerings to you that I may have power throughout eternity. . .[41]

"Come to this bread that is warm, and to this [beer or wine]. Be here and stay honored, be and stay endowed with *Ba*, be and stay powerful, be and attend to my words. Smite the enemies with your staff; govern with your disk. Rise up, O Amun-Ra. Rise up and enter in to this, your bread and to these, your divine offerings in your place and in your temple, unwavering for ever."[42]

The priest places the offerings on the altar table. If the offerings include meat, as the platter is elevated the following shall be said:

"The Eye of Heru is refreshed for him. The testicles of Sutekh [Set] are refreshed for him. As Heru is content with his two Eyes, as Sutekh is content with his two Testicles, so Amun-Ra is content with these choice meats, as a gift to you. May I be given life, stability, and good fortune, like Ra, forever!"[43]

Any meat offered is placed together with the other foods on the altar table.

PRAYER OF PRAISE

Raising his two hands in the *Dua*/adoration position, the priest recites the following:

"Hail, one who makes himself into millions
whose length and breadth are limitless,
power in readiness, who gave birth to himself,
uraeus with great flame,
great of *heka*-power [magic] with secret form,
secret *Ba*, to whom reverence is shown.

39

King, Amun-Ra, (life, prosperity, health!)
who came into being himself,
Akhty, Heru of the east,
the Rising One whose radiance illuminates
the light that is more luminous than the *Netjeru*.

You have hidden yourself as Amun the great;
you have withdrawn in your transformation as the sun disk,
Tatenen, who raises himself above the *Netjeru*.
The Ancient One forever young, travelling through eternity,
Amun, who remains in possession of all things.
This god has established the earth by his providence."[44]

II

"Hail, Amun-Ra!
Every face says, 'We belong to you,'
strong and weak alike;
rich and poor from one mouth,
all things equally.
Your loveliness fills their hearts,
no body is devoid of your beauty.
Do not the widows say, 'You are our husband,'
while others say, 'Our father and our mother'?
The rich boast of your beauty,
the poor turn their faces to you.
Prisoners turn to you,
the sick call upon you.
Your name is an amulet for the lonely,
prosperity and health for those on the water,
a saviour from the crocodile.
To think of whom is good in times of distress,
who rescues from the mouth of the hot-blooded.
Everyone turns to you to implore you,
your ears are open to hear them and fulfil their wishes.
You are our Ptah, who loves his handiwork,
our shepherd, who loves his flock.

His reward is a 'beautiful burial'
for a heart that is satisfied with Ma'at."[45]

The priest extends his hands, palms downward, over the offerings. As he does so, the following shall be said:

"Hail to you, O Atum! Hail to you, O Khepri! Place your arms around me and cause my *Ka* to flourish for eternity. Even as flourishes the name of Heru, flourishing eternally. Even as flourishes the name of Sutekh, flourishing eternally. Even as flourishes your name, O Amun-Ra, together with your Ennead, flourishing eternally.

"I give these choice offerings to you and to the *Netjeru* of this, your temple. These *Netjeru* shall be endowed with *Ba*; they shall have honor, they shall be alert, they shall have power. To them shall be given every good thing that I give to you, my father, O Amun-Ra, together with your Ennead, flourishing eternally!"[46]

THE TWENTY-NINETH CEREMONY
Chapter of Scattering the Sand*

* *"By virtue of its early appearance from the receding flood waters [of the Nile], sand was intimately associated with the creation of the Egyptian cosmos, and hence with all creative acts. As a purifying substance, sand is thus used in the foundations (and foundation deposits) of temples and sanctuaries, is ritually strewn during processions of the gods and private magical rites, is offered to deities, and even serves in the composition of divine figures and as a platform for magical images . . . ." Robert Ritner,* The Mechanics of Ancient Egyptian Magical Practice, *155-56.*

The image of the god is now returned to its place in the *Kar*-shrine. The double doors of the shrine are closed. The priest picks up fresh sand and scatters it on the ground before the closed *Kar*-shrine. The following shall be said:

"Heru, you have found your Eye. Amun-Ra, lord of *Ipet Sut* [meaning "The Most Select of Places," called Karnak today], **you have found your Eye. You have removed it, you have removed it.**

You have sprinkled with sand from your hand the Eye of Heru which makes the gift of life, stability, strength, and health as the sun, forever!"[47]

THE THIRTIETH CEREMONY
Chapter of the *Seman* Fragrance

The priest circles the statue four times with a bowl of natron identified as the *seman* fragrance. With each circumambulation he sprinkles natron in his path. The following shall be said:

"The fragrance, the fragrance opens your mouth! You taste its taste, O leader of the Divine Pavilion. O Amun-Ra, lord of Ipet Sut [Karnak], I present to you the Eye of Heru. You have tasted the outpouring of Heru [which is] the *seman*, the outpouring of Sutekh [which is] the *seman*. It has established the heart of Heru and of Sutekh [which is] the *seman*. Your purification is the purification of the *Netjeru*, the servants of Heru. Pure, pure is Amun-Ra, lord of Ipet Sut!"[48]

* Notice that the text above refers to the "heart" of Heru and Sutekh, a single heart, showing that now, at the conclusion of the ritual, Heru and Sutekh are united, reconciled, and at peace. The ancient Egyptians artistically represented this as a being with a single body having the two heads of these gods, the falcon and Set head. They referred to this as "Antywey." This profound belief in the reconciliation of these two opposing forces showed itself in the priestly title "shtp ntrwy" ("who reconciles the two gods") and in the ceremonial name for the capital of the 10th nome of Upper Egypt, "hwt shtp," (house of reconciliation). This also extended to a temple dedicated to Heru-Sutekh. For further information see Herman te Velde's important work, Seth, God of Confusion, *69-72.*

THE THIRTY-FIRST CEREMONY
Spell for Extinguishing the Candle or Oil Lamp

The priest, using a candle snuffer, extinguishes the flame. The following shall be said:

"This is the Eye of Heru by which you have become great, by which you live, and by which you have power, O Amun-Ra. This is the Eye of Heru which you consume and through which you enchant your body. The *Wedjat* Eye now enters into the West, into *Manu*, but it shall return. Truly, the Eye of Heru returns in peace!"[49]

THE THIRTY-SECOND CEREMONY
Spell for "Removing the Foot"

In sweeping the floor the priest/ess obliterates his/her own footprints and thus returns the temple room to its pristine condition. A second purpose of the act is to "sweep" the area free from any negative influences that might have accompanied the participants. The Liturgist, impersonating Djehuty, Lord of Heka-Magic, "whose words are truly effective," establishes and affirms the continued pristine purity of the Temple Chamber.

Then with the broom the priest ritually sweeps the area beginning at the altar as he and any assistants, all bowing, back out of the Temple Chamber. Upon leaving the ritual area the broom is set aside, all bow and the following shall be said:

"The distress that causes confusion has been driven away, and all the *Netjeru* are in harmony. I have given Heru his Eye, I have placed the *Wedjat* Eye in the correct position. I have given Sutekh his testicles, so that the two Lords are content through the work of my hands."[50]

"I know the sky, I know the earth. I know Heru, I know Sutekh. Heru is appeased with His eyes, Sutekh is appeased with His testicles. I am Djehuty, who reconciles the *Netjeru*, who makes offerings in their correct form."[51]

CONCLUDING UTTERANCE

The Utterance accompanying this action of closing the doors of the Temple Chamber is a declaration that the lord of sacred ritual, Djehuty, has in fact restored the Balance—he has filled the Eye of Heru and restored the Testicles of Sutekh. As the previous Utterance had just proclaimed, "all the Netjeru are in harmony." The whole intent and purpose of the divine service has been to restore the Balance. Every action in the ritual is designed to renew and restore and maintain the equilibrium of human and divine life.

The broom is set aside. Facing the doors to the Temple Chamber, all bow, touching the palms of their hands to their knees. As the priest closes the double doors of the Temple Chamber, the following shall be said:

"Djehuty has come. He has filled the Eye of Heru; He has restored the testicles of Sutekh. No evil shall enter this temple. Ptah has closed the door, Djehuty has set it fast. The door is closed, the door is set fast with the bolt."[52]

Once again all bow, touching the palms of their hands to their knees. The priest and assistants withdraw.

One final ceremonial act remains: the removal of the food offerings from before the Naos housing Amun-Ra, followed immediately by their reversion for distribution and consumption by the servants of the god.

THE REVERSION OF OFFERINGS

One priest and as many assistants as necessary enter the Temple Chamber a final time. While he and any assistants lift up the offerings before the sacred image, the priest shall say:

"O Amun-Ra, your enemy withdraws for you.* Heru has turned himself to his Eye in its name of 'Reversion-of-Offerings.' I am Djehuty. I come to perform this rite for Amun-Ra, king of the *Netjeru*. These, your divine offerings revert, they revert to your servants for life, for stability, for health and for joy! O that the Eye of Heru may flourish for you eternally!"[53]

Everyone shall withdraw, carrying away all food offerings.

*When a meat offering is removed, the Liturgist exclaims, "O (name of the Netjer), your enemy withdraws for you." Meat offerings bore a dual meaning—

as a food offering and also as a symbol of the defeated enemy. In Egypt we find no ritual focused on the sacrificial slaughter of animals. In fact, animals were not killed anywhere near the Netjer's altar. Unlike Israelite practice, there is no animal holocaust or burnt offering. Meat was offered solely as an item of the divine banquet. But because of the necessary slaying of the animal and the shedding of its blood, there is associated with every meat offering a connection with the slaying and defeat of the cosmic enemies, Apep and his brood.

APPENDIX A

ITEMS NEEDED FOR
THE MORNING RITUAL

The following articles should be assembled for the foregoing rite.

Items for use in front of the closed doors of the Temple Chamber:

- an unlighted candle or oil lamp
- censer with incense cup (with a lighted charcoal briquette)
- frankincense*

Items needed within the Temple Chamber, listed in order of their use:

- the *Ib* or heart symbol (The hieroglyph for "heart" resembles a vase with handles on each side, flat on top, and rounded sides. A suitable model can be crafted with clay and then gilded.)
- either a small mound of clean sand or a white linen cloth on which the god's image is to be placed after it is removed from the *Kar*-shrine [known as the "Naos" in Greek]
- the Ma'at symbol (a statue of the goddess, or an ostrich feather, real or fabricated)
- honey (for any feast of Amun-Ra)
- 4 white *Nemset* vases filled with fresh water
- 4 red *Teshert* vases filled with fresh water
- bowl of Natron**
- unguent (made by combining an odorless base such as jojoba or almond oil with a pure essential oil. A high quality oil of frankincense or myrrh would be appropriate.)***
- the god's apparel: two white linen cloths or ribbons; one green linen cloth or ribbon; a red linen cloth or ribbon

- linen mantle (the *Atma* bandlet)—blue or white
- myrrh incense
- a variety of food offerings (solid as well as liquid; for example, bread, fruit, cooked meats, fresh produce, together with wine, beer and water)
- bowl of sand
- *seman* natron—regular natron made fragrant with a few drops of essential oil
- candle snuffer
- ritual broom

* When selecting an incense, it is important to avoid the commonly available incense sticks made in India. They typically contain materials such as cow dung which make them unacceptable and impure for worshipping the *Netjeru*. Other incenses may contain urea, a compound of urine, and thus ritually impure. Many stores that stock herbs and spices in bulk also carry pure frankincense, myrrh, and other suitable incenses.

** Natron is a naturally occurring salt found in Egypt. It was used for purification rites. For information on making your own Natron, please see the notation in the Twentieth Ceremony in this chapter or refer to Kerry Wisner's *Eye of the Sun: The Sacred Legacy of Ancient Egypt* (Nashua, New Hampshire: Hwt-Hrw Publications, 2000).

*** For an informative treatment on the actual recipes used for a variety of sacred unguents, the reader is referred to Lise Manniche's *Sacred Luxuries: Fragrance, Aromatherapy, and Cosmetics in Ancient Egypt* (Ithaca, New York: Cornell University Press, 1999). Frankincense was one of the ingredients in six of the nine sacred unguents whose composition is recorded in the temple of Heru at Edfu (see Manniche, 108). Myrrh, according to Manniche, was in fact the important *Madjet* unguent applied by the priest to the sacred image throughout pharaonic times. Later, during the era of the Greek Ptolemies, *Madjet* became instead a composite preparation [see Manniche, 43 and 81]. Both frankincense and myrrh, therefore, played important roles in the temple rituals of Egypt.

Contemporary worshippers using these fragrances to honor the gods and goddesses can be confident that they are continuing within the spirit of the ancient tradition. The present state of knowledge does not allow us to identify all the botanical terms appearing in the recipes. If that day arrives, some future Kemetic priest or priestess may be able to duplicate or more closely approximate the sacred unguents once used throughout ancient Egypt.

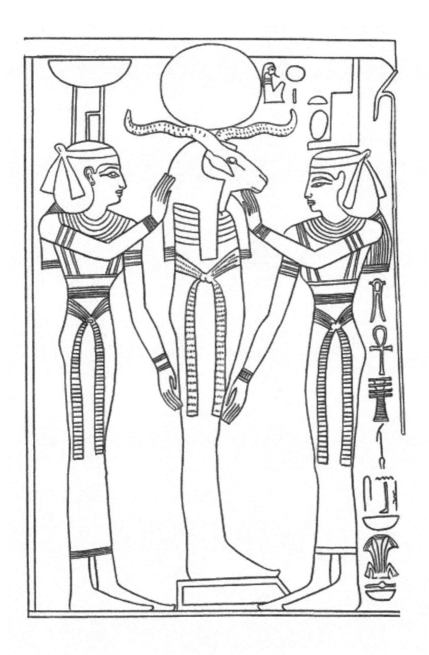

*The Mystical Union of Ra with Ausir, flanked by Nebet Het
(Nephthys) and Aset (Isis)*
*Drawing Based on a Relief from the Tomb of Nefertari,
wife of Ramses II*

CHAPTER TWO

The Nighttime Ritual of the Mystical Union of Ra with Ausir

Introduction

This is the second installment in the series *Eternal Egypt: Ancient Rituals for the Modern World*. The first chapter provides the Morning Ritual in the Temple of Amun-Ra. Like its predecessor, this second section presents ancient texts for contemporary use. Specifically the objective is to give the Kemetic Reconstructionist community authentic and workable texts for celebrating a nighttime ritual honoring Ra in his nightly journey and transformations through the *Duat* (netherworld).

In conducting this rite we bear witness to our own ultimate destiny as *akhu*, that is, radiant spirits in the realm of the West. Second, we witness to the indissoluble bond between ourselves and our beloved dead, who live on in reality as well as in our memories and hearts. Third, we honor the creator Ra as the fountain of life and the source of the renewal of life. And last, as expressed in the magical texts following the seventy-five acclamations (the latter are referred to as the Great Litany), we identify ourselves with Ra, the Lord of Life. We identify ourselves with the netherworld forms of Ra, even as His "second Self." I am reminded of spouses and lovers who refer to each other as their "other half." The term "second Self" conveys a similar sense of intimate union with the beloved.

In accordance with ancient practice those participating in this or any rite should first purify themselves with water and natron, according to the usual manner (see Kerry Wisner's *Eye of the Sun*, 17 ff.). This honors the divine beings whom we then approach in a state of physical cleanliness just as we would for any important meeting with others. Such ritual cleansing can help us begin focussing on the upcoming encounter with deity.

Since this is a nocturnal rite, it should be conducted after sunset. In as much as the repetitive nature of the acclamations is very conducive to creating in participants a semi-trancelike state, lighting should be minimal. The ritual itself calls for rekindling a single lamp or candle. To facilitate reading, of course, you will want to provide some additional lighting for each participant.

A final note: This ritual is not about running a race. The pace of recitation needs to be slow and measured. Let your body's quiet natural rhythm of breathing be your guide. Read slowly and reflectively so the great priestly wisdom of Egypt can reveal to you the deep meaning behind your words. Don't worry if some of the images appear unusual or even strange. As we grow by means of regular reading about ancient Egyptian spirituality, the words of the Litany will begin to reveal their deep meaning. Our spiritual eyes will adjust, as it were, to the hidden and veiled realities contained in this profoundly mystical text.

San Francisco, 7 August 2003,
Rising of Sopdet,
Festival of the Opening of the Year
RICHARD J. REIDY

Commentary
on The Nighttime Ritual
in Honor of the Mystical Union
of RA with AUSIR

"Merely by listening to a myth, man forgets his profane condition, his 'historical situation,' as it is nowadays called. . . . For the Australian as well as the Chinese, the Hindu, and the European peasant, myths are true, because they are sacred—they speak of sacred beings and events. Consequently, in narrating or listening to a myth, one resumes contact with the sacred and with reality and in so doing transcends the profane condition, the historical situation." Mircea Eliade,"Time and Eternity in Indian Thought," in Man and Time, *Henry Corbin, editor, (Princeton University Press, 1949), 174.*

The text known as the "Litany of Ra" originally bore the more descriptive title of the "Book of the Adoration of Ra in the West and of the Adoration of the One-Joined-Together-in-the-West" (i.e., Ra united with Osiris). In his scholarly work *The Cult of Ra,* Stephen Quirke states: "Among the finest of Egyptian religious compositions, the Litany of Ra provides perhaps the most explicit demonstration of the unity of creation in its creator."[54]

The Litany of Ra consists first in a series of seventy-five recitational acclamations of the great creator-*Netjer* Ra as he progresses through his nighttime journey in the *Duat* (netherworld), the realm of Ausir (the Egyptian name for Osiris). It is a stately, poetic and profound vision of the mystical union that recurs nightly between the two great *Netjeru* who rule the polarities of the existent, that is, daylight and darkness, life and death. Each of the seventy-five acclamations invokes a specific form (*ir,* plural *iru*) or manifestation (*kheper,* plural *kheperu*) of Ra in creation, with creation including the netherworld as well as the visible world. This is Ra as "Lord to the Limit," (i.e., lord to the very limit of all that exists). Ra is united with Ausir; life enters the realm of the dead and brings life to its inhabitants.

Following the seventy-five acclamations there are a number of magical formulations equating the reciter with those in the following of Ra and, finally, with Ra Himself. This is classic ancient Egyptian magic–to identify oneself with a god or goddess. The present volume includes an important recapitulation text immediately following the Great Litany. Subsequent and very lengthy texts preserved in the tombs are appropriate for the blessed dead, and so are omitted in this volume. I have edited these concluding magical formulations for ritual recitation, substituting the appropriate first-person pronouns (I, me, my) to replace the name of the tomb's deceased occupant. Readers interested in reviewing a complete English translation of the Great Litany as well as all the accompanying texts are referred to Alexandre Piankoff's *The Litany of Re*, Bollingen Series 40/4 (New York, 1964).

By implication, the Litany of Ra is a song of hope–death is not destruction; what once lived shall most assuredly have life again. The Lord of Life, the creator god, does not abandon his creation to the tomb. Instead he himself enters the realm of the dead–called variously "the Silent Region," "the Secret Region," "the Mysterious Caverns"–and, as the fifty-fifth acclamation proclaims, he "unites himself to the Beautiful West, at whom those of the Netherworld rejoice when seeing him." The "uniting" of himself with death is revealed as more than a figure of speech. It is not like a living person's visit to a cemetery. The ancient Egyptians saw it as a true mystical union, and throughout the seventy-five acclamations and the accompanying recitations which follow them, they attempted to plumb the depths of that union of life with death. Life cannot be defeated. Life will not be permanently separated from those who once lived. All die, both gods (*Netjeru*) and humans. But the Lord of Life himself travels to the limits of all that exists, even to the depths of death, and it is he "for whom the awakened ones arise" (acclamation 67).

It is no wonder that such a message of hope found receptive hearts among the ancient Egyptians. Copies of the Litany of Ra are preserved in a number of papyrii of the nobility as well as on the walls of temples built at Abydos by Sety I and Ramesses II, an edifice constructed by Taharqa at Karnak, and a chapel built by Hakoris, also at Karnak. Of special importance are examples of the Litany in the tombs of numerous pharaohs including Sety I, Thutmosis III, Ramesses II, Merenptah, Amenmes, Siptah, Sety II, Ramesses III, Ramesses IV, and Ramesses IX.[55]

It is central to the ancient Egyptian understanding of the nightly journey of Ra into the *Duat* that Ra himself does not die. He enters the realm of the dead. He revivifies it. He unites mystically with Ausir (Osiris) in a genuine and profound union while always remaining the Lord of Life, the lord who brings life because he is the font of life. Like the caterpillar in its cocoon, appearing dead, but in reality undergoing a transformation, Ra enters the Silent Region, bringing life to its inhabitants and renewing his own being, to emerge at dawn as the Child-in-the-Lotus, having begun his descent the previous sunset as the aged Ra-Atum, shown bent over and leaning on a staff. But Ra-Atum had not died. As one evening hymn used in the daily cult attests:

Hail Ra, as you set in life, when you have merged with the horizon of the sky. You have appeared on the western side as Atum who is in the dusk, arrived in your might, without flinching. You have taken sovereignty over the heavens as Ra.[56]

The statement *"Arrived in your might, without flinching"* clearly contradicts any notion that Ra somehow dies. His entry is at all times triumphant and life-giving. Unlike Ausir, Ra is not pictured "fallen on his side," that is, lying prostrate in death. He is depicted either sitting or standing. He lives even in the midst of death.

In the majority of the seventy-five acclamations the verb forms are boldly active: Ra makes transformations of himself; he protects; he gives light; he gives air to the *Bas*; he decrees; he gives orders; he punishes the evildoers; he opens the roads in the *Duat* [the Underworld or Afterlife Realm]; he repulses his enemies; he judges the very *Netjeru*. This does not sound like a god who has died!

And yet Ra clearly is shown entering the realm of the dead. And he unites with the lord of the dead. This union of Ra with Ausir, as well as in each of the seventy-five transformations, is graphically depicted with individual drawings of seventy-five figures intended to illustrate the subject of each acclamation. The vast majority of these figures are mummiform, with differences indicated in a figure's head or even simply limited to a change in its name. These figures were not an afterthought. The directions for reciting the Litany of Ra stipulate that the figures are to be traced on the ground. Of course, in the tombs preserving the text of the Litany these figures have been painted on the walls, thus magically acquiring an enduring and eternal existence.

The fact that the forms are predominantly mummiform highlights the centrality of belief that Ra does indeed effect transformations of himself into a multiplicity of forms. The use of the mummiform does not so much refer to lifeless corpses as it does to the hidden transformations taking place in the realm of the dead. Recall that *Netjeru* such as Ptah, Min and Khonsu appear mummiform as well. They are not regarded as dead or as lords of the dead. The mummiform, then, is here a *visual metaphor* for profound and recurring transformation. Cocooned in mummy-wrappings, Ra is like a chrysalis, potent with life and preparing to emerge rejuvenated and restored. Ra, the source of life, enters the *Duat*, descends into the depths, the "Mysterious Region," and there embraces Ausir, effecting a temporary "merging of the two opposites who become a Twin Soul."[57] Truly this is a mystical union that strains our ability to take in its full importance.

As Alexandre Piankoff points out in his important study of the Litany, "The first ten Invocations apply to Re in his two aspects, the solar and the Osirian ... Invocations 1, 3, 5, 7, and 9 are addressed to the Osirian forms."[58] Numbers 2, 4, 6, 8, and 10 refer to solar elements. It is in the very first acclamation that we encounter the name of "Deba-of-the-One-Joined-Together" (i.e., Ra united to Ausir). The drawing which accompanies this name is of a mummiform Ausir complete with his hallmark Upper Egyptian crown. Certainly this shows Ausir imbued with the *Ba* or soul of Ra. This is a very dynamic god, passing from life through death and back to life again. How different from the classical Greek philosopher's uninspiring conception of a static, unchanging "First Cause," ultimately uninvolved and untouched by his own creation. The ancient Egyptians on the other hand saw the creator Ra as intimately and continuously involved in what he has made–a dynamic vision of a creator who is both imminent in his creation and in the cyclic processes of creation. Radiating life, Ra's very presence reawakens the blessed dead.

After the first ten acclamations, alternately focusing on Ra and then on the united Ra-Ausir, the next ten acclamations proceed to glorify Ra as he manifests himself in those *Netjeru* reflecting successive stages of creation. These begin with Atum (the All), and Khepri (the Becoming One), and go on to Shu and Tefnut, Geb and Nut, Aset (Isis), and Nebet Het (Nephthys), culminating in Heru (Horus). In each case the acclamation concludes with the statement, "You are the body of . . ." followed by the name of the *Netjer* or *Netjeret*. We would be mistaken to read into this an underlying monotheism in which the *Netjeru* are merely aspects of the one Ra. Rather, as Stephen Quirke explains, "all creation derives from the one creator, and, in a certain sense, remains a part of that divine being, even if the individual elements take on lives of their own."[59]

The remaining fifty-five acclamations present snapshots as it were, of "forms" or "transformations" of Ra moving in the cycle of creation. The text does not proceed as would a systematic and sequential description of an event in time. Rather we are in a mythic place; we enter into a mystical state where images come and go more in a dreamlike fashion than in a linear, temporal one. In a certain sense we are outside the confining parameters of a strictly logic-bound presentation. The images proceed not in an illogical but rather in a supralogical manner. The central point of these acclamations is that they reveal Ra in a multiplicity of his "forms." This is not simply an Eastern style of verbose exuberance. For as Erik Hornung explains in *Conceptions of God in Ancient Egypt,* "Everywhere and at all periods the gods thrive on an abundance that tolerates no dogmatic restriction. The multiplicity of names, of manifestations, and of possible ways of encountering these deities is an outward sign of this abundance."[60] Elsewhere the noted Egyptologist expands on this concept, "These are not mere glorifying phrases for the god who is being worshiped; behind every name and every epithet there is a reality of myth or cult, which is often incorporated more directly into the invocations by means of wordplay."[61] In many cases modern research has yet to uncover the full significance behind certain epithets. But over time we are progressively recovering the mythic depths beneath many an ancient text.

In order to derive a clearer understanding of what the ancient Egyptians had in mind Alexandre Piankoff would have us look at four key words that regularly reappear in the Litany: 1) *Ba*—the visible manifestation of a deity; 2) *iru*—the "forms" of this divine manifestation; 3) *kheperu*—the stages through which the *Ba* passes in its cyclical "transformations" from life to death and back to life again; 4) *h3t* [pronounced "hot"] or "body," what Piankoff calls "a kind of divine personality, a hypostasis which the supreme divinity may assume at a certain moment."[62]

And so as most of the acclamations end with the statement "truly you are the body of . . ," it helps to recall the common expression heard in describing a child: "He/she is the *spitting image* of his/her mother or father." That physical resemblance, of course, reflects the underlying genetic inheritance from the parent. The ancient writers saw the reflection of Ra in his own divine offspring. Just as we distinguish a child as a separate being from its parent, so the ancient Egyptians distinguish each *Netjer* as a unique individual, separate from his or her divine originator, but carrying a divine imprint, as it were, attesting to its heritage.

Returning now to that central image of Ra's union with Ausir, Erik Hornung points out, "A well-known relief in the tomb of Nofretiri [wife of Ramses II] . . . shows a ram-headed mummy between Isis and Nephthys captioned 'This is Re when he has come to rest *(htp)* in Osiris' and 'This is Osiris when he comes to rest in Re.'"[63] A variant of this formula appears in Theban Tomb 290 in which "the text is followed by the adverb "daily," thus showing how it should be understood: Re enters into Osiris and Osiris enters into Re daily, and the combination is dissolved again daily."[64]

For readers familiar with ancient Egyptian liturgical forms, it will come as no surprise that the Litany of Ra celebrates mythic events as they recur daily in the unfolding cycle of existence, from birth through old age and then, having passed through the region of the dead, Ra emerges reborn and rejuvenated. Through ritual this divine cycle is commemorated daily—here, nightly—and through verbal recitations, coupled with specific ritual acts (here involving pictoral drawings of Ra's *kheperu* or "manifestations"), humans participate in the ongoing actions of the gods and goddesses.

Instructions included in copies of the Litany direct that "when this Book is being recited, these figures should be done in ... color on the ground, at night. This is the victory of Ra over his enemies in the West. It is profitable for a man upon earth; it is profitable for him after his burial."[65] A rubric appearing later in the text of the Litany gives the following direction: "This spell is to be recited to every god ... these being depicted ... while two portions [offerings] are to be placed on them as a divine action."[66] Another rubric states: "This book is to be read every day when Ra goes to rest in the West, correct a million times."[67]

These rubrics reveal a number of important points: 1) Although extant copies appear in a funerary context, the Litany is for the use of the living as well as the dead. 2) The Litany or some portion of it may have been in regular use in the ordinary cult of certain temples, particularly solar temples. In some cases it may have been recited regularly and perhaps even daily. 3) The cultic act of food offerings are to accompany the recitation. 4) Recitation of the Litany is specifically a nocturnal rite.

With the foregoing commentary as background, we come to the purpose of this book, namely, the ritual performance of the Litany in the modern era. Like so many rituals from ancient Egypt, we may possess the texts that were recited but we lack exact and complete step-by-step instructions for enacting the rite. For the student of ancient religions or even modern creeds this should come as no surprise. Ceremonial texts seldom contain more than general rubrics or instructions to guide the priest or ritualist. A significant proportion of "how-to" information was–and continues to be—transmitted by word of mouth. Seminarians and clergy-candidates, as well as members of esoteric orders, typically receive detailed *verbal* instruction in ritual from their seniors.

In terms of reviving the rites of ancient Egypt we are fortunate to have important and substantial texts preserved on the walls of both temples and tombs as well as on scrolls of papyrus. Such texts often are accompanied by graphic depictions called "vignettes" that illustrate in picture form one or another ritual action, for example, offering incense, presenting food offerings, body posture and gestures for a whole host of ritual activities. We also know that Egyptian rituals contained such standard opening and closing ceremonies as various purificatory lustrations or sprinklings with water, presentation of pellets of natron, censings, an initial lighting and a final extinguishing of a lamp or candle. As Kemetic Reconstructionists we can with some confidence, like Ra, revive and rejuvenate the ancient rites of Egypt. We can do this without introducing customs or practices from other religious traditions. In fact, as Kemetic Reconstructionists, that is our goal. This is not in any way whatsoever to criticize other forms of worship. It is, though, our attempt to be faithful to a profound and rich heritage, one which is complete and integral in itself.

Postscript

In an effort to provide the reader with the tools needed for celebrating this rite, illustrations of the seventy-five forms of Ra are included in Appendix A. Photocopies of these pages can be used effectively in ritual in place of actually drawing the figures, much as permanent tomb paintings or papyrus scrolls with these or similar images were originally created by the ancient Egyptians. As with any object for use in sacred rites, handle and store them with special care. The series of drawings is small enough to be convenient for placing on a small table before the *Kar*-shrine. The "double portion" of offerings called for in the rubrics can also be placed on the same or on an adjacent table.

This set of illustrations is based on wall paintings discovered in the tomb of the great pharaoh Seti I. The originals line the left and right sides of an interior corridor. By numbering each drawing a 19th century publisher has attempted to identify each figure with its corresponding acclamation. (In this case only seventy-four figures appear. The exact number could vary, depending on space and precision by the ancient copyist.) The interested student can refer to G. Lefébure's *Les Hypogées Royaux de Thèbes* (Paris, 1886, pt. i., pl. 15 ff), as well as to E. A.Wallis Budge's *The Gods of the Egyptians* (London, 1904, vol. 2, 317-320).

This book is intended primarily as a working text for conducting ritual. It is not meant to serve as an exhaustive analysis or scholarly commentary. The preceding remarks are provided as an overview and guide for both the reader and ritualist. The subject of the Litany of Ra is a deeply mystical one, not easily conveyed in words or in the familiar categories of logical discourse with which we normally grapple when trying to understand difficult phenomena or concepts. But we can be confident that, with practice, the unfamiliar can become familiar and that which is veiled can eventually be seen with clarity. Mystical truths, no doubt among the most important of all truths, can be experienced in these ancient rites of divine rebirth.

As you celebrate this important ritual may you, like Ra, be renewed, restored, and rejuvenated both in this world and in the next!

The Nighttime Ritual
of the Mystical Union of Ra with Ausir

After the sun has set those gathered for this rite shall begin by entering the Temple Chamber, each holding a lighted taper or oil lamp.

THE FIRST CEREMONY
Spell for Entering the Sanctuary

The priest and all attendants kneel in adoration before the closed *Kar*-shrine housing the statue of the principal *Netjer* or *Netjeret* (god or goddess). An attendant shall place the threefold image of Ra on the empty table before the shrine. The following shall be said:

"Adoring Amun-Ra, king of the *Netjeru*. Hail to you, who came into being on the First Occasion. I have come to you that I may adore your beauty, for I know your beneficence towards me."[68]

"There wait for you the Great Ones of the sky, who have come from heaven, who descend from the horizon. You enter into the hall as Ausir, having appeared as Lord of All."[69]

"Hail to you, master of endless repetition, Atum, great one of endless duration. You have come in peace. You have reached land and joined the arms of Manu [the western mountain]. **Your Majesty has received venerableness, moored at your place of yesterday.**

"The arms of your mother [Nut] **protect you, Sutekh** [Set] **slays your enemies. The western *Bas* [spirits] tow you on every path in the Holy Land** [necropolis/underworld] **so that you may illuminate the face of those in the *Duat*, and resurrect those who are prostrate. May you give me transfiguration in your retinue to take the tow rope of the *Mesketet* boat** [the evening boat] **and the landing rope of the *Mandjet* boat** [the morning boat].

"I have come to you with my arms full of Ma'at, Ma'at spread out on my fingers, I have rowed the 'Majesty-of-the-Thousand-Feet.' I have performed the transfiguration in the tent daily, every day."[70]

THE SECOND CEREMONY
Spell for renewing the candle of every day

Rising to his feet, the priest lights a single candle or oil lamp which he places in front of the closed doors of the *Kar*-shrine. As he does so the following shall be said.

"The candle has come to your *Ka*, O Amun-Ra, lord of Iunu [Heliopolis]. There has come one who proclaims night after day. The second self of Ra has come; it has appeared gloriously in this sanctuary. I have caused it to come. I have brought it, even the Eye of Heru, arisen upon your forehead, hale upon your brow.

"To your *Ka*, O Amun-Ra, lord of the thrones of the Two Lands, O Amun-Ra, lord of Iunu! The Eye of Heru is your protection, she spreads her protection over you, and she overthrows your enemies. Pure, pure is this beautiful one! She has come, the Eye of Heru, the beautiful one, the Proclaimer, a candle of new fat and of cloth of the launderers, a candle for Amun-Ra, lord of the thrones of the Two Lands, for Amun-Ra, lord of Iunu, for Amun-Ra, Bull of his Mother, who is upon His Great Seat, for Hwt-Hrw in the midst of Dendera, for Montu, for Atum, for Shu, for Tefnut, for Geb, for Nut, for Ausir, for Aset, for Sutekh, for Nebet-Het, for Heru, for Sekhmet and for Bastet, for the great bark 'Displayer-of-his-Beauty,' Amun-Ra, lord of the thrones of the Two Lands, and Amun-Ra, lord of Iunu, and for the *Netjeru* and *Netjerut* who are in Ipet-sut [the temple of Ra in Heliopolis], for the *Ka* of every king and every queen of Upper and Lower Egypt who have made monuments for Amun-Ra, lord of the thrones of the Two Lands, and for Amun-Ra, lord of this land."[71]

THE THIRD CEREMONY
Spell for a Libation (Offering of Water)

Taking a vase of fresh water, the priest pours it into a bowl or receptacle positioned in front of the closed *Kar*-shrine. The following shall be said:

"O Amun-Ra, take to yourself this your libation which is in this land, which produces all living things. Everything, indeed, comes forth from it, upon which you live, upon which you exist."[72]

THE FOURTH CEREMONY
The Offering of Incense

The priest places grains of khyphi, the incense for the evening rite, on the censer. Lifting and lowering the smoking censer with slow, repetitive movements before the *Kar*-shrine, the priest shall say the following:

"The incense comes, the perfume of the *Netjer* comes towards you. The perfume of the Eye of Heru comes towards you, the perfume of Nekhbet coming forth from Nekheb [El-Kab]. It washes you. It adorns you."[73]

THE FIFTH CEREMONY
Spell for Renewing the Divine Offerings

The priest or his/her assistant presents a tray on which is arrayed a variety of food and drink offerings. Slowly elevating and lowering the offering tray four times (see page 331 in Gardiner regarding this ritual action), the priest shall say the following:

"Hail to you, O Atum! Hail to you, O Khepri! You ascend on high by the High Stairway, you shine forth on the pyramidion [benben] in the House of the Benben in Iunu. You spit forth as Shu and Tefnut. You place your arms around me and you cause that my *Ka* may be flourishing for eternity.

"IT FLOURISHES, IT FLOURISHES, the name of Atum, the lord-of-the-Two-Lands of Iunu, even as flourishes the divine offerings given by me to my father Amun-Ra, lord of Iunu, together with his Ennead, flourishing eternally;
EVEN AS FLOURISHES the name of Shu, flourishing forever;
EVEN AS FLOURISHES the name of Tefnut, flourishing forever;
EVEN AS FLOURISHES the name of Geb, flourishing forever;
EVEN AS FLOURISHES the name of Nut, flourishing forever;
EVEN AS FLOURISHES the name of Ausir, flourishing forever;
EVEN AS FLOURISHES the name of Aset, flourishing forever;
EVEN AS FLOURISHES the name of Heru, flourishing forever;
EVEN AS FLOURISHES the name of Sutekh, flourishing forever;
EVEN AS FLOURISHES the name of Nebet Het, flourishing forever;
EVEN AS FLOURISHES the name of Djehuty, flourishing forever.

"'AN OFFERING WHICH THE KING GIVES' to Geb, choice offerings for these *Netjeru*. They shall be endowed with *Ba*, they shall have honor, they shall be alert, they shall have power, to them shall be given bread and beer, incense and ointment, and every good thing that I give to my father Amun-Ra, together with his Ennead, flourishing eternally."[74]

THE SIXTH CEREMONY
Words of the "Song of the Two Regions"
to be recited in the evening

All present sing or recite the following:

FIRST STANZA. "Amun unites himself to the horizon of heaven, having appeared gloriously on the western side. Atum who is in the eventide has come in his power; there are none disaffected towards him. He has assumed rulership of the sky as Ra; he has illumined the earth as Amun. His heart becomes joyful, for he has dispersed the gloom and the rain-storm, having descended from the body of his mother Nut, his father Nun bows before him; and the *Netjeru* make jubilation to him. The dwellers in the *Duat* are in joy, when they see their lord long of stride, Amun-Ra, the lord of the world, the goodly stripling, joyful in his shrine."

SECOND STANZA. "The *Netjeru* partake of your beauty, their hearts revive when they see you, Sia following you and Hu in front of him. Great is your might, lord of the thrones of the Two Lands, who came into being aforetime in Ipet-sut. Every *Netjer* and every *Netjeret* propitiate you. May your beautiful face be pleased with me; may I be given life. Jubilating crowds make your beauty. May I be a favored one. May Amun favor me, love me, perpetuate me, and overthrow my enemies whether dead or alive."[75]

THE SEVENTH CEREMONY
Spreading forth the scroll of the Transfigurations of Ra

An assistant unrolls or uncovers the drawn figures of the seventy-five forms of Ra on a stand or table set before the *Kar*-shrine.

An assistant shall say the following:

"Beginning of the Book of the Adoration of Ra in the West and of the Adoration of the One Joined Together in the West. This book should be recited at night . . . . This is the victory of Ra over His enemies in the West. It is beneficial for a man upon earth; it is beneficial for him after he has died."[76]

THE EIGHTH CEREMONY
Elevating the Double Portion of Offerings for Ra
in his Seventy-five Forms

Once again the priest elevates offerings four times before the figures of the seventy-five forms of Ra. The offerings are then placed before the forms of Ra. The following shall be said:

"Elevating the offerings to Ra, setting out provisions for his *Ka* [spirit]. **Your bread belongs to you, your provisions belong to you. I am pure. May you make for me a 'granted life.'"**[77]

THE NINTH CEREMONY
Recitation of the Great Litany

The priest and as many assistants as are present shall say the following:

1) "Homage to you, Ra, high of power, Lord of the Caverns, with hidden forms, He who rests in the secret places when He makes transformations [*kheperu*] **of Himself into Deba-of-the-One-Joined-Together.**

2) Homage to you, Ra, high of power, this Khepri [the Becoming One] **who flutters His wings, who descends into the *Duat*, as He makes transformations of Himself into He-Who-Comes-Forth-from-His-Own-Members.**

3) Homage to you, Ra, high of power, Tatenen [lit. "The Earth Which Rises"], **who fashions His *Netjeru*, He who protects those among whom He is, He who makes transformations of Himself into He-at-the-Head-of-His-Cavern.**

4) Homage to you, Ra, high of power; who makes the earth visible, who gives light to those in the West, He whose forms are His becomings [*kheperu*], **as He makes transformations of Himself into His Great Disk.**

5) Homage to you, Ra, high of power, with a *Ba* who speaks to those in the *Duat,* He who is content with His speech, who protects the spirits [*akhu*] of those in the West while they breathe through Him.

6) Homage to you, Ra, high of power, Unique One, Powerful Heart, who is joined to His body, He who calls His *Netjeru* while passing through His secret caverns.

7) Homage to you, Ra, high of power, who calls His Eye, who addresses His Head, He who gives air to the *Bas* in their places in order that they may receive their breaths.

8) Homage to you, Ra, high of power, He who attains His *Ba,* who annihilates His enemies, He who decreed the punishment of the damned.

9) Homage to you, Ra, high of power, the one who is dark in His cavern, He who decrees that there be darkness in the cavern which hides those who are in it.

10) Homage to you, Ra, high of power, who gives light to the bodies, who is on the horizon, He who enters His cavern.

11) Homage to you, Ra, high of power, who approaches the hidden cavern of He-at-the-West; truly you are the body of Atum.

12) Homage to you, Ra, high of power, who comes to what Anpu hides; truly you are the body of Khepri [the Becoming One].

13) Homage to you, Ra, high of power, whose lifetime [i.e., existence] is longer than that of the West, She-Who-Hides-Her-Images; truly you are the body of Shu.

14) Homage to you, Ra, high of power, sparkling star for the dead; truly you are the body of Tefnut.

15) Homage to you, Ra, high of power, who gives orders to the time-gods at their times; truly you are the body of Geb.

16) Homage to you, Ra, high of power, the great one of reckonings of what is in Him [i.e., the stars in the sky]; truly you are the body of Nut.

17) Homage to you, Ra, high of power, Lord of Journeyings for those who are before Him; truly you are the body of Aset [Isis].

18) Homage to you, Ra, high of power, with head more luminous than those before Him; truly you are the body of Nebet Het [Nephthys].

19) Homage to you, Ra, high of power, Filler of the Members [i.e, intact in body], the Unique One, with sinews joined; truly you are the body of Heru [Horus].

20) Homage to you, Ra, high of power, shaper, He who shines in the flood; truly you are the body of Watery Abyss [i.e., Nun].

21) Homage to you, Ra, high of power, whom Nun protects, He who comes forth from that which He has been; truly you are the body of the Weeper [i.e., reference to humankind's being created from the tears of Ra].

22) Homage to you, Ra, high of power, He of the two cobras, the one ornamented with two plumes; truly you are the body of the Decomposed One.

23) Homage to you, Ra, high of power, He who enters and comes forth, and He who comes forth and enters, who belongs to His mysterious and hidden Cavern; truly you are the body of the *Abdju* [Abydos] **fish** [a species that is lapis blue in color, and which mythically guide the boat of Ra].

24) Homage to you, Ra, high of power, *Ba* to whom is presented His missing Eye; truly you are the body of the Divine Eye.

25) Homage to you, Ra, high of power, *Ba* who stands, Unique One, who protects what He has engendered; truly you are the body of Netuty.

26) Homage to you, Ra, high of power, with a raised head, with high horns; truly you are the Ram, Great of Transformations [*kheperu*].

27) Homage to you, Ra, high of power, He who shuts off light in the Silent Region; truly you are the body of the West.

28) Homage to you, Ra, high of power, with a *Ba* who sees in the West; truly you are the body of the Cavern-dweller.

29) Homage to you, Ra, high of power, He of the wailing *Ba*, the Weeper; truly you are the body of the Mourner.

30) Homage to you, Ra, high of power, the one with the arm which comes out, who is praised for His Eye; truly you are the body of the One-with-Hidden-Members.

31) Homage to you, Ra, high of power, the one who descends into the Mysterious Region; truly you are Khentamenti [He-at-the-Head-of-the-Westerners].

32) Homage to you, Ra, high of power, the one rich in transformations *[kheperu]* in the Holy Chamber (i.e., the Hidden Place); truly you are the body of the Sacred Beetle [i.e., the Becoming One] [*kheperer*].

33) Homage to you, Ra, high of power, who places His enemies in their bonds; truly you are the body of the Feline One [i.e., Ra as the Great Cat of Iunu].

34) Homage to you, Ra, high of power, who shines in the Secret Place; truly you are the body of the Ejaculator [of semen, the seed of life].

35) Homage to you, Ra, high of power, with wrapped body and breathing throat; truly you are the body of He-Who-is-in-the-Coffin.

36) Homage to you, Ra, high of power, who calls the bodies who are in the *Duat*; they breathe and their decay is arrested; truly you are the body of He-Who-Causes-to-Breathe.

37) Homage to you, Ra, high of power, with mysterious face, Image of the Divine Eye; truly you are the body of Shay [Fate].

38) Homage to you, Ra, high of power, Lord of Arising, He who comes to rest in the *Duat*; truly you are the body of Resting *Ba*.

39) Homage to you, Ra, high of power, whose body is more hidden than those among whom He is; truly you are the body of Hidden Bodies.

40) Homage to you, Ra, high of power, stouter of heart than those who are in His Following, who orders heat [i.e., flames] into the Place of Annihilation; truly you are the body of Flaming One.

41) Homage to you, Ra, high of power, who decrees annihilation, who creates breath by means of His forms *[kheperu]*, the one who is in the *Duat*; truly you are the body of He of the *Duat*.

42) Homage to you, Ra, high of power, you with lifted head who presides over His time [or oval, i.e. the *Duat*], shining one in the Mysterious Region; truly you are the body of Shining One.

43) Homage to you, Ra, high of power, with reassembled members, the body of He-Who-Is-Prominent-in-the-Earth; truly you are the body of He-with-Reassembled-Members.

44) Homage to you, Ra, high of power, who creates Secret things and generates bodies; truly you are the body of Secret One.

45) Homage to you, Ra, high of power, He who has provided for those in the *Duat* when passing the Mysterious Caverns; truly you are the body of He-Who-Provides-for-the-Earth.

46) Homage to you, Ra, high of power, the one whose flesh jubilates when seeing His bodies, . . . with *Ba* honored when passing by His members; truly you are the body of Jubilating One.

47) Homage to you, Ra, high of power, elevated one, with exudations from His Whole Eye, the Ensouled One for whom His Glorious Eye is being filled; truly you are the body of Elevated One.

48) Homage to you, Ra, high of power, He who makes passable the ways in the *Duat* and opens the roads in the Mysterious Region; truly you are the body of He-Who-Makes-Passable-the-Ways.

49) Homage to you, Ra, high of power, the *Ba* who travels with passing steps; truly you are the body of the Traveller.

50) Homage to you, Ra, high of power, who gives orders to His stars when He illuminates the darkness in the Caverns, with mysterious forms; truly you are the body of Illuminating One.

51) Homage to you, Ra, high of power, who has made the Caverns and who causes the bodies to come into being by what He Himself has decreed; may you decree, O Ra, for those who

exist and for those who do not exist, for the *Netjeru*, the spirits, and the dead; truly you are the body of He-Who-Causes-Bodies-to-Come-into-Being.

52) Homage to you, Ra, high of power, mysterious, mysterious, this Hidden One whose *Bas* of the Head are like His very image, who causes those in His Following to move on; truly you are the body of Hidden One.

53) Homage to you, Ra, high of power, Shining Horn, Pillar of the West, with darkened locks, who is in the boiling pot; truly you are the body of the Shining Horn.

54) Homage to you, Ra, high of power, with exalted forms when He traverses the *Duat* and causes the *Bas* in their Caverns to jubilate; truly you are the body of the One-with-Exalted-Forms.

55) Homage to you, Ra, high of power, who unites Himself to the Beautiful West, at whom those of the *Duat* rejoice when they behold Him; truly you are the body of Jubilating One.

56) Homage to you, Ra, high of power, Great Cat, who protects the *Netjeru*, Judge, presiding over the Tribunal, He at the head of the Holy Cavern; truly you are the body of Great Cat.

57) Homage to you, Ra, high of power, He whose Eye rescues and whose Brilliant Eye speaks while the bodies are in mourning; truly you are the body of He-Whose-Brilliant-Eye-Speaks.

58) Homage to you, Ra, high of power, whose *Ba* is on high and whose bodies are hidden, He who illuminates when He sees His hidden things; truly you are the body of the High *Ba*.

59) Homage to you, Ra, high of power, with exalted *Ba*, when He repulses His enemies, and when He decrees the flame against His transgressors; truly you are the body of the Exalted *Ba*.

60) Homage to you, Ra, high of power, Decomposing One, who hides the decomposition, He who has power over the *Bas* of the *Netjeru*; truly you are the body of the Decomposing One.

61) Homage to you, Ra, high of power, the Great Elder in the *Duat*, Khepri who becomes the child; truly you are the body of the Child.

62) Homage to you, Ra, high of power, Great Traveller, who repeats His travels, *Ba* with bright body and dark face; truly you are the body of the Dark-faced One.

63) Homage to you, Ra, high of power, who protects His body, who judges the *Netjeru* as Blazing One, Mysterious One who is in the Earth; truly you are the body of the Blazing-One-Who-Is-In-The-Earth.

64) Homage to you, Ra, high of power, lord of bonds for His enemies, Unique One, Great One, chief of long-tailed monkeys; truly you are the body of the One-Who-Binds.

65) Homage to you, Ra, high of power, who orders fire into His cauldrons, who severs the heads of the annihilated ones; truly you are the body of He-of-the-Cauldrons.

66) Homage to you, Ra, high of power, generator with completed forms, Unique One, who lifts up the earth by His *heka* power; truly you are the body of Tatenen [The-Earth-Which-Rises].

67) Homage to you, Ra, high of power, for whom the Watcher-gods rise, while those who on their biers do not see their secrets; truly you are the body of the Watchers.

68) Homage to you, Ra, high of power, Djenty of the sky, star of the *Duat*, who causes the bodies of His deceased ones to come forth; truly you are the body of the One-Who-Causes-Bodies-to-Come-Forth.

69) **Homage to you, Ra, high of power, the cheering baboon, You of Wetjenet** [i.e., the desert homeland of the sun in the east], **Khepri, you with just forms; truly you are the Baboon of the** *Duat.*

70) **Homage to you, Ra, high of power, He who renews the earth and opens up what is therein, you with the** *Ba* **who speaks and extols His members; truly you are the body of He-Who-Renews-the-Earth.**

71) **Homage to you, Ra, high of power, Nehi, who burns His enemies, flaming one, with fire-spitting tongue; truly you are the body of Nehi.**

72) **Homage to you, Ra, high of power, traveller with passing glance, one who causes darkness to come into being after His light passes; truly you are the body of the Traveller.**

73) **Homage to you, Ra, high of power, Lord of** *Bas,* **He who is in His Benben-house, chief of the** *Netjeru* **who are in the Forecourt; truly you are the body of the Lord of** *Bas.*

74) **Homage to you, Ra, high of power, He-of-the-Benben-House, Great God who ties time together; truly you are the body of He-of-the-Benben-House.**

75) **Homage to you, Ra, high of power, Lord of Darkness, who speaks from His mysteries,** *Ba* **who calls to those who are in the Caverns; truly you are the body of Lord of Darkness."**

The priest shall recite the following:

"O Ra of the Caverns; O Ra who calls those of the Caverns; O Ra, He in His Caverns! Homage to you, Ra, the Wanderer! *(Repeat four times.)*

"Those of the Caverns pay homage to you, *Ba* of the Wanderer! They pay homage to His *Ba*, they adore your bodies among which you are. Homage to the great Wanderer! *(Repeat four times.)*

"Homage to you, *Ba* of the Wanderer, in your seventy-five Forms, coming to being in your seventy-five Caverns!

"I, (*Name*), know them by their names; I know their Forms completely. I know what is in their bodies, all their mysterious forms; I, (*Name*), call them by their names; I convoke them in their forms. They open for me the *Duat*, they throw open the gates of the Mysterious Region for my *Ba* as for your *Ba*. You protect them, you also protect me so that my body breathes like you, for I am one of those who are in your following, who are at the Head of their Caverns, who speak in the dark place, who are glorious under your protection and who breathe when You call them.

"I, (*Name*), am like one of them speaking in the hidden Caverns.
    Hail to you! Prepare me a way! I pass by in the following of the *Ba* of Ra.
    Hail to you! Prepare me this way of Khepri!
    Hail to you! Prepare me a way!

"I, (*Name*), know the substance of those of the West.
Hail to you! Prepare me a way among you while praises are given to the *Ba* of the Wanderer! *(Repeat four times.)*

"O Ra in the West, placed into the earth, He who gives light to those of the *Duat*, O Ra, He-in-His-Disk!
    You lead me towards the roads of the West on which pass the *Bas* of the West. You lead me towards the roads of a mysterious nature.
    You lead me toward the roads of the West that I may pass the Caverns which are in the Silent Region.

You lead me towards the roads of the West, so that I may adore that which is in the Hidden Chamber.

You lead me towards the roads of the West; you elevate me to the caverns of the Watery Abyss.

Hail to you, Ra! I am the Watery Abyss.

Hail to you, Ra! I am yourself, and you are myself.

Hail to you, Ra! Your *Ba* is the *Ba* of myself.

My *Ba* is the *Ba* of yourself.

Hail to you, Ra! May my resting place be in the *Duat* when I traverse the Beautiful West.

Such as you are, such am I. Your glory, O Ra, is my glory.

"I, (*Name*), adore those of the West, I exalt their *Bas*.

Your course, O Ra, is truly my course.

Your passage is truly my passage.

O One-of-the-Disk, great of rays!

Homage to the *Ba* of the Wanderer!"

THE TENTH CEREMONY
Spell for Extinguishing the Candle or Oil Lamp

The priest, using a candle snuffer, extinguishes the flame. The following shall be said:

"This is the Eye of Heru by which you have become great, by which you live, and by which you have power, O Amun-Ra. This is the Eye of Heru which you consume and through which you enchant your body. The *Wedjat* Eye now enters into the West, into Manu, but it shall return. Truly, the Eye of Heru returns in peace!"[78]

THE ELEVENTH CEREMONY
Spell for "Removing the Foot"

Then with the broom the priest ritually sweeps the area beginning at the altar as he and any assistants, all bowing, back out of the Temple Chamber. As he does so the following shall be said:

"The distress that causes confusion has been driven away, and all the *Netjeru* are in harmony. I have given Heru his Eye; I have placed the *Wedjat* Eye in the correct position. I have given Sutekh his Testicles, so that the two Lords are content through the work of my hands."[79]

"I know the sky, I know the earth; I know Heru, I know Sutekh. Heru is appeased with his Eyes, Sutekh is appeased with his Testicles. I am Djehuty, who reconciles the *Netjeru*, who makes offerings in their correct form."[80]

CONCLUDING UTTERANCE

The broom is set aside. Facing the doors to the Temple Chamber, all bow, touching the palms of their hands to their knees. As the priest closes the double doors of the Temple Chamber, the following shall be said:

"Djehuty has come. He has filled the Eye of Heru; He has restored the Testicles of Sutekh. No evil shall enter this temple. Ptah has closed the door, Djehuty has set it fast. The door is closed, the door is set fast with the bolt."[81]

Once again all bow, touching the palms of their hands to their knees. The priest and assistants withdraw. One final ceremonial act remains: the removal of the food offerings from before the Naos housing Amun-Ra, followed immediately by their reversion for distribution and consumption by the servants of the god.

THE REVERSION OF OFFERINGS

One priest and as many assistants as necessary enter the Temple Chamber a final time. While he and any assistants lift up the offerings before the shrine housing the sacred image the priest shall say:

"O Amun-Ra, your enemy* withdraws for you. Heru has turned himself to his Eye in its name of 'Reversion-of-Offerings.' I am Djehuty. I come to perform this rite for Amun-Ra, king of the *Netjeru*. These, your divine offerings revert, they revert to your servants for life, for stability, for health and for joy! O that the Eye of Heru may flourish for you eternally!"[82]

Everyone shall withdraw, carrying away all food offerings. Ancient practice calls for food offerings to be consumed and not thrown away. Just as a generous landowner or noble would provision his servants and their dependents, so the *Netjer*, as lord of his temple, provisions his servants, the priests.

* To the ancient Egyptian priesthood an offering can possess more than one single meaning. For example, meat can represent the slain enemies of the god— moral enemies such as evil and lawlessness, or actual physical enemies—and at the same time the offering can represent the gift of rich bounty, the produce of the land blessed by the gods, given back by humankind to the gods, only in the end to "revert" back to the offerers. This polyvalence of meaning reflects the complexity and depth of the world of the existent, and is quite typical of the Egyptians' viewpoint of a deeply multifaceted reality.

81

APPENDIX B

Forms of Ra from the Litany of Ra in the Tomb of Seti I

Each drawing of a form of Ra is numbered in accordance with the numbering sequence presented by Marshall Clagett in his *Ancient Egyptian Science*, Vol. One, Tome Two, 860-61. The numbers identify each form of Ra with its corresponding numbered acclamation. The reader is advised that, in general, the numbering system alternates odd and even, from side to side. But upon close inspection the reader will see that this method was not rigidly applied throughout the entire seventy-five images. Also, in two instances a single image served for two separate forms of Ra (see image 68/72 and image 70/74).

Trying to fully explain this would require an extended digression that is well beyond the scope of the present book. Perhaps it is enough to note that upon occasion the original artisans had to contend with limitations of wall-space, and so they seem to have taken the liberty of making certain adjustments to their work. Be that as it may, the reader will notice that there are really only seventy-four images–thirty-seven on each side. The seventy-fifth and last image actually served as a title illustration for the entire composition. It brings together in one striking image the solar oval (representing Ra, the noontime sun) together with the familiar images of the Kheper beetle (symbol of the morning sun) and the ram-headed human figure (Atum, or the evening sun).

In addition to including a special page with the Forms of Ra for use in ritual, this book also includes a separate insert with the tripartite form of Ra. This may be positioned so as to serve as the focal point of the table on which lay the scroll of the Forms of Ra and the double portion of food offerings. This will be particularly useful when no statue of Ra is available.

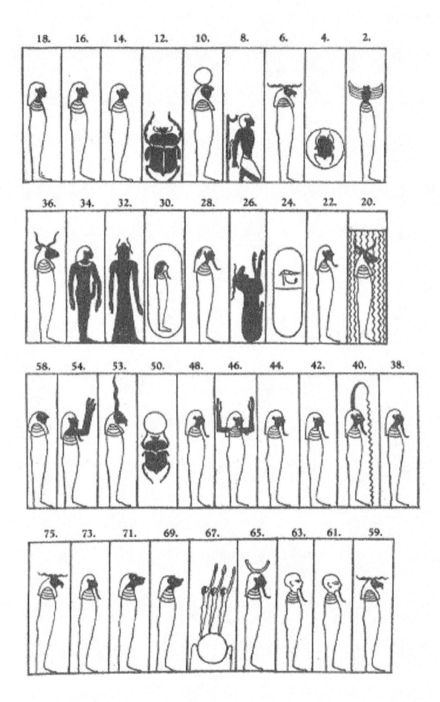

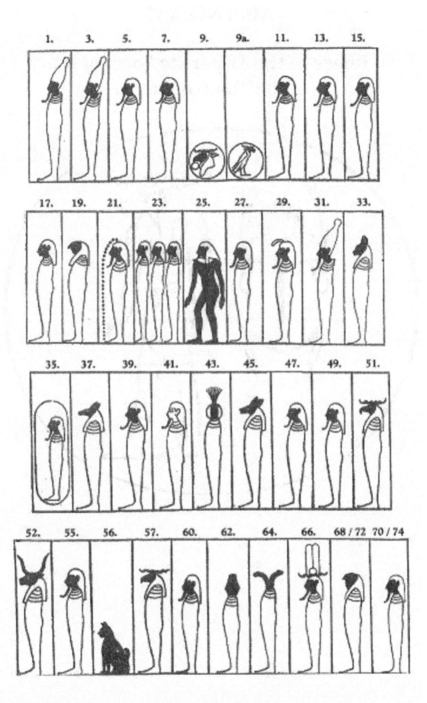

1.   3.   5.   7.   9.   9a.   11.   13.   15.

17.   19.   21.   23.   25.   27.   29.   31.   33.

35.   37.   39.   41.   43.   45.   47.   49.   51.

52.   55.   56.   57.   60.   62.   64.   66.   68 / 72   70 / 74

APPENDIX C

Image of the Tripartite Form of Ra in the Tomb of Seti II

APPENDIX D

Items Needed for Celebrating the Nighttime Ritual

The following articles will be needed for this rite.

- a new candle or freshly filled oil lamp for placing before the Naos-shrine (This is for the ceremonial lighting "Renewing the Candle of Every Day.")
- a candle or oil lamp to be carried by each participant (optional) (This is intended for sufficient lighting to permit ease of reading.)
- a vase or urn of fresh water (for the libation offering).
- a bowl or receptacle to receive the poured libation
- lighted charcoal in the censer
- Kyphi incense (For recipes recorded in the temples at Edfu and Philae see Lise Manniche's *Sacred Luxuries: Fragrance, Aromatherapy, and Cosmetics in Ancient Egypt*, 51, or refer to Kerry Wisner's *Eye of the Sun*, 76.)
- tray with food offerings
- a small stand or table to hold the open scroll and double portion of offerings
- scroll of the Forms of Ra
- image of Ra (or use the insert showing the tripartite form of Ra)
- a double portion of food offerings (e.g., two offering loaves, plus two portions of another food offering)
- a candle snuffer
- broom for "Removing the Foot"

A relief on a stela showing a relative offering incense and a libation of water to the deceased who is pictured seated, holding the lotus of rejuvenation so that he might breathe in the life-renewing scent. Such reliefs were common on funeral stelae commemorating the beloved dead. Special offering formulae would accompany such inscriptions with the request that passersby recite the offertory spell on behalf of the departed. These monuments were normally set up in the necropolis, with some persons receiving the special honor of having their stela placed within temple precincts.

CHAPTER THREE

Two Transfiguration Liturgies for the Radiant Spirits of the Blessed Dead

Introduction

This is the third installment in the series *Eternal Egypt: Ancient Rituals for the Modern World*. The first presents the morning ritual in the temple of Amun-Ra, and the second gives the special nighttime rite celebrating the mystical union of Ra with Osiris (originally "Ausir" in Egyptian). Together they provide the foundational rites for the daily, recurring cycles of day and night. As surely as the sun would rise, cross the sky, and set in the evening, so each day the priesthood of ancient Egypt would worship the divine powers with offerings and hymns of praise, commemorating divine events, and both renewing and re-establishing the vital links between the world of the gods and the world of humankind.

The third chapter addresses the profound mystery of death, that visible cessation of human life which inexorably affects and claims each of us. Every student of history is at least vaguely aware of the ancient Egyptians' mortuary monuments and artefacts. But far fewer persons are familiar with the great body of mortuary literature created by the ancient Egyptians that give evidence of their beliefs, their hopes and fears, and ultimately attest to their confidence in the triumph of life over death.

An axiom among theologians is *"lex orandi, lex credendi"*– the rule of prayer is the rule of belief. In other words, if a person wants to know what a particular group actually believes, then study the prayers and rituals of that group. The key to understanding a group's religious beliefs is contained in its prayers, songs, and rites. The important themes, the underlying hopes and fears, the very vision, perception, and experience of the sacred will reveal themselves in the words and actions of those rites and rituals. Religious spokespersons, whether clerics or theologians, may come and go–each having their unique but limited interpretation of what they think their group believes. Such clerics or theologians, regardless of their good intentions, can be influenced and therefore limited by either personal bias or preference, including numerous outside influences such as alien theologies or philosophical and sociological trends peculiar to their own nation and era. But it is in the actual prayers and rites of the group that we shall discover the genuine, underlying core of beliefs.

Thus, in attempting to understand how the ancient Egyptians viewed post-mortem existence, we turn our gaze to the substantial body of funerary as well as mortuary writings that have come down to us. These ancient texts come to us not through the accident of having been preserved in one solitary copy, but they appear in a variety of manuscripts dating from across the millennia of pharaonic history. These texts document for us the recurring themes, the enduring beliefs, and the persistent hopes of a deeply spiritual people. As modern-day Kemetic Reconstructionists we can do no better than adopt these ancient texts for assisting and honoring our own beloved dead.

Funerary texts such as the Book of Opening the Mouth highlight the conviction that a deceased person can be restored to a true and lasting form of life in the *Duat* (the next world, or afterlife) and that all the human faculties such as sight, speech, and movement can be reconstituted in that new dimension of existence. And not only such "earthly" abilities as these, but even greater powers, specifically those ascribed to divine beings, in particular the power to accompany the sun god in his barque "Millions of Years."

Only those who share in the divine nature can accompany the Lord of Life in his sun-boat, that is to say, in the creator-god's passage through cyclic time and existence. Only those who have been divinized themselves can accompany the gods. That is *the* central point, *the* core truth in the Egyptian vision of humankind's destiny—to become gods/goddesses, and to join the company of the *Netjeru*.

The Book of Night inscribed in the Osireion built at Abydos by the great pharaoh Seti I, and repeated in many Ramessid royal tombs, shows in parallel drawings the twelve hours of the nocturnal journey undertaken by the sun god, Ra. In the upper or "celestial" register, one sees the divinities associated with each hour. In the lower register one sees portrayed the successive stages of post-mortem experience destined for the justified dead. Finally, as Alison Roberts points out in *My Heart My Mother: Death and Rebirth in Ancient Egypt,* in the tenth hour all the human figures are "defined by a single feature–the divine beard which each one wears. It symbolizes the divinized state they have attained here, the realization of their divine nature. . . ."(2000, 156) Deification is the dynamic state of existence destined for those "true-of-voice" (*ma'a kheru*), whose hearts are found to be "justified" in the Balance.

In addition to such funerary texts as the Book of Opening the Mouth–intended for use in the rites following death (i.e., preparation of the deceased's body, the funeral service and, finally, the burial itself)–the ancient Egyptians created a corpus of mortuary texts for use by priests or family members intended to assure the continued existence and well-being of the departed. These mortuary texts were designed for special feasts, celebrated both annually as well as at specific times each lunar month.

The ancient Egyptian did not regard death as an unbreachable divide or as a tragic end to the human connectedness with the deceased person. Death was a passage. But a type of life existed on the other side of that passage. That type of life was not a totally spiritualized existence limited to disembodied "souls."

Unlike certain Greek philosophers or Gnostic thinkers, the ancient Egyptians did not disdain the physical body or the material world. Much to the contrary, they affirmed the intrinsic goodness of material creation. That world was not "fallen" or corrupt. It was not to be "overcome" through ascetic effort. Rather, it was to be treasured, guarded, supported, renewed, protected, and preserved. So, too, with human beings. The mortuary rituals reveal that every deceased man and woman was to be treasured and guarded, supported and renewed, protected and preserved. Human relationships, whether through birth or marriage, were not dissolved by death. The system of mutual support and sustenance operative among human families endured even after death. Children and spouses took care to regularly provide for their beloved dead. Through rituals and offerings the continued welfare of the deceased was assured.

This third part of *The Emanations of Ra* contains two mortuary rituals–one for the annual Beautiful Feast of the Western Valley, and the other being a *s3ḥw* ("transfiguration") liturgy (pronounced "sakhu") intended for recitation at specified times each month on behalf of the deceased. Both rituals are based upon extant texts preserved on papyri from the pharaonic era. They have not been shortened or abridged to accommodate the modern taste for brevity. Unlike modern day memorial services, they are not intended simply to console the living. Based upon critical theological insights and grounded in a uniquely Egyptian vision, they are designed to be of genuine benefit to the blessed dead–to sustain them, to rejuvenate them, and, ultimately, to help effect their divinisation. The two mortuary rituals in this booklet present for the contemporary Kemetic community key foundational texts for reviving and restoring the authentic practices of ancient Egypt, not just in honoring our beloved dead, but in assisting them in their transformation into *akhu*, that is, "transfigured spirits of light," the divine destiny of every man and woman.

The ancient Egyptian word for "emanations" is *bau*, meaning "all-powerful effectiveness." Sacred writings were regarded as themselves the *bau* of Ra. Words and their accompanying ritual actions were seen, and are still seen, to contain the immense, transformative power of the creator-god himself. As humans we participate in this transformative power when we recite the words and perform the actions handed down to us by the priesthood of ancient Egypt. Having been preserved through the past two millennia, the power-filled words recited for over three thousand years prior to our own Common Era once again are accessible for humankind. Once again they can assist our beloved dead on their journey to divinity.

San Francisco, 19 May 2004
(day 1 in the month *Hnt-Htj*, in the season of *Shomu*)
Beautiful Feast of the Western Valley
RICHARD J. REIDY

Commentary
for The Beautiful Feast of the Western Valley

An important annual festival celebrated for the departed is known as the "Beautiful Feast of the Western Valley." Evidence for this festival dates as far back as the Eleventh Dynasty (c. 2040 B.C.E.), and it continued to be celebrated throughout the entire pharaonic and Græco-Roman eras, covering a span of over twenty-three centuries. The valley referred to is located on the western side of the Nile across from the great city of Thebes. The festival lasted for two days, beginning with the new moon in the second month of the Egyptian summer. (The Egyptian name for this month is *Hnt-Htj*, later called *Payni* by the Greeks.)

Amidst much pageantry the statue of the creator god Amun was brought forth from his vast temple at Ipet-Sut [Karnak], placed aboard a special festival barque, and rowed across to the funeral temples and cemetery complexes serving the population of Thebes. The pharaoh himself would ceremonially accompany the god on this pilgrimage to the royal ancestors. The physical movement of the god from east to west repeated on the terrestrial plane what occurred daily on the celestial plane, with the sun, or Ra, crossing the sky, finally to descend to the west, that is, to the netherworld. The theme of the movement of the creator god who renews life by his personal visitation is a central, recurring motif in Egyptian theological thought.

As if to emphasize the importance of this insight, but on a much less elaborate scale, the life-endowing visitation by Amun–crossing from Thebes to the necropolis took place *every ten days*, that is, once every Egyptian week.[83]

As Egyptologist Fayza Haikal explains, during the Beautiful Feast of the Western Valley, "While the god visited the dead kings in their temples, the Theban families celebrated the feast in the streets of the necropolis and in their tombs . . . . [They] visited their tombs and spent the day there with their dead ancestors among relatives and friends, and singers and priests came from the temples to greet the population. . . . These festivities culminated in a banquet during which the tomb owners and their dead ancestors were presented with bouquets coming from the temples, which were a sign of the favor of the god."[84]

While the pharaoh presided over the cult in the royal funerary temples, Theban families gathered at their family tombs for a series of prayers and offerings to their beloved dead. As pharaoh would present offerings to his deceased ancestors not merely to honor their memory but in fact to renew the vitality of each royal *Ka*-spirit, so, too, Egyptian families would enlist the assistance of a lector-priest and a priestess to preside over rites intended to renew the vital force of their own deceased ancestors.

The link between family members was not severed at death. The dead were not set adrift in a "spiritual" realm unconnected from this world. To the ancient Egyptian the dead were not "beyond help." Quite to the contrary, the beloved dead could benefit from the earthly ministrations of their families. Vestiges of this nearly instinctual intuition regarding the real, indissoluble link between the living and the dead can even now be seen in the custom of tending gravesites, decorating graves with flowers, and the practice of praying for the dead found in many religions across the world.

Despite denials by materialists, men and women continue to behave in ways that point to the realization that ultimately death does not defeat love, it does not vanquish life, and it does not destroy our loved ones. Of all ancient civilizations it was that of Egypt which affirmed most eloquently the mutual interdependence of human with human, both in this life and in the afterlife. The life-spirit was not destroyed at death. The individual did not cease being a unique person, fated to blend somehow into an ocean of nothingness. On the contrary, the uniqueness of each individual remained and endured after death. The personality of each individual not only survived, but its scope of action and abilities took on qualities and powers exercised by the gods themselves. In short, the individual could join the ranks of divine beings. But just as the gods depend in a real sense upon humans to provide for them upon the earth by means of offerings and sacred rites in order to affirm and maintain that divine/human contact, so, too, the blessed dead rely upon the living to provide offerings and sacred mortuary rites aimed at renewing and sustaining their spirits.

This part of the book offers for contemporary Kemetic use, a rite based solely upon authentic texts used in ancient Egypt. The major portion of this rite comes from a papyrus currently in the possession of the British Museum and identified as Papyrus BM. 10209. It dates from the fourth century B.C.E., and, based upon internal textual evidence, is clearly a text intended "as a manual for the glorifications to the dead made at the Festival of the Valley."[85] The term *"sakhu,"* or "glorifications," refers to various recitations and offerings aimed at assisting the departed in becoming or in continuing to be an *"akh,"* that is, a "transfigured and equipped spirit of light." The destiny of every man and woman, according to ancient Egyptian thought, is precisely to become such a transfigured, radiant spirit, a divinized human being. [For an extensive treatment of the concept surrounding the state of being an *"akh,"* the reader is referred to R. J. Demarée's *The 3h ikr n Rc-stelae: On Ancestor Worship in Ancient Egypt,* Leiden: Nederlands Instituut, 1983. The epithet *3h ikr n Rc*–pronounced *akh iqer en Ra*–translates as "effective spirit of Ra." It appears on memorial stelae and is used to describe revered ancestors whose names also appear on the stelae.]

In ancient times the ceremony which makes up the preponderance of the ritual contained in these pages would have been performed at the family gravesite where typically multiple generations of ancestors had been interred. Since the custom of having multi-generational burial plots is very seldom the case for modern families, the ritual has been adapted for celebration in a Temple Chamber dedicated to one of the *Netjeru.* Likewise, since we no longer employ the mortuary "false door"–intended as a gateway between the worlds–replete with statues of our beloved dead, we are faced with the necessity of substituting a special photograph of the departed, or, lacking even that, simply writing their names on paper or papyrus. In either case, the photo or the paper should be used exclusively for these ceremonies and not returned to ordinary use. In order to activate the item so it becomes a genuine abode for the spirit of the deceased and a point of contact between the worlds of life and afterlife, it is recommended that you perform the "Opening of the Mouth" ritual as was done in traditional ancient

Egyptian practice for every statue or wall rendering of a deity, royal person, or tomb occupant. For more on this important ceremony, including the ritual text, please refer to Book Two in the present volume.

So as not to get lost in or be overwhelmed by the myriad details of this ancient technology, whose aim is nothing less than the revivification and rejuvenation of a deceased individual, the reader should be familiar with three basic concepts that are the groundwork for the ritual acts as well as the specific sequence of those acts.

The first principle to keep in mind is that Egyptian ritual focuses on divine activities and not human activities. It is the gods and goddesses who act and are acted upon. As Egyptologist Jan Assmann points out in his important work *The Search for God in Ancient Egypt*:

> . . . the ritual–and this is probably its most distinctive characteristic–*was not conceived of as a communication between the human and the divine, but rather as an interaction between deities.* [Assmann's italics] In the spells with which the priest regularly accompanied his actions, and which were evidently as important to their success as the actions themselves, he assumes the role of such deities as Horus, Thoth, Anubis, and Harsaphes.[86]

It was by identifying earthly events, individual persons, and material items with the "timeless time" of the gods, with the enduring and timeless Eternal Present of the divine dimension, and even with the gods themselves that humans could "enter into" that divine, everlasting reality. All the various cultic acts, from offerings of various kinds to other ritual activities, rest on what Assmann calls "the principle of explanatory transposition of what is happening into the divine realm."[87] Ritual activities are designed to bridge the gulf between the two spheres of existence–the divine and the human. The words spoken by the priest and priestess are divine utterances filled with miraculous power. Every cultic act, accompanied by specific verbal recitations, transposes a mundane action into the world of the *Netjeru*. As Assmann explains, "Speech established a relationship between this and the other world . . . . by interpreting cultic acts as divine or celestial events. Thus was accomplished what the Hermetic text designates *translatio*, the transference of celestial events to the terrestrial realm."[88]

In the mortuary ritual this is evident in the identification of the deceased with the god Ausir (Osiris). The deceased person is repeatedly referred to as Ausir, followed by his/her name. And all the recitations continually link the departed person with Ausir, with the various events in the post-mortem mythic history of that god, with his embalming, burial, rejuvenation, and finally with his total divinisation as lord of the Westerners (the blessed dead). As if to sum up and definitively reaffirm this identification with Ausir, a priestess in the role of the great *Netjer*'s sister and spouse Aset (Isis) addresses the deceased as if he/she were the goddess's beloved spouse.

Every act Aset performed for her spouse is now stated to have been performed for the deceased. The triumph of Ausir becomes the triumph of every man and woman. His victory over death becomes their victory. The gulf between the divine and human realms has been bridged. As Kemetic followers we once again are able to use the ancient words of power—what the Egyptians called "divine words"—to assist our beloved dead in their transformation into *"akhu,"* "transfigured and equipped spirits of light."

The second principle one needs to keep in mind so as not to get lost in the forest of details is that this festival *"sakhu"* ritual was carefully structured by the ancient priesthood to progress in an order reflecting both logic and propriety. To begin with, offerings of seven specific foods are made first to the *Netjeru*—the idea being that the great *Netjeru* should be the first to whom offerings are presented. Then the *"akhu"* are invited to come forth, followed by offerings of three types of liquid made to the divine doorkeepers who are asked to open up the gates of the netherworld (*Duat*). Again the *"akhu"* are urged to come forth and "turn back toward life." A candle is lit to help illumine the way for the blessed dead. Libations of water, so necessary for life, are offered again and again. Incense is offered and burned for the *"akhu."* Specific food offerings are presented. The goddess Aset herself pours libations and pronounces spells for the deceased. Then, on behalf of the deceased, offerings are made to various *Netjeru* associated with Ausir.

Finally, a bouquet of scent-emitting flowers is presented to the rejuvenated *"akhu."* This concludes the *"sakhu"* ritual proper. Each of the rites enumerated above is accompanied by verbal references to events and divine personages associated with Ausir. The deceased is at one and the same time identified closely with Ausir and yet distinguished from the god by the repeated use of his/her proper name, followed by the name of his/her mother. The individual's identity does not somehow "dissolve" into the god's person. The individual is in the retinue of the god–he or she does not merge with or *become* the god.

The third principle informing this and every ancient Egyptian rite is the "narrating power" of the words spoken. The words pronounced are efficacious in achieving their end. The verbal references to mythic events make these events present in the here and now, and it is by ritually connecting the present situation with a mythical precedent that the priest or priestess imbues the "ordinary" time and space of the present with the "extraordinary" power of its parallel mythic antecedent.[89] In the present case the parallel is drawn between Ausir and the blessed dead. As Ausir was revived and assisted by a host of deities, so, too, the blessed dead are revived and assisted by them. As the scholar G. Van der Leeuw expresses it,

> An event that occurred in prehistoric times, and which now possesses a mythical eternity and typicalness, is by the power of the formula rendered present in the literal sense and *made actual and fruitful.* [Italics mine.][90]

"... *made actual and fruitful*"–this was the insight of ancient Egypt for over three millennia. It is now at the very heart of the current Kemetic revival. We believe and we experience the power of the spoken word and the accompanying ritual actions as both sacred and efficacious.

With study and reflection, the modern Kemetic ritualist can discover that neither the number nor the sequence of ritual actions is superfluous or arbitrary. Each combined action/recitation is designed to bring about a specific result. It is no accident that precisely seven food/drink offerings are made. Or that multiple libations of water are poured. Or that certain offerings are named "An-Offering-Which-the-King-Gives." These and other details of the cult reflect the ancient Egyptians' understanding of how to revivify and restore the *Ka*-spirits of their beloved dead. The theology underlying this ritual is complex, mystical, and nuanced. It surely runs counter to the current tendency to seek simple–or simplistic–answers to profound theological questions, or to design "minimalist" rituals or practice a streamlined spirituality.

The challenge and the promise call out to us in the very first Utterance spoken in this rite: "Rejoice, O *Netjer/Netjeret* of this temple, for a perfect offering, complete in word and in substance, is accomplished in accordance with what has been done before." Through these words the ancient priesthood speaks to us today, calling us to restore the sacred rites and to celebrate the great festivals. Through patience and dedication we can take part in this rebirth.

The Yearly Ritual of bringing the *Ba* to the glorifications of the Beautiful Feast of the Western Valley

On the day of the New Moon in the tenth lunar month (*Payni*), in the second month of summer (*Shomu*) the lector-priest/ess and his/her assistants shall enter the Temple Chamber bearing aloft an image of Ausir (Egyptian for the Hellenized name "Osiris"), followed by images of the blessed dead. The sacred images are preceded by a priest/ess carrying a smoking censer, as well as a priest/ess sprinkling pure water in front of the images. As many as possible of those present are softly and slowly shaking sistrums and *menat* necklaces as the procession makes its way into the Temple Chamber. After everyone has entered the Chamber, all bow, touching the palms of their hands to their knees.

THE FIRST CEREMONY
Spell for Entering the Sanctuary

The lector-priest steps forward and raises his/her arms in the *nis* position–arms stretched out and elbows bent, hands open with the palms facing toward each other–and he/she recites the following:

"Rejoice, O *Netjer/Netjeret* [god/goddess] of this temple, for a perfect offering, complete in word and in substance, is accomplished in accordance with what has been done before."[91]

The image of Ausir is placed on a table in front of the *Kar*-shrine [Naos]. The other images are placed to the right and left of Ausir.

THE SECOND CEREMONY
Spell for Lighting the Four Torches for the Ceremonies
Which are Carried out for a *Ka*

The priest lights the first of four red candles which had previously been anointed with frankincense oil* and placed in front of the sacred images.

Frankincense oil is here used as a substitute for the yet unidentified "Libyan oil," one of the seven sacred unguents used in funeral rites. Frankincense oil has been selected because it was an ingredient in six of the nine sacred oils whose composition is recorded in the temple of Heru at Edfu. See page. 108 in Lise Manniche's Sacred Luxuries.

The following shall be said:

"**The torch comes to your *Ka*, O Ausir, Foremost of the Westerners** [the blessed dead], **and the torch comes to your *Ka*, O Ausir N. There comes he who promises the night after the day; there comes the two sisters from Ra; there comes she who was manifested in Abdju** [Abydos], **for I cause it to come, even that Eye of Heru which was foretold to you, O Ausir, Foremost of the Westerners.**"

The priest lights the second red candle:

"**The Eye of Heru is your protection, O Ausir, Foremost of the Westerners. It spreads its protection over you; it defeats all your adversaries. Truly your adversaries are fallen.**

"**The Eye of Heru is your protection, O N. It spreads its protection over you; it defeats all your adversaries. Truly your adversaries are fallen.**"

The priest lights the third red candle:

"To your *Ka*, O Ausir, Foremost of the Westerners! The Eye of Heru is your protection. It spreads its protection over you; it defeats all your adversaries for you. Truly your adversaries are fallen.

"To your *Ka*, O N! The Eye of Heru is your protection. It spreads its protection over you; it defeats all your adversaries for you. Truly your adversaries are fallen."

The priest lights the fourth red candle:

"The Eye of Heru comes intact and shining like Ra in the horizon. May the four torches go in to your *Ka*, O Ausir, Foremost of the Westerners. May the four torches go in to your *Ka*, O N.

O you children of Heru—Imsety, Hapy, Duamutef, and Qebehsenuef—as you spread your protection over your father Ausir, Foremost of the Westerners, so spread your protection over N so that he/she might live with the *Netjeru*.

"To your *Ka*, O Ausir, Foremost of the Westerners! The Eye of Heru is your protection. It spreads its protection over you; it defeats all your adversaries for you. Truly your adversaries are fallen.

"To your *Ka*, O N! The Eye of Heru is your protection. It spreads its protection over you; it defeats all your adversaries for you. Truly your adversaries are fallen.

"It is Ausir, Foremost of the Westerners, who causes a torch to be bright for the potent *Bas* in Nekhen [Heracleopolis]. May you make the living *Ba* of N strong with his/her torch so that he/she may not be repelled or driven off from the portals of the West. Then there will be brought to him/her offerings of things good and pure; you will send up thanks for this power, for N will be restored to his/her true shape, his/her true god-like form."[92]

PRESENTATION OF OFFERINGS IN FRONT OF the image of Ausir and images of the ancestors, and in front of the image of Ausir N, justified, born of N (justified*), and for the excellent Bas in the West.

* *The word "justified" is added after the name if that parent is deceased. The theological significance of the term "justified"–literally "true of voice" [in Egyptian "ma'a kheru"–underscores the deceased's status as having been found righteous and morally upright before Ausir (Osiris) and thus in accord with Ma'at.*

THE THIRD CEREMONY
Recitation of Words for a Sevenfold Offering
to All Divine and Divinized Beings

The priest or his/her assistant presents the offering tray on which are arrayed seven types of offerings: bread, beer, "water from the inundation," wine, milk, incense, and cool water. In the customary manner the priest slowly elevates and then lowers the offering tray four times in front of the images of Ausir and the ancestors. The following shall be said:

"'An-Offering-Which-the-King-Gives'* to those who are in the *Duat,* to the Great Ennead and the Small Ennead, to the followers of Ra and the followers of Ausir, to those watchmen who protect their Lord, and to the attendants who are beside the bier of Ausir-Wennofer ["He who lasts in perfection"] justified, that your *Ba* and your *Ka* may receive the offerings of food: bread, beer, "water from the inundation" by which the *Netjeru* [the gods] live, wine, milk, incense and cool water. O excellent *Bas* in the West, and Ausir N, justified, born of N [Add the word "justified" if the parent or stepparent is deceased.], these offerings are for you."[93]

* In ancient Egyptian thought the single individual in whose person co-existed and co-mingled both the human and the divine was the reigning pharaoh, the one responsible for maintaining Ma'at in the land. He was regarded as "the living Horus" (Heru), and thus any offering which he presented to the Netjeru (the deities) was by implication a perfect offering, complete and capable of pleasing the Netjeru. It became customary for every funerary offering to be named as "An-Offering-Which-the-King-Gives" (Hotep-dee-Neesoot) even though the social rank of the deceased did not necessarily justify such a royal favor. Nevertheless, because of the firm belief that the verbal declaration itself had the power to bring about or make real the words uttered, this tradition persisted over the course of Egyptian history.

Note that this first offering consists of seven items. As Kerry Wisner explains in *Song of Hathor: Ancient Egyptian Ritual for Today,* "This number is one of the most potent numbers in Egyptian magic. This number has the combined effects, and meanings, of three and four. Thus such concepts as plurality, completeness, and universality are conveyed. The number is strongly connected to Ausir." (page 19) Note that the seven items offered are symbolic of both rejuvenating and sustaining life. For further information the reader is referred to "The Number Seven in Egyptian Texts," by Warren R. Dawson, in the scholarly journal *Aegyptus* VIII, 7 (97-107).

The bread, wine and beer were staples of the Egyptian diet. Milk was intended to give sustenance to the newborn spirit(s) of the blessed dead. And lastly, water, especially water from the yearly inundation which made Egypt fertile, was manifestly essential for all life. Even in climates dissimilar to that of Egypt the items offered carry very similar meanings of sustenance, nourishment, and renewal.

THE FOURTH CEREMONY
Spell for Calling Forth the Transfigured
Spirit(s) [*akh;* plural *akhu*] of the Blessed Dead

The priest/ess extends his/her arms in the *nis* position employed for invocations–arms stretched out and elbows bent, hands open–and the following shall be said:

"**O Ausir, chief of the Westerners, great *Netjer* [god], lord of Abdju [Abydos], Ausir N justified, born of N (justified), if you are in heaven, come to your *Ba*. If you are on earth, come to your shining spirit (*Akh*). If you are in the south, the north, the west or the east, come so that you may be content. Be strong in your body, so that you may come therefrom, you having become an incarnated *Ba* and a shining spirit (*Akh*), mighty as Ra and equipped as a *Netjer*. Come to this your bread, your beer, and your cool water so that you may become strong through every good and pure offering, O Ausir, chief of the Westerners, great *Netjer*, Lord of Abdju [Abydos], Ausir N justified, born of N (justified).**"[94]

THE FIFTH CEREMONY
Spell for a Threefold Libation Offered to
the Doorkeepers of the "Sacred Land"
(i.e., the necropolis or cemetery)

The lector-priest shall announce the following:

"**Praising Ausir, chief of the Westerners, great *Netjer*, lord of Abdju [Abydos], and bringing the *Ba(s)* of the transfigured spirit(s) to the ritual of the Festival of the Valley.**"[95]

Taking up in succession a vessel with water, the second with wine, and the third with milk, the priest pours a quantity from each vessel into three separate bowls–one for each fluid–stationed before the sacred images. The following shall be said:

"It is pure, it is pure, 'An-Offering-Which-the-King-Gives.'
Accept this libation as a libation of the coolest water, wine
and milk. O doorkeepers, lords of the Sacred Land, lords of
burial, receive what is given to you and pull open the gates of
the *Duat*. Open the gates of the West. Open the double doors
of the Silent Region."[96]

THE SIXTH CEREMONY
Spell for Summoning the Blessed Dead

The priest/ess once again extends both arms in the *nis* position
used for invocations–arms stretched out and elbows bent, hands
open–while the following shall be said:

"Come forth, O Ausir N, justified. Come forth, Ausir N,
justified, born of N (justified). Awake! Turn yourself about,
back toward life! O Ausir N, justified, raise yourself up. Bring
yourself to me. Arise and receive offerings from my hand. I
will be a helper for you!"[97]

"May you emerge from the earth and behold Ra. May
you follow Amun in this, his beautiful festival of the desert
valley."[98]

THE SEVENTH CEREMONY
The Offering of Incense

The priest places grains of myrrh–the customary incense
accompanying food offerings–on the censer. Lifting and lowering
the smoking censer with slow, repetitive movements, first in front
of the image of Ausir, and then in front of each of the other images
surrounding Ausir, the priest shall recite the following:

"Crossing the river you see heaven, while the fragrance of
incense is in front of you and you ferry across heaven adorned.
As a transfigured and equipped spirit [*Akh*] you are adorned
most richly, and you eat bread and offerings in front of Ra,
from the altars of Djehuty while your intelligence is given to

108

you in the House of Intelligence and your heart in the House of the Heart and an offering is made for you and for your *Ka* and for your body. Your *Ba* is in heaven and your body is in the *Duat,* twice great and twice mighty. You wake up sound and intact in heaven and in your resting place, Ausir, chief of the Westerners, beneficent one, who has no failure in his deeds , Ausir N justified, born of N (justified)."[99]

The priest places more grains of incense on the censer and resumes censing the sacred images while the following is said:

"O Ausir chief of the Westerners, great *Netjer,* lord of Abdju [Abydos], Ausir N justified, born of N (justified), heaven is open for you. Earth is open for you. The ways of your resting place are open for you, so that you may go out and come in with Ra, so that you may walk freely like the Lord of Eternity.

"May you receive bread from what is offered on the altar of the *Bas* of Iunu [Heliopolis], your food being like that of the Great Ennead. May you accept offerings from what is put out for you, pure bread on the altar of Heru, so that your flesh becomes alive and your muscles flourishing, so that you may be clear-sighted on the dark way. Hapy will give you water; Nepyt will give you bread; Hwt-Hrw [Hathor] will give you beer; and Hesyt will give you milk.*

"You cleanse your feet in a basin of silver and turquoise, with a cloth from the hands of Tayet.** You drink water from the shore of the Nile, and offerings are given to you beside Ausir. A seat is prepared for you, and you assume the form of a *Netjer.* You alight at every place according to your desire, like the Great Noble in Djedu [Busiris] [i.e., Ausir]. Your *Ba* goes to heaven and your body rests in the *Duat.*"[100]

---

* Each of these four deities is connected with rebirth and rejuvenation. Hapy is Netjer of the life-giving inundation. Nepyt, as a harvest goddess, brings forth life from the grain buried in the earth. Hwt-Hrw (Hathor) is here in her aspect as the goddess of sacred intoxication. Last, Hesyt is the cow goddess of Atfih who nurses the Netjeru and royal offspring.

** *Tayet—or Tait—is the Netjeret (goddess) of weaving, specifically weaving the linen wrappings for the body of the deceased.*

THE EIGHTH CEREMONY
Spell for Lighting the Candles Which Illumine
the Way in the *Duat*

The priest lights a candle or oil lamp in front of each image, including that of Ausir. The following shall be said:

"**When you are justified in your resting place, you raise your face to the heaven of Ra and you see Heru as his steersman. A luminous disk is made for you in your resting place, in front of your image so that it may light up for you the darkness in the *Duat*, so that it may shine as Shu on your head. A boat is placed in front of you. The two sisters glorify you and Djehuty spreads out for you his writing equipment so that you may become divine like the *Netjeru*. He leads you through the mysterious gates, and when you pass by 'He-who-protects-the-dead'** [a doorkeeper of the *Duat*], **Ra comes to you and gives you his brightness. His rays flood through your eyes while the arms of Tatenen*** **are prepared to receive you. Those in the West rejoice greatly. All plans against you are abolished. They are abolished.**

"**You receive illumination from the disk of Ra, being placed beside Ra in his barque in the Room of Awakening. He opens your face. He illumines your seat so that you may be like Deba-of-the-One-Joined-Together** [i.e., a nightly form of Ra]. **Sepulchral meals are presented to your *Ka* beside Ausir–Wennofer** ["He who lasts in perfection"]. **You receive justification from those who preside over your resting place, and your *Ba* lives for ever and for ever. Your seat is established and your name flourishes even like that of the Great Noble in Djedu** [Busiris]."[101]

*Tatenen—a primordial creator-god—is viewed as a manifestation or form of Ptah. His role is that of a protector of the blessed dead.

THE NINTH CEREMONY
Spell for Another Offering of Incense

More myrrh is placed on the censer and the sacred images are then censed. The lector priest recites the following:

"Raise yourself up so that you may feel joy again; and your *Ba* is alive for ever like *Sah* [Orion] in the womb of Nut. Aset transforms herself into a bier. She receives you as a couch while your son Heru, his arms carrying the crown of justification, adorns your head. May your beautiful face be content for you have received your bread and you have inhaled the scent of the incense–they shall be pure for your *Ka*, O Ausir chief of the Westerners, lord of Abdju [Abydos], in heaven, on earth, on your seat in Upper *Kemet* [Egypt] or on your seat in Lower *Kemet* [Egypt]."[102]

THE TENTH CEREMONY
Spell for a Sevenfold Libation of Water

With each of the seven declarations "to you belongs water", the priest pours a quantity of water into a single basin or bowl, for a total of seven separate pourings. The following shall be said:

**(1) "To you belongs water,
(2) to you belongs water, O Ausir N justified, born of N, (justified);
(3) to you belongs water,
(4) to you belongs water of millions of millions,
(5) to you belongs water of millions of *nemset* jars and a hundred thousands of *meker* jars,
(6) to you belongs water of the Great River [the Nile] from the waters of Heru in the region of Iunu [Heliopolis],
(7) to you belongs water from the beginning of infinity to the end of eternity, O possessor of honors, chief of the Westerners, who awakens intact, O lord of infinity, king of the Two Lands, sovereign, ruler of eternity, O lord of the cool water, great one**

of the two sources, in heaven, in his resting place and in his tomb, great being of the first generation, beautiful of face; first of the five *Netjeru*; heir of infinity for whom the time has come; beneficent *Ba* among every *Ba* and every tomb-chapel, excellent of heart, who has fixed the two uraei on his head, enduring for ever and for all eternity."[103]

THE ELEVENTH CEREMONY
A Lustration Spell for the Blessed Dead's
Restoration to Life and Vitality

The priest takes four *nemset* jars and elevates them four times before the sacred images as an offering. The following is recited:

"May Water be given to the noble *Ka* who rests in the eternal residence of Shu in Iunu [Heliopolis] and in Mennefer [Memphis]. Your horizon is in the Castle of the Prince [in Iunu]. The *Bas* foremost in Iunu come to you. They present Ma'at to you as an offering every day. Your father Shu and your mother Tefnut come to you bearing *nemset* jars of turquoise, filled with water the color of faience, their content being pure water. . . .

The priest now sprinkles water from the first *nemset* jar as he walks around the sacred images for the first time and the following is said:

" . . . and they give you this water which you desire, your body being received into their hands while your forebears and those who have begotten and given birth to you come to you; they loosen the bonds of your funeral wrappings daily like those of the Great Noble (Ausir).

The priest sprinkles water from the second *nemset* jar and walks a second time around the sacred images while the following is said:

"Hapy comes to you from his cavern. He moistens the fertile land for you. The *Netjeru* of the First Time come to you every day, carrying offerings for you. Aset and Nebet Het come to

you; they raise you up into the horizon. The lord of the *Duat* comes to you, accompanied by his retinue, his female mourners preceding him. Equipped with the spells of Aset and Nebet Het, the Great Mourner, they unite your limbs. Djehuty reads the Book of the Opening of the Mouth for you, while Heru, your *sem*-priest, pronounces magic spells for you. Seshat opens for you the 'House of Life.' Aset and Nebet Het make you divine, and Hu and Sia adore you.

The priest sprinkles water from the third *nemset* jar as he walks for a third time around the sacred images. The following is said:

"Ptah prepares for you a burial cloth with his hands, with the garments of Tayet. He washes your body and he purifies you. Then Shu and Tefnut reanimate you with their hands with milk of Hesat [the cow goddess], and water is poured for you in front of the excellent *Bas*. They say to you, 'Stand up, because your heart lives and we have fashioned your flesh.' They make your heart healthy. They place you into the earth and they protect you. They protect you. They receive your spirit in your resting place like that of Tatenen, the great *Netjer*.

The priest sprinkles water from the fourth *nemset* jar as he makes a final circuit around the sacred images and the following is said:

"Heru comes to you, having assumed the white crown, with the red crown shining upon his head. Aset rejoices at his sight, her son, an *Akh* [a transfigured and equipped spirit] who comes forth justified and who establishes Ma'at in her place, near the beauty of Nut. Water is given to you, O noble *Akh*, so that the heart of your *Akh* rejoices. Give water to this noble *Akh* when his *Ba* comes to see him. Rejoice, O Great Noble, for Heru is given his office; he comes forth justified from the 'Hall of the Two Truths,' he comes forth triumphant."[104]

The lector-priest/ess announces the following:

"Decree for the majesty of Aset, issued by the *Netjeru*: 'We shall not stand between you and your brother Ausir so that he may hear what you have said and praise you on account of what we have done. May you remember all our good deeds.'"[105]

THE TWELFTH CEREMONY
The Address of Aset [Isis], Great of Magic, to Her Brother and Spouse

Taking the part of Aset, a priestess shall say the following:

"I have made for you your house with my sister Nebet Het. I have caused you to enter the 'left Eye' and become the moon. Heaven rejoices, while Djehuty, protector of the moon, fills the *Wedjat* Eye in the Great Mansion [the residence of Atum and Ra in Iunu]. Your effigy is holy and the 'Mansion of the Prince' bears your mystery. You are *Sah* [Orion] in the southern sky while I am *Sopdet* [Sirius] as your protectress."

The priestess pours a libation before Ausir, and the following shall be said:

"O Ausir, may you receive water from my hands, for I am your sister Aset. O lord of the *Netjeru*, may every joy be with you. I have healed for you your son Heru and I have placed your *Ba* in the horizon. I have established for you your son on your seat of eternity; O Ausir N, justified, born to N (justified)."

Another libation is poured before Ausir, and the following shall be said:

"Receive for yourself this libation from your sister, in accordance with what you desire. I am your sister. I am your wife. I am the daughter of your mother. I have caused your beautiful face to see.

"O my good lord, say what I should do in front of you so that I may please your heart through it. I have placed your son Heru

114

upon your seat.I have done it because of your love before your father Geb. May your protection be in the Mysterious Place for I know your excellent form. I have presented to you offerings consisting of barley cakes; they will last forever and forever. I have assembled for you the world into one single city and they make for you the 'linen of one day' [i.e., a special funeral linen woven on the 20th /21st of Khoiak]. I have caused you to rise upon the throne; I have caused you to rest in your palace. I have caused that your images appear in every land while you are in the horizon of Ra, your boat remaining beside his boat. Your statues appear in the temples while the *Netjeru* and *Netjerut* are with you as an Ennead; the divine lord of every temple offers to you even his own temple throne. I have placed the sky under your *Ba* and the *Duat* under your effigy. Every region has your statues, they being pure, while they praise you, Ausir Wennofer ["He who lasts in perfection"] justified. You are rejuvenated for ever and ever, O Ausir N justified, born of N (justified)."[106]

THE THIRTEENTH CEREMONY
Spell Confirming that the Rejuvenation of the
Blessed Dead has been Completed

"You are rejuvenated, O Ausir, you are rejuvenated in heaven. You appear in the eastern horizon of the sky, having spent days and passed hours, and you come in accordance with the proper time every year, and you rise as the moon at the time of the festival of illuminations. Your name endures in the 'Mansion of the Prince' [the palace of Ra in Iunu] and you come as Hapy to cover the fertile lands, so that all the world may live through your *Ka*. Your phallus is strong and you repeat your forms of yesterday. Aset safeguards you and protects you as lord of the uraeus, O Ausir Wennofer ["He who lasts in perfection"] justified. You are rejuvenated for ever and ever, O Ausir N, justified, born of N (justified)."[107]

THE FOURTEENTH CEREMONY
Spell Confirming that a Royal Offering and the Appropriate
Libations Have Been Made to the Rejuvenated, Divinized Dead
Who is now Fully Identified With Ausir Himself

Standing before the offerings and libations previously made, the priest/ess holds his/her arm outstretched, with palm facing up and open (i.e., the *henek* gesture), pointing toward the table of offerings. The following shall be said:

"'An-Offering-Which-the-King-Gives.' O Ausir, I have poured for you, water which comes out from Elephantine [in the south, near the First Cataract, and regarded as the source of the Nile], and milk from Athribis [in the north, an important Delta city]. I have brought to you *nemset* jars full of fresh offerings from the estate of Ra so that you may receive that which Tatenen was given and loaves from what is offered. I have done this so that your *Ba* is able to come out to worship your god, there being no one who can turn you out from heaven or from earth. Your *Ba* lives and your limbs flourish. You are rejuvenated as the ruler of 'the living ones' [the justified deceased]. You are great and you are elevated in Djedu [in Greek, Busiris, in Upper Egypt] and your seat is noble in To-Wer [in Lower Egypt]. A libation of cool water is poured for you consisting of the best liquid on the offering table in the middle of the mound of Tjeme. Rejoice, for you have joined gladness in the noble *ished* tree and your *Ba* is divinized in the realm of the dead. Receive for yourself offerings of every kind, and rejoice for you have joined Manu (the western horizon). Your father Shu praises you, O Ausir, chief of the Westerners, great *Netjer*, lord of Abdju [Abydos]."[108]

THE FIFTEENTH CEREMONY
Spell for an Offering to Various *Netjeru*
on Behalf of the Transfigured Dead

"Ausir of Coptos who is first in the 'Mansion of Gold,' Ausir-Sokar, Ausir, lord of Djedu [Busiris], Wennofer ["He who lasts in perfection"], **Ausir the beloved one, ruler of eternity, Imsety, Hapi, Duamutef, Qebehsenuf,** *Netjeru* **[gods] and** *Netjerut* **[goddesses] who are in the mound of Tjeme,** *Netjeru* **and** *Netjerut* **who are in the mansion of Sokar,** *Netjeru* **and** *Netjerut* **who are in the 'Mansion of Gold,'** *Netjeru* **and** *Netjerut* **who are in the 'Great Place,' great and noble bull, Great Ogdoad, oldest of the very primeval times, Ausir, Heru, Aset and Nebet Het, enneads and divine bodies: may you receive, may your** *Ba* **receive and may your** *Ka* **receive offerings and provisions–bread, beer, wine, milk and 'water from the inundation' by which the** *Netjeru* **live."**

The priest/ess pours a libation. The following shall be said:

"Accept the Eye of Heru, I offer to you the water which is in it, fresh water as of love and praise for Ausir, N justified, born of N (justified)."[109]

THE SIXTEENTH CEREMONY
A Threefold Libation Spell Addressed First to
Sokar-Ausir, then to Ausir and Other Deities, and,
finally, one to the Transfigured Spirit(s) of the Blessed Dead

The priest/ess pours a libation of fresh water. The following shall be said:

"Sokar-Ausir, accept this, your libation. Your libation belongs to you throughin your name of 'Fresh Water.' Accept this vital fluid which comesfrom you and which Heru restores to you. The Eye of Heru is given to you, for the children of Heru recognize you as divine. The sky is given to you in your name of Ra and your enemies are fallen beneathin your name of *Netjer*; **Heru recognizes you as 'the Rejuvenated One.' Rejuvenate! Rejuvenate in your name 'Rejuvenated Waters.' The waters exist as the strength of Ausir. He is great, he is noble, he is strong, he is free and he is powerful through this living water. He has encircled for himself and he has given to himself,**

pervading each and every land. Sokar-Ausir, you are great and you are noble. You are strong and you are free through this your libation of life-giving water."

The priest/ess pours a second libation of water. The following is said:

"Ausir, Heru, Aset and Nebet Het, enneads and divine bodies, accept the Eye of Heru; I offer the water which is in it, fresh water as of love and praise."

The priest/ess pours a third libation of water. The following is said:

"O Ausir, N justified; born of N (justified), may you receive a libation of fresh water after the *Netjer* [Ausir] becomes satisfied, each day and every day."

"May you live and may your *Ba* live both now and for ever!"[110]

THE SEVENTEENTH CEREMONY
Presenting the Bouquet

A bouquet of fresh, fragrant flowers, or even a single such flower, is placed before the images of the blessed dead. The following shall be repeated four times:

"Khonsu [son of Amun] causes Amun to be your protection as you live eternally. May Amun fulfill what you desire, O beloved one. May you be a favored one, and may Amun favor you for all your good deeds. May he favor you and love you. May he perpetuate you and overthrow your adversaries whether dead or alive."[111]

"May you live and may your *Ba* live both now and for ever!"

All present exclaim the following:

"May you live and may your *Ba* live both now and for ever!"

The mortuary recitations for bringing the *Ba* to the Beautiful Feast of the Western Valley are now at an end. The participants shall now fulfil the usual concluding rites for leaving the Temple Chamber:

THE EIGHTEENTH CEREMONY
Spell for Extinguishing the Candle or Oil Lamp

The priest, using a candle snuffer, extinguishes the flame. The following shall be said:

"This is the Eye of Heru by which you have become great, by which you live, and by which you have power, O [name of the god or goddess in whose temple this rite takes place]. This is the Eye of Heru which you consume and through which you enchant your body. The *Wedjat* Eye now enters into the West, into Manu, but it shall return. Truly, the Eye of Heru returns in peace!"[112]

THE NINETEENTH CEREMONY
Spell for "Removing the Foot"

Then with the broom the priest ritually sweeps the area beginning at the altar as he and any assistants, all bowing, back out of the Temple Chamber. As he does so the following shall be said:

"The distress that causes confusion has been driven away, and all the *Netjeru* are in harmony. I have given Heru his Eye, I have placed the *Wedjat* Eye in the correct position. I have given Sutekh his Testicles, so that the two Lords are content through the work of my hands."[113]

"I know the sky, I know the earth; I know Heru, I know Sutekh. Heru is appeased with His Eyes, Sutekh is appeased with His

Testicles. I am Djehuty, who reconciles the *Netjeru*, who makes offerings in their correct form."[114]

CONCLUDING UTTERANCE

The broom is set aside. Facing the doors to the Temple Chamber, all bow, touching the palms of their hands to their knees. As the priest closes the double doors of the Temple Chamber, the following shall be said:

"Djehuty has come. He has filled the Eye of Heru; He has restored the Testicles of Sutekh. No evil shall enter this temple. Ptah has closed the door, Djehuty has set it fast. The door is closed; the door is set fast with the bolt."[115]

Once again all bow, touching the palms of their hands to their knees. The priest and assistants withdraw.

One final ceremonial act remains: the removal of the food offerings from before the *Kar*-shrine [Naos] housing the statue of the god/dess, followed immediately by their reversion for distribution and consumption by the servants of the deity.

THE REVERSION OF OFFERINGS

One priest and as many assistants as necessary enter the Temple Chamber a final time. While he and any assistants lift up the offerings before the sacred image the priest/ess shall say:

"O [name of deity], every adversary withdraws for you. Heru has turned himself to his Eye in its name of 'Reversion-of-Offerings.' I am Djehuty. I come to perform this rite for [name of deity]. **These, your divine offerings revert, they revert to your servants for life, for stability, for health and for joy! O that the Eye of Heru may flourish for you eternally!"**[116]

Everyone withdraws, carrying away all food offerings which now become the memorial meal honoring the transfigured spirits of the blessed dead. Food offerings presented to the spirits of the departed are treated in the same manner as food offerings to the *Netjeru*. They are consumed and not discarded. After all, the blessed dead are "equipped, radiant spirits" who have been divinized, and, therefore, sharing their food is a blessing and a form of celebratory communion with them. This reflects the ancient temple practice of the Reversion Offering in which the foods offered to the main *Netjer* were then offered to the temple's other resident deities, and then offered before images of deceased pharaohs, and finally to various deceased personages (government officials, priests, scribes, pious laymen, etc.) who had the honor of having their personal stele or statue located within temple precincts. In the end the food offerings reverted to the priests and their dependents.

A traditional toast for this festive meal is:

"For your *Ka*! Drink the good intoxicating drink, celebrate a beautiful day!"[117]

APPENDIX E

Items Needed for Celebrating the Annual Ritual for the Beautiful Feast of the Western Valley

The following articles will be needed for this rite.

- four red candles previously anointed with frankincense oil (Second Ceremony)
- the Sevenfold Offering: bread, beer, spring water (i.e., "water from the inundation"), wine, milk, incense, and cool water (Third Ceremony)
- the Threefold Libation: water, wine, and milk (Fifth Ceremony)
- grains of myrrh incense (Seventh and Ninth Ceremonies)
- a candle or oil lamp to be placed before each image (Eighth Ceremony)
- a Sevenfold Libation of water (Tenth Ceremony)
- four *nemset* jars filled with water (Eleventh Ceremony)
- Aset's libation of water (Twelfth Ceremony)
- a water libation (Fifteenth Ceremony)
- a threefold libation of water (Sixteenth Ceremony)
- a bouquet of fragrant flowers (Seventeenth Ceremony)
- candle snuffer (Eighteenth Ceremony)
- broom for "Removing the Foot" (Nineteenth Ceremony)

Commentary
for the Great Recitation Ritual
for Transfiguring the *Ka* spirit

The following rite is a *s3ḫw* (pronounced *"sakhu"*) liturgy attested on four papyri. The title *"sakhu"* means "glorification" or "transfiguration." Its goal is the transfiguration of the *Ka*-spirit of a deceased person into a deified state, into being an *akh*, that is, a "transfigured and equipped spirit of light." Egyptologist Mark Smith sums up the characteristics of the *sakhu* liturgy:

> *s3ḫw* are spells addressed to Osiris or to deceased persons with the aim of securing their elevation to a particular state of existence. Important features of this elevation are the complete restoration of mental and physical faculties and integration within the hierarchy of gods and blessed spirits.[118]

According to Jan Assmann the full title of this liturgy reads:

> Beginning of the great *s3ḫw* to be recited at the 6th day festival, the festival of the mid-month and the month, and at every festival of Osiris, by the chief lector priest of this temple.[119]

In the four extant papyrus copies of this rite the text flows on without any indication of rubrics (i.e., instructions to the officiant pertaining to the ritual acts to be performed while reciting the text). Compared to other ritual compositions where rubrics do indeed occur throughout the text, it seems that the *sakhu* rituals were primarily, although not exclusively, intended to be recited. An examination of the text supports this view since the vast majority of the spells make reference to mythic events among the *Netjeru*, in particular, events relating to Ausir (Osiris), Heru (Horus), Aset (Isis), and Nebet Het (Nephthys). The number of spells referring to specific ritual actions, such as libations, censings, or food offerings, are rare. These *sakhu* recitations, then, are, as Mark Smith states, "manifestations of a belief in the 'performative' power of speech."[120] Please see the previous "Commentary for the Beautiful Feast of the Western Valley" for more on this important principle in Egyptian spiritual thought.

In discussing this *sakhu* liturgy, the noted Egyptologist Jan Assmann remarks, "The most striking feature of this liturgy is that (excluding spell 1) it consists exclusively of Pyramid and Coffin Texts."[121] He goes on to state that this particular liturgy–although the four extant copies date only to the Ptolemaic era–actually goes back "at least 1700 years to the MK" (Middle Kingdom).[122] This liturgy appears in four different contexts:

1. inscribed on Middle Kingdom (2022-1650 BCE) coffins–hence the name "Coffin Texts"–where they appear in the same set sequence;
2. on leather rolls from the Eighteenth Dynasty (1593-1293 BCE), having been used as liturgical manuscripts in the library at Abydos;
3. inscribed upon the walls and door jambs of tombs in the Theban necropolis dating to the Saite Period (656-525 BCE);
4. in four liturgical papyri of the Ptolemaic Period (305-31 BCE).[123]

In his article "Egyptian Mortuary Liturgies," Assmann breaks down this liturgy into its constituent parts by identifying each Pyramid Text or Coffin Text used in composing the rite.[124] The original manuscripts had simply transcribed the text as one long continuous piece, a procedure that makes sense if the lector-priest was expected to read the rite aloud with a minimum of specific cultic actions. By means of the empowered verbal utterance such recitational liturgies link the deceased with the various gods and goddesses participating in the timeless events surrounding Ausir.

Conspicuous by their absence are references to the many items of specialized cultic equipment or elaborate offering sequences that are the hallmark of many ancient Egyptian rites. It would appear that our liturgy would have been conducted with a modest array of cultic actions: one food offering, one libation, and a single censing. Quite frankly this would greatly help to make this liturgy a "doable" rite, keeping preparation time and cost to a minimum.

Recall that this liturgy was intended to be performed three times each month as well as at each Osirian festival. Even at that, we can see that it requires genuine commitment on the part of a family to carry out such a rite on a regular and long-term basis. This in itself speaks volumes as to the importance given to maintaining contact with and supporting the departed members of one's household. Our own surprise or even unease with such substantial time commitments may reveal more about our own era's preoccupations and underlying beliefs. Again, the vision of the ancient Egyptian priesthood can challenge us to reassess our own era's priorities and suppositions. The end result may help not only our departed loved ones, but it may help us to reprioritize our own goals in light of spiritual realities.

It is important to remember that this present edition of the Great Recitation Ritual has the Pyramid and Coffin Texts identified by the standardized numbering system in use among scholars. They are provided solely for the benefit of any reader who may wish to locate individual texts making up the Ritual. Textual divisions do not occur in any of the original manuscripts. When this ritual is contrasted to the previous one for the Beautiful Feast of the Western Valley, one can see that there is much less concern with the temporal sequence of specific cultic actions and much more a free-flowing, extra-temporal, contemplative visiting and re-visiting of mythic events that are not time-dependent. The rite is meditative, repetitive to the point of being at times almost antiphonal or hymn-like, and utterly above and outside the restrictive confines of the space-time boundaries of this world. In fact, it would not come as a surprise if some day it is discovered that this liturgy was cadenced in a musical or semi-musical fashion. Be that as it may, it remains that our Western mind, accustomed to the press of what we regard as "logical" and "sequential", may need to familiarize our spirits with other ways of being, with other dimensions of experiencing and interacting with transcendent realities.

The format for the present liturgy has been structured so that the Great Recitation Ritual is preceded by a brief set of cultic acts we label "Preliminary Rites." Then, following the Great Recitation Ritual, the service is brought to an end with a final series of actions we identify as "Concluding Rites." In ancient times this ritual in some cases would be performed in an open chamber within the tomb itself. However, there also is archaeological evidence showing that some rites could have been performed within the home, before a special niche containing a shrine with the image(s) of the ancestor(s). Such practices would substantiate the ancient belief that the *Ka*-spirits of the ancestors are not confined to the preserved body or even to the burial chamber itself.

Like the *Netjeru* themselves, the transfigured *akhu*-spirits are seen as quite capable of abiding in many dwelling places. After all, the transfigured *akhu*-spirits have themselves been divinized, and, like the *Netjeru*, can benefit from the ministrations of their human family. In turn, these glorified human beings provide a genuine and enduring link with the transcendent realm of the *Netjeru*. And, thus, the gulf between the worlds is bridged. By means of an enduring love coming from their human families, a love made manifest through the maintenance of these sacred memorial rites, the bond is reaffirmed and strengthened. As a lover does not cease to express his or her love through words and gestures, repeating again and again the words, "I love you," so the living repeat for their beloved dead the words that bring renewal and life, words that bridge every gap, even between death and life.

The Great Recitation Ritual
for Transfiguring the *Ka* spirit
of the Blessed Dead

Traditionally this ritual is performed on the evening of the sixth lunar day (six days following the New Moon), on the festival of the mid-month (the evening of the Full Moon), and, finally, at month's end (the evening of the day prior to the New Moon. Rubrics in the original of this as well as other *sakhu* liturgies indicate that it is appropriate to perform this rite at festivals honoring Ausir (Osiris).

This ritual may be conducted by a priest or priestess or a family member or friend of the deceased. The location might be graveside or in one's home shrine or altar. In the later case a special photo of the person or persons being remembered can be dedicated for this exclusive use. In keeping with ancient practice the image can be ritually prepared to serve as an abode or dwelling place for the spirit of the deceased by performing an Opening of the Mouth ritual. (For the text of this important rite please refer to Chapter Five.)

As with every rite performed for the *Netjeru*, mortuary rituals begin by the participants preparing their bodies and minds by means of a purifying bath. This also reminds us that what we are about to do is to contact the divine, to pronounce sacred words, and to assist our beloved dead in their transformation into "transfigured and equipped spirits of light."

PRELIMINARY RITES

The participants approach the gravesite or home shrine while gently shaking sistrums and menats. All bow, placing both hands on their knees while doing so.

THE FIRST CEREMONY
The Chapter of Lighting the Fire

The priest or priestess lights a candle or oil lamp and the following shall be said:

"Come, come in peace, O glorious Eye of Heru,
Be strong and renew your youth in peace.
For the flame shines like Ra on the double horizon.
I am pure, I am pure, I am pure, I am pure."

THE SECOND CEREMONY
The Chapter of Offering Incense

The priest/ess places incense on the burner. The following shall be said:

"The fire is laid, the fire shines;
The incense is laid on the fire, the incense shines.
    Your perfume comes to me, O Incense;
May my perfume come to you, O Incense.
    Your perfume comes to me, you *Netjeru*;
May my perfume come to you, you *Netjeru*.
    May I be with you, you *Netjeru*;
May you be with me, you *Netjeru*.
    May I live with you, you *Netjeru*;
May you live with me, you *Netjeru*.
    I love you, you *Netjeru*;
May you love me, you *Netjeru*."

THE THIRD CEREMONY
Spell for Summoning the Blessed Dead

The priest/ess extends both arms in the *nis* position used for invocations—arms stretched out and elbows bent, hands open—while the following shall be said:

"Come forth, O Ausir N [name], justified. Come forth, Ausir N, justified, born of N (justified). Awake! Turn yourself about, back toward life! O Ausir N, justified, raise yourself up. Bring yourself to me. Arise and receive offerings from my hand. I will be a helper for you!"[125]

THE GREAT RECITATION RITUAL

THE FIRST UTTERANCE
Title from the Manuscript Copies of the Ritual

"Beginning of the Great *s3hw* [*"sakhu,"* or "Ritual of Glorification"] to be recited at the 6th day festival, the festival of the mid-month and the month, and at every festival of Ausir [Osiris], by the chief lector priest of this temple."[126]

THE SECOND UTTERANCE
Pyramid Text 373

"Raise yourself, O N [name]. Receive your head, collect your bones, gather together your limbs, throw off the earth from your flesh, receive your bread which does not grow stale and your beer which does not grow sour . . . . *Khenty-menutef* [Heru) comes out to you and grasps your hand. He takes you to the sky, to your father Geb. He is joyful at meeting you. He sets his hands upon you, he kisses you and caresses you; he sets you at the head of the spirits, the Imperishable Stars. Those whose seats are hidden worship you. The Great Ones care for you. The Watchers wait upon you. Barley is threshed for you, emmer wheat is reaped for you, and an offering thereof is made at your monthly festivals, an offering thereof is made at your half-monthly festivals, according to what was commanded to be done for you by your father Geb. Rise up, O N, for you have not died."[127]

THE THIRD UTTERNACE
Pyramid Text 721

"O N [name], raise yourself so that you may eat figs and drink wine. Your face is that of a jackal, even as the face of Anpu . . . . Those in the realm of the dead serve you; chamberlains make purification for you, and the Great Mooring-Post [the Pole Star] calls to you. Your two divine mothers caress you; your two mothers kiss you. Your house upon the earth is strengthened for ever and for ever."

THE FOURTH UTTERANCE
Pyramid Text 422

"O N, go, so that you may be a *Ka* spirit and have power as a god, as the successor of Ausir. You have your *Ba* soul within you, you have your *sekhem*-power about you, you have your *Wrrt* crown [of Lower Egypt] upon you, you have your *Mizut* crown [of Upper Egypt] upon your shoulder. Your face is before you, worship of you is before you, the followers of the *Netjer* are behind you, the nobles of the *Netjer* are in front of you. They recite, 'The god comes, the god comes, this N comes on the throne of Ausir.' Aset speaks to you, and Nebet Het calls to you. The *Ka* spirits come to you bowing and they kiss the earth at your feet because they are in awe of you, O N. Ascend to your mother Nut. She will take your hand, she will give you a road to the horizon, to the place where Ra is. The doors of the sky are opened for you. The doors of the firmament are thrown open to you, and you will find Ra standing as he waits for you. He will take your hand and guide you to the two Conclaves of the sky. He will set you on the throne of Ausir.

"O N, the Eye of Heru comes to you. It addresses you. Your *Ba* which is among the *Netjeru* comes to you, your *sekhem* power which is among the spirits comes to you. The son has protected his father; Heru has protected Ausir. Heru has protected N from his foes. May you arise, O N, protected and provided as a *Netjer*, equipped with the form of Ausir upon the throne of the Foremost of the Westerners [Ausir].

"O N, there is given to you what is yours by Ra. May you speak of yourself when you have received the form of a *Netjer*. May you be great thereby with the *Netjeru* (gods) who preside over the Lake [of Rushes].

"O N, may your *Ba* stand among the *Netjeru* and among the *Ka* spirits, for it is the awe of you which is in their hearts.

"O N, succeed to your throne at the head of the living, for it is the awe of you which is in their hearts. May your name live upon earth. May your name endure upon earth, for you shall not perish, nor shall you be destroyed for ever and ever."

THE FIFTH UTTERANCE
Pyramid Text 374

"Be great, O N, and cross over! May your name be announced to Ausir. You are surefooted and strong, so come across the Great Bed of the sky to us. You will not be seized by powers of the earth; you will not be opposed by powers of the sky. The doors of the sky will be opened for you so that you may go forth from them as Heru and the jackal beside him who conceals his shape from his foes, for there is no father of yours among humankind who could sire you, and there is no mother among humankind who could give you birth. You are of the gods! You are of the gods!"

THE SIXTH UTTERANCE
Pyramid Text 424

"O N, you possess freedom in your movements even as Heru is free in his movements. Your arms are those of Anpu [Anubis], your face is that of Wepwawet."

The priest/ess raises up the food offerings, slowing raising and then lowering the tray upon which they are arrayed four times. The following shall be said:

"O N, 'An-Offering-Which-the-King-Gives' is made for you, that you might occupy the Mounds of Heru and the Mounds of Sutekh, that you might sit upon your throne of iron and judge their affairs at the head of the Great Ennead which is in Iunu [Heliopolis] . . . . Take this god's-offering of yours with which you are content each day, a thousand of all things good and pure! O N, you are provided with water, even water from the inundation, and you have every good thing which has been brought to you by your brother the Old One, even Atum."

THE SEVENTH UTTERANCE
Pyramid Text 366

"O Ausir N, arise! Lift yourself up! Your mother Nut has borne you. Geb has wiped your mouth for you. The Great Ennead protects you . . . . Aset and Nebet Het come to you that they may make you vigorous, and you are complete and great . . . . Your sister Aset comes to you rejoicing for love of you. You have placed her on your phallus and your seed issues into her, she being ready as *Sopdet,* and Heru has come forth from you. It is well with you through him in his name 'Spirit who is in the *Djendru* barque' [the barque of Ausir]. He protects you in his name of Heru, the son who protects his father."

THE EIGHTH UTTERANCE
Pyramid Text 367

"O Ausir N, Geb brings Heru to you that he may protect you and bring you to the hearts of the *Netjeru.* May you neither languish nor groan. Heru has given to you his Eye that you may take possession of the *Wrrt* crown by means of it at the head of the *Netjeru.* Heru has reassembled your limbs and he has restored your body. Nothing in you shall be disturbed."

THE NINTH UTTERANCE
Pyramid Text 368

"O Ausir N, this is Heru in your embrace, and he protects you. It is well with him and again with you in your name of 'Horizon-from-which-Ra-goes-forth.' Clasp your arms about him, about him, and he will not be separated from you. Heru will not let you perish. May you live! For Heru has given you his children

132

so that they may go beneath you and none of them will turn back when they carry you. Your mother Nut has spread herself over you in her name of *'Shet-pet.'* She has caused you to be a *Netjer* to any foe in your name of *'Netjer.'* She will protect you from all things evil in her name of 'Great Well,' for you are the greatest of her children. Geb is gracious to you; he has loved you and protected you. He has restored for you your head; he has caused Djehuty to reassemble you so the evil [death and decay] which was upon you comes to an end."

THE TENTH UTTERANCE
Pyramid Text 369

"O Ausir N, stand up! Heru has caused you to stand up, for Geb has caused Heru to see his father in you in your name of 'Mansion of the Monarch.' Heru has given you the *Netjeru.* He has caused them to go up to you so that they may make you glad. Heru has given you his Eye that you may see with it. You shall come to your former condition, for the *Netjeru* have knit together your face for you. Heru has opened* your eye for you so that you may see with it in its name of 'Opener of Roads.' Heru has struck* your mouth for you; he has adjusted your mouth to your bones for you. Heru has split open* your mouth for you, and it is your well-beloved son who has re-set your eyes for you. Heru will not let your face be sightless in your name of 'Heru-at-the-head-of-his-people.'"

*Reference to the ritual actions of touching the mouth and eyes with the adze-tool during the funeral ceremony of Opening the Mouth.

THE ELEVENTH UTTERANCE
Pyramid Text 423

The priest/ess pours a libation of water. The following shall be said:

"O N, receive this your cold water, for you have coolness with Heru in your name of 'Him-who-issued-from-cold-water.'"

The priest/ess lifts up an offering of natron. The following shall be said:

"Receive your natron that you may be divine, for Nut has caused you to be a *Netjer* in your name of 'god.'"

THE TWELFTH UTTERANCE
Pyramid Text 370

"O Ausir N, Heru has caused the *Netjeru* to join you and to be brotherly to you in your name of '*Senut* shrines.' Go up to Heru. Betake yourself to him. Do not be far from him in your name of 'Sky.' Heru has attached himself to you and he will never depart from you, for he has made you live. Run, receive his word and be pleased with it. Listen to him, for it will not harm you. He has brought to you all the *Netjeru* at once and there is not one of them who will depart from him. Heru has attached himself to his children. Join yourself with those of his body, for they have loved you. Heru has acted on behalf of his *Ka* spirit in you so that you may be content in your name of 'Contented *Ka* spirit.'"

THE THIRTEENTH UTTERANCE
Pyramid Text 371

"O Ausir N, Heru has placed you in the hearts of the *Netjeru*; he has caused you to take possession of all that is yours. Heru has found you, and it goes well with him through you. He has protected you as one who is to be protected in due season. Geb has seen your nature and has set you in your place. You are the father of Heru, having begotten him in your name of 'Begetter,' and Heru is pleased with you in your name of 'Foremost of the Westerners.'"

THE FOURTEENTH UTTERANCE
Pyramid Text 365

"Raise yourself, O N. Run, you who are greatly strong! You shall sit at the head of the *Netjeru*. You shall do that which Ausir did in the Mansion of the Prince [the temple of Ra] which is in Iunu. Receive your dignity, for your foot will not be obstructed in the sky. You will not be opposed upon the earth, for you are a spirit whom Nut bore, whom Nebet Het suckled, and it is they who restored you. Arise in your strength and do what formerly you used to do, for you are more spirit-like than all *Ka* spirits. You shall do what Ausir did, for you are he who is upon his throne. Arise, O *Ka* spirit, greatly strong, adorned as a great wild bull. You will not be opposed in any place where you walk. Your foot will not be obstructed in any place where you desire to be."

THE FIFTEENTH UTTERANCE
Pyramid Text 332

"You are one who escaped from the coiled serpent. You have ascended in a blast of fire, having turned yourself about. The two skies [east and west] go to you, and the two earths [south and north] come to you. You have trodden upon the *kad* plant under the feet of Geb. You have travelled the roads of Nut."

THE SIXTEENTH and
SEVENTEENTH UTTERANCES
Pyramid Text 468

"O N, raise yourself! Stand up! The Great Ennead which is in Iunu has assigned you to your great throne, so that you may sit at the head of the Ennead as Geb, most senior of the *Netjeru*, as Ausir at the head of the Powers, and as Heru, Lord of both humankind and *Netjeru*.

"O N, whose form is as mysterious as that of Anpu [Anubis], receive your jackal-face. The Herdsman waits upon you, even you who are at the head of the Conclaves as Anpu who presides over the God's Booth [the embalming tent], **and you make the Followers of Heru content. May Heru protect you, O N. May Heru make you content with the offering with him. May your heart be content with it in the monthly festival and in the half-monthly festival. May the rejoicing woman rejoice at you as at Anpu who presides over the God's Booth. May Aset cry out to you. May Nebet Het call to you as Heru who protects his father Ausir. The son has protected his father; Heru has protected N. As Ausir lives, as the spirit who is in Nedit** [the place of Ausir's murder] **lives, so does N live. O N, may your name live at the head of the living. May you be a *Ka* spirit at the head of *Ka* spirits. May you have power at the head of Powers.**

"**O N, the awe of you is the intact Eye of Heru, namely the White Crown, the serpent-goddess of Nekheb. May she set the awe of you in the eyes of all the *Netjeru*, in the eyes of the spirits of the Imperishable Stars and those whose seats are hidden** [those in the afterlife, or *Duat*], **and in the eyes of everything that shall see you and hear your name.**

"**O N, I provide you with the Eye of Heru, the Red Crown rich in power and many-natured, so that it may protect you just as it protects Heru. May it set your power at the head of the Two Enneads as the two serpent-goddesses on your brow, that they may raise you up, that they may guide you to your mother Nut so that she might take your hand. May you not languish. May you not groan. May you not suffer. Heru has caused you to be a *Ka* spirit at the head of the *Ka* spirits and to have power at the head of the living. How good it is, what Heru has done for N, for this *Ka* spirit whom a *Netjer* fashioned, whom two *Netjeru* fashioned!**"

The priest/ess places two spoonfuls of myrrh on the censer. The following is said:

"**O N, I am Djehuty. 'An-Offering-Which-the-King-Gives': There is given to you offerings of food and drink and all things good and pure, and these two portions of incense which came forth from Heru, so that he may make your heart content for ever and ever.**"

THE EIGHTEENTH UTTERANCE
Pyramid Text 723

"O N, raise yourself upon iron bones and golden members, for this body of yours belongs to a *Netjer*. It will not waste away; it will not be destroyed; it will not decay. The warmth which is on your mouth is the breath that issued forth from the nostrils of Sutekh, and the winds of the sky will be destroyed if the warmth on your mouth be destroyed. The sky will be deprived of its stars if the warmth on your mouth be lacking. May your flesh be born to life, and may your life be more than the life of the stars in their season of life."

THE NINETEENTH UTTERANCE
Pyramid Text 690

The priest/ess offers in his/her hands two strips of woven cloth or ribbons. They may be draped around the image or photograph of the departed. The following shall be said:

"Ausir awakes. The languid *Netjer* awakes. The *Netjer* stands up. The *Netjer* has power in his body. N awakes. The languid *Netjer* awakes. The *Netjer* stands up. The *Netjer* has power in his body. Heru arises and clothes this N in the woven fabric which went forth from him. This N is provided as a *Netjer*.

"O N, stand up and come in peace to Ra, you who are the messenger of the great *Netjer*. Go to the sky. Come forth from the gate of the horizon. May Geb guide you, you having a *Ba* soul as a *Netjer*, you being strong as a *Netjer*, and having power in your body as a *Netjer*, as a *Ba* soul at the head of the living, as a Power at the head of the *Akhu* [transfigured spirits].

"This N comes provided as a *Netjer*, his bones are knit together as Ausir. This Ausir comes to you in Iunu [Heliopolis] and you are protected. Your heart is placed in your body for you. Your face is that of a jackal. Your flesh is that of Atum. Your *Ba* is within you, and your *Sekhem* power surrounds you.

Aset is in front of you, and Nebet Het is behind you. You go round the Mounds of Heru and you go round the Mounds of Sutekh. It is Shu and Tefnut who guide you when you go forth from Iunu.

"O N, rise up for Heru, that he may make you an *Akh* [glorified spirit], and guide you when you ascend to the sky. May your mother Nut receive you. May she take your hand. May you not languish. May you not groan. May you live as the *Kheper*-beetle [the morning form of Ra], being stable as a *djed* pillar [symbol of Ausir].

"O N, you are clad as a *Netjer,* your face is that of a jackal as Ausir, this *Ba*-soul who is in Nedit [the place where Ausir died], this Power is in the Great City. The sky trembles, the earth quakes at the feet of the *Netjer,* at the feet of N. Your power is that of Ra; you make humans tremble in the night as does a *Netjer,* a lord of awe. Govern the *Netjeru* as a Power at the head of the Powers.

"O N, I have wept for you. I have mourned for you. I will not forget you. I will not rest until my voice speaks the words of offering for you each day, in the monthly festival, in the half-monthly festival, and at every memorial festival of the year. This is done to sustain you throughout the year, in accordance with your desire so that you may live as a *Netjer.* O N, may your body be adorned so that you may come to me."

THE TWENTIETH UTTERANCE
Pyramid Text 674

"I come to you for I am your son; I come to you for I am Heru. I set your staff for you at the head of the glorified spirits (*akhu*), and I place your sceptre at the head of the Imperishable Stars. I have found you knit together; your face is that of a jackal and your hind-parts are the Celestial Serpent. She freshens your heart in your body in the house of her father Anpu. Be purified and sit at the head of those who are greater than you. Sit on your iron throne, on the seat of the Foremost of the Westerners [Ausir] . . .

"The Mourning Woman calls to you as Aset, and the Joyful One rejoices over you as Nebet Het. You stand before the *senut* shrines as Min. You stand at the head of the people of Athribis as Apis. You stand in *Pedu-esh* as Sokar. You stand at the great processional way with your sceptre and your crown, with the plumes on the arms of Djehuty and the sharp knife of Sutekh. You shall extend your hand to the dead and to the spirits who shall grasp your hand for the Foremost of the Westerners."

THE TWENTY-FIRST UTTERANCE
Pyramid Text 462

"O N, mighty in waking and great in sleeping, for whom sweetness is sweet, raise yourself, O N, for you have not died."

THE TWENTY-SECOND UTTERANCE
Pyramid Text 675

"O N, come in peace to Ausir! O messenger of the great *Netjer*, come in peace to the great *Netjer*! The doors of the sky are opened for you, the starry sky is thrown open for you. The Jackal of Upper *Kemet* [Egypt] comes down to you as Anpu [Anubis] at your side. . . .

"O N, you have no human father who could beget you. You have no human mother who could bear you. Your mother is the Great Wild Cow who dwells in Nekheb–white of headcloth, long of hair, whose breasts are full. She suckles you and does not wean you.

"Raise yourself, O N, and clothe yourself in this cloak of yours which comes from the Mansion [the house of Ra], with your mace on your arm and your scepter in your hand; with your scepter on your arm and your mace in your hand -standing at the head of the Two Conclaves so that you may judge the *Netjeru* [the gods].

"O N, you belong to the stars which shine in the train of the Morning Star, and truly no *Netjer* will be absent because of what has been said to him. He will offer to you your thousand measures of bread, your thousand of beer, your thousand of oxen and your thousand of fowl, and your thousand of everything on which a *Netjer* lives!"

THE TWENTY-THIRD UTTERANCE
Pyramid Text 676

"You have your water. You have your flood. You have that stream issuing forth from Ausir. Gather together your bones and make ready your bodily members. Throw off your dust and loosen your bonds. The tomb is open for you, and the doors of your resting place are drawn back for you. The doors of the sky are thrown open for you.

"Aset says, 'Greetings!' and Nebet Het proclaims, 'In peace!' when they see their brother in the Festival of Atum. This cool water of yours, O Ausir, is that which is in *Djedu* [Busiris]. Your *Ba* is within you and your power surrounds you. It has been established at the head of all the Powers.

"Raise yourself, O N. May you travel across the Southern Mounds. May you travel across the Northern Mounds. May you have power by means of the powers within you. There has been given to you your *Ba* spirits, the jackals which Heru of Nekhen has given to you.

"Raise yourself, O N. May you sit on your iron throne, for Anpu who presides over the God's Booth has commanded that you be purified with your eight *nemset*-jars and your eight *aabet* jars which came forth from the Great House of the *Netjer*. You indeed are god-like, for you have shouldered the sky and you have raised up the earth. The Mourning-Woman cries out to you; the Great Mooring-post calls to you. Hands are clapped for you and feet are stamped for you. You ascend as a star, as the Morning Star!

"O Geb, N comes to you his father. He comes to you. Take his hand and let him sit on the great throne . . . . His mouth is cleansed with natron, and he is purified on the thighs of *Khenty-irty* [Heru of Khem (Letopolis)]. The nails on his hands and feet are purified. Do for him what you did for his brother

Ausir on that day of putting his bones in order, of making good the soles of his feet, and of traveling the causeway.

"The *Netjeru* come to you, bowing in homage to you. You summon the Conclave for Upper *Kemet* [Egypt], and the Conclave for Lower *Kemet* comes to you bowing."

THE TWENTY-FOURTH UTTERANCE
(Section One)
Pyramid Text 477

"The sky reels and the earth quakes. Heru comes and Djehuty appears. They raise Ausir from upon his side and they make him stand up in front of the Two Enneads. . . . Raise yourself, O Ausir. Aset has your arm and Nebet Het has your hand. The sky is given to you. The earth is given to you. The Field of Rushes together with the Mounds of Heru and the Mounds of Sutekh are given to you. The towns are yours and the provinces assembled by Atum are yours. He who declares this is Geb."

". . . I have come to you, my lord. I have come to you, Ausir. I will wipe your face, and I will clothe you with the clothing of a *Netjer.* I will do you priestly service. . . . I have come to you, my lord. I have come to you, Ausir. I will wipe your face. I will do for you this which Geb commanded me to do for you. I will make firm your hand over the living, and I will lift up your hand bearing the *was* staff."

THE TWENTY-FOURTH UTTERANCE
(Section Two)
Coffin Text 837

"Opening the doors of the sky, throwing open the doors of the firmament, Heru appears and Djehuty approaches. They come to Ausir and they cause him to go forth at the head of the Enneads.

"Rise up, Ausir, onto your side. Aset holds your arm and Nebet Het takes your hand, so go forth between them. The sky and the earth are given to you. The Field of Rushes is given to you. Travel throughout the Mounds of Heru and the Mounds of Sutekh in the presence of these two *Netjeru*, the two lords who give judgement.

"Live, Ausir! Being purified, I am holy. I have come that I may make for you the abundant food offerings which your son Heru made for you. I have come that I may make for you the great meal that Geb has commanded. Lift up your hand which bears the *ankh* sign of life, and make firm your hand which bears the *was* staff, so that you may be the *djed* pillar of the *Netjeru*. You shall go forth for you have gone forth as Lord of the horn.

"I have come to you, my lord. I have come to you, my god. I have come to you, Ausir, so that I may clothe you with your apparel. May you be pure in *Djedet*. It is your daughter *Sopdet* [the stellar form of Aset] who sits for you and who prepares for you your yearly sustenance [food offerings] in her name of 'Year.' It is she who guides me.

"I have come to you, my lord, I have come to you, Ausir, that I may wipe your face and clothe you with the clothing of a *Netjer*.

"I have come to you, my lord, I have come to you, my god, I have come to you, Ausir, that I may wipe your face and clothe you with the clothing of a *Netjer*. Priestly service will be done for you by Heru your son whom you fashioned. I will remove you from the dead and I will put you at the head of your runners who are *akhu* [transfigured spirits] in the West and who transform into *akhu* those in the West. My bread is the bread of the *Netjeru*, and my beer is the beer of the *Netjeru* on which the *Netjeru* live, and I will live thereon. What Heru did for his father, so will I do for you."

THE TWENTY-FIFTH UTTERANCE
Coffin Text 839

"The Great One falls on his side. He who is in Nedit quakes. 'Raise your hand,' says Ra, and your hand is taken by his

Enneads. O my father, see, this is Ausir . . . . Go down onto the deck of that barque in which Ra rows to the horizon. O my father Ausir, go down onto the bow of this barque of Ra. You and Ra shall go aboard her; you and Ra shall sit in her. You and Ra shall take your seat in her. You shall sit on this throne of Ra. Heru on your south side, and Sutekh on your north side. Shu on your east side, and Tefnut on your west side. They will cause you to take possession of the *werret* crown at the head of the Enneads just as they caused Ra to take possession of the *werret* crown at the head of the Enneads. They will lead you to the seats of Ra. They will receive you as a spirit.

"I have come, O my father Ausir, for I am your son. I am Heru. I am your heir upon your throne, while you are perpetuated in front of your shrine upon the earth. May you speak with the great and mighty *Netjeru*. May your power be even greater than that of the *Netjeru* of the Westerners. May the awe of you be mightier than that of the *Netjeru* of the Westerners. May the Silent Ones go to you, Ausir; may the awe of you be upon them and the awe of you on their hearts. May your bonds be cut by Heru who is in his house, and may your cords be hewn asunder by Sutekh who is in *Henet*. O my father, Ausir, be a *Ka* spirit, be awake, be wise, be effective, and walk the earth by day in full stride. May you travel by day. May you open up a path. May you go to rest on the pillow of Ra which separates the Day-barque from the Night-barque in which Ra sails. The darkness of the two *Netjeru* [Ra and Ausir] in which they go to rest is what the two *Netjeru* seek when they go to rest. Go aboard the Day-barque on the day when the Lord of the Horizon is transfigured so that he may row you in the Night-barque and the Day-barque like Ra every day. Stand up, Ausir, living for ever and ever!"

CONCLUDING RITES

THE FOURTH CEREMONY
Extinguishing the Candle or Oil Lamp

Using a candle snuffer, the priest/ess extinguishes the flame. The following shall be said:

"This is the Eye of Heru by which you have become great, by which you live, and by which you have power, O N. This is the Eye of Heru which you consume and through which you enchant your body. The *Wedjat* Eye now enters into the West, into Manu, but it shall return. Truly, the Eye of Heru returns in peace!"[128]

One final ceremonial act remains: the removal of the food offerings, followed immediately by their reversion for distribution and consumption by those who participated in this rite.

THE REVERSION OF OFFERINGS

Standing before the image of the deceased a final time, the priest/ess shall lift up the offerings and shall say:

"O N, every adversary withdraws for you. Heru has turned himself to his Eye in its name of 'Reversion-of-Offerings.' I am Djehuty. I come to perform this rite for N. These, your divine offerings revert, they revert to your servants for life, for stability, for health and for joy! O that the Eye of Heru may flourish for you eternally!"[129]

The food offerings are removed and they now may be used as part of a memorial meal for the blessed dead.

APPENDIX F

Items Needed for Celebrating the Great Recitation Ritual for Transfiguring the *Ka* spirit of the Blessed Dead

The following articles will be needed for this rite.
- a candle or oil lamp (for the 1st Ceremony)
- *kyphi* incense (for the 2nd Ceremony)–for a recipe see Kerry Wisner's *Eye of the Sun*, 76, or Lise Manniche's *Sacred Luxuries: Fragrance, Aromatherapy, and Cosmetics in Ancient Egypt*, 47-60.
- tray with food offerings (for the 6th Utterance)
- water for a libation offering (for the 11th Utterance)
- natron (also for the 11th Utterance)
- myrrh incense (for the 16th Utterance)
- two strips of woven cloth or ribbon (for the 19th Utterance)
- candle snuffer (for the 4th Ceremony)

Sutekh (Set) is shown stationed at the prow of the divine barque, spearing the cosmic foe Apep with his iron lance. For most of ancient Egypt's history the great Netjer Sutekh was regarded in a positive light as the one chosen by Ra to protect the divine barque called "Millions of Years" on its nightly journey through the Duat (Underworld) as well as during the day as Ra crossed the sky. As Egypt fell again and again under the domination of foreign powers—the Hyksos, Persians, Greeks, and Romans—as well as long-term exposure to foreign ideologies which required some sort of evil being to explain the hardships and misfortunes of life, it became increasingly difficult for Egyptians to comprehend the truly beneficial role that Sutekh plays in maintaining Balance or ma'at in the cosmos. This resulted in a fatal impoverishment of the original Kemetic vision.

Illustration based on the funerary papyrus of Herweben. (Museum of Fine Arts, Boston)

CHAPTER FOUR

The Book of Overthrowing Apep

Introduction
to The Book of Overthrowing Apep

The official religious rituals of ancient Egypt included a combination of what we in the modern era would regard as positive and negative, constructive and destructive. On the positive side we find in the temple services daily worship and praise, replete with a multitude of offerings, in particular, the central cultic act of the offering of *Ma'at*, that is, an offering of that which is right and just, that which is in full accord with goodness, beauty, and divine order. *Ma'at*, in fact, was so esteemed that it was regarded as that upon which the *Netjeru* (gods) live.

Ma'at was their sustenance and their joy. Modern philosophers–in much less compelling language–might term *Ma'at* the "ground of being," that is, the essence of that which makes something good. No single word in English adequately translates or conveys the full meaning of this core concept. In his *The Priests of Ancient Egypt*, Serge Sauneron describes *Ma'at* as:

> The equilibrium of this entire cosmos, the harmonious rapport of its elements, the indispensable cohesion that maintained the entities that had been created–this was what the Egyptians called Ma'at, the very appearance of the world as willed by the divine, the order of the universe as the divine had established it. . . .[130]

The ancient Egyptians did not take the condition of *Ma'at* in their world for granted. It was always seen as an effort, indeed, as an ongoing, daily struggle engaging both humans as well as the *Netjeru*. A central theme in the mythic vision of Ra crossing the sky in his day-barque was the danger confronted and overcome in the person of the chaos-serpent, Apep or Aapep (referred to in Greek as "Apophis"). It was this cosmic enemy of creation who was utterly opposed to all that exists. It was he who threatened the equilibrium of *Ma'at*. As Dimitri Meeks and Christine Favard-Meeks explain:

From the moment of its creation, the world was threatened by the Forces of the uncreated, forces that the mere existence of a world drove back toward its periphery. There was no escaping these forces, even if they were pushed further and further back as the domain of the created expanded. Because they had not been brought into being by the act of creation, they could not be definitively destroyed. They could only be defeated periodically; their repeated onslaughts made it necessary to wage unending battle to maintain the integrity and equilibrium of creation.[131]

The ancient Egyptian experienced the civilized, orderly world as fragile and in need of continual maintenance, defence, and renewal. Each new day brought fresh opportunities as well as new challenges and struggles. It was humankind's responsibility to share in the struggle to maintain the creator's creation. The battle was waged on both the divine as well as human plane. The reality of this deep cosmic struggle permeates the mythic vision of ancient Egypt. In the three great dimensions of the existent–in the celestial realm or sky, on the earth, and, finally, in the *Duat* or netherworld–the lord of creation, the sun god Ra, is repeatedly threatened by the hostile action of that embodiment of the nonexistent, the chaos serpent. As Egyptologist Erik Hornung explains in *Conceptions of God in Ancient Egypt*:

Egyptian ontology is based on the insight that the nonexistent is not simply transformed into the existent and thus eliminated. Creation does not remove what was there before it; as well as the sum total of existence there is a remainder which is endless and which is never transformed into existence.[132]

Creation was seen as an ongoing, eternal process–a cycle of light and darkness, a cycle of life and death, renewal and rebirth. But, in the words of Stephen Quirke,

The process never freed itself from the risk of collapse, the danger that the forces of disintegration would engulf the bark of the sun, and this threat was pictured by the Egyptians in the form of the serpent Aapep on whose coils Ra might founder like a boat on a sandbank in the Nile.[133]

When the Egyptians dug into the soil, the shallow water table brought to the surface the waters below, recalling the underlying, hidden waters of Nun, those limitless, primordial waters from which all life would spring. When the Nile flooded each year and the land was covered with water, the Egyptians were reminded of those primordial waters from which the primeval hill emerged. It seemed then that the whole of the created world was surrounded by the primeval flood. In the event of too much water from the annual flooding of the Nile, the people would witness the collapse of mud brick buildings into the rising waters, melting back into the formless, watery depths. Life was tenuous. The nonexistent penetrates the existent, pulling at it as if to sink back once and for all into nothingness, shapeless and formless and without life.

In our own times astronomers see the universe as expanding, growing ever larger–creation expanding as it fills the void. But they also see black holes with gravitational fields so intense that they are capable of sucking into themselves entire galaxies that venture near. As stars age they grow red and large, only to collapse in upon themselves in ever recurring cycles of birth and death. But we need not look to the stars to find the growth and collapse of natural phenomena. Our own planet serves up numerous examples of events in nature that underscore the cycles of life and the ongoing struggle to maintain it. Likewise, at the level of moral action we see individuals as well as nations struggle with issues of justice and right behaviour. *Ma'at* continues to be endangered and in need of humanity's assistance to overcome a host of dark and very real forces.

And just as a deep sense of this cosmic struggle helped shape the mythic universe in ancient Egyptian thought, so, too, official temple rituals reflected this awareness of the daily battle to sustain the cosmos in the face of repeated and unrelenting attack. In a very illuminating passage from the Teaching for King Merikare (c.2060 BCE), the author advises his young royal reader:

> Shepherd the people, the cattle of God,
> for it is for their sake that He created heaven and earth.
> He stilled the raging of the waters,
> And created the winds so that their nostrils might live.
> They are His images who came forth from His body,
> And it is for their sake that He rises in the sky.
> . . . .
> For their sake He creates the daylight,
> And voyages (across the sky) to observe them.
> . . . .
> And when they weep, He hearkens.
> For them He has made rulers from the egg,
> Leaders to raise up the backs of the weak.
> *He has ordained for them magic*
> *As weapons to fend off the impact of what may come to*
> *pass* . . . . [Italics mine][134]

Again and again the rituals and rites of Egypt reinforce the fact that magic–or what the Egyptians called *heka*–was a gift of the creator god to humankind. Magical practice was part and parcel of official temple worship. *Heka*-power was to be used as a weapon "to fend off the impact of what may come to pass." In this passage we see the creator's gifts to humanity: he created the universe for humankind; he appointed leaders for them, and he has given them the gift of magic to enable them to ward off dangers.

To the ancient Egyptian the image of the snake represented both positive and negative forces. The cobra could stand for the goddess Wadjet whose image adorned the forehead of pharaoh in the form of the sacred uraeus, protecting the king from harm. On the other hand the snake, no doubt due to certain of its characteristics, came to represent the uncanny and eerie forces of the nonexistent, becoming the very personification of the unseen, malevolent forces that sought to destroy life. The primitive reptilian appearance of the snake, its lightning-fast ability to deliver a poisonous bite, its habit of emerging from underground, its ability to travel effortlessly through the water–each of these traits prompted the Egyptians to see in the snake the epitome of all that was negative, destructive, and threatening.

Just as the *Netjeru* could be manifest in animal form–recall the sacred ram of Amun, the Apis bull of Ptah, the ibis of Djehuty, as well as many other instances–so too the great enemy was seen in animal form as a huge serpent, unlike any real serpent because it represents both the source and totality of nonexistent and chaotic forces. But more than being just a symbol or personification such as Uncle Sam or the statue of Liberty, Apep was understood as a conscious entity. Just as *Ma'at* at the opposite extreme was a living deity, the daughter of Ra, with her own temples and priesthood, so Apep was apprehended as the malevolent embodiment or hypostasis of the anti-life, anti-creation energies of the nonexistent. Its reptilian form serves to reinforce its image as one of fearfulness and powerful malevolence.

In keeping with their understanding of the active role humankind plays in the cosmic struggle to increase *Ma'at* and to destroy *isfet* (evil or that which is wrongful), the ancient priesthood performed powerful magical rituals to destroy the chaos-serpent. Several examples of such rites are preserved in the Bremner-Rhind Papyrus, dating to around the fourth century BCE. The following titles appear in this very lengthy papyrus:

- The book of the felling of Apep the foe of Ra . . . which is performed daily in the temple of Amun-Ra, Lord of the Thrones of the Two Lands, who dwells in Ipet Sut
- The first book of felling Apep the foe of Ra
- The book of felling the foe of Ra daily
- The book of the repelling of Apep the great enemy which is done at morning-tide
- The book of knowing the creations (*kheperu*) of Ra and of felling Apep
- The book of felling Apep
- Another book of felling Apep

□   The Names of Apep[135]

The manuscript gives instructions on preparing models and drawings of the chaos-serpent as well as containing the recitational texts used during the ritual destruction of those models or drawings. Surely here we see *heka*-power used as we saw described earlier in the Teaching for King Merikare–as a weapon. Wielding magic, the priests of Egypt engage in the continuing cosmic struggle using the gift with which the creator god has endowed humankind. The means of activating that *heka*-power aimed at destroying Apep were manifold: spitting, trampling, cursing, binding, stabbing, burning, and burying the wax image or image drawn on papyrus. All aspects of the cosmic foe were targeted: its name, body, spirit, shadow, and *heka*-power. These are not rituals for the squeamish. By means of words infused with *heka*-power the priests brought to bear a battalion of powerful deities with the sole intention of fulfilling the command of the creator-god:

> O you wise ones who are in this land, and you Nine Netjeru (gods) who came into being from my flesh, be vigilant in felling Apep! Exorcise him and destroy his name. May your arms fell him. May you not permit his name to be spread abroad. His children shall not exist. His seat shall not exist, and he shall have neither Ba (double) nor body nor Ka (spirit), for he is given over to the Eye of Ra and it has power over him. It devours him.[136]

Some readers may feel uncomfortable with the starkly aggressive tone of these rites. And certainly not everyone will feel called to enact them. That is a very personal decision best left to each individual. The incontrovertible fact is these rituals were a regular part of formal worship in ancient Egypt. Internal textual evidence as well as graphic depictions on temple walls show that these and similar rites for combating spiritual enemies were among the corpus of liturgical rituals performed throughout Egypt. In our present effort to reclaim and restore the authentic rites of ancient Egypt such rituals can reveal important insights and attitudes that helped shape the spiritual vision of this ancient culture. In our own contemporary society there often is a tendency to gloss over things we are not comfortable with in studying ancient spiritual traditions.

Much like a Chinese take-away meal, some will pick and choose what suits their fancy or what they might at first glance be attracted to. The end result is a makeshift spirituality–a little of this, a bit of that. But experience shows that spiritual patchworks eventually fail to sustain a compelling interest–and a lasting dedication in the hearts and minds of spiritual seekers. However, the spirituality of ancient Egypt is neither easy nor simple. It is nuanced, expansive, and presents a wholistic and integrated vision of the world of spirit. It does not deny the existence of evil or chaos. It acknowledges it and deals with it by means of what the ancient Egyptians recognized as a divine gift–*heka*-power, rites of magic that address the root cause of the chaotic energies tearing at the fabric of an orderly universe.

Typical of Egyptian magical practice, the rituals of *The Book of Overthrowing Apep* place the action within a mythological context. Two of the rituals (the two lengthiest) contain what Egyptologists refer to as creation stories, spoken by the creator god himself. The divine narrator describes how the Lord of All had come into being and how he created each generation of *Netjeru* until we come to the main point, namely, that "They (the children of the gods) made conjuration in my name that they might fell their foes; they created the magic spells for felling Apep." And just so there is no doubt about the divine authorization for such magic, the creator god is made to say, "O you wise ones who are in this land, and you Nine *Netjeru* (gods) who came into being from my flesh, be vigilant in felling Apep! Exorcise him and destroy his name . . . ." By divine mandate the children of Ra are counselled to utilize *heka*-power to battle the chaos serpent. Thus the entire proceeding is taken from the mundane world and it is transformed into a cosmological event. As noted Egyptologist Jørgen Podemann Sørensen explains:

> By far most Egyptian magical formulae state some argument in favor of the efficacy of the formula itself or

the rite that it accompanies. . . . One of the most prominent
varieties of Egyptian magical argument is found in the so-
called epic formulae. . . . In the epic formula, a *historiola*
is cited as exemplar of the handling of the situation in
question. . . . By identifying the present situation as the
parallel mythical one, the formula subjects the case in
question to the rules laid down in primeval time . . . .[137]

In the case of *The Book of Overthrowing Apep* we see that the
recital of the creation story followed by the god's command to "be
vigilant in felling Apep" pierces, as it were, the veil covering day-
to-day life to reveal the great underlying cosmic war that must be
waged against the serpent of non existence.

Who, we may ask, is to undertake such a task? Immediately
following the god's command the reciter states, "I am he who has
been sent to fell him, to destroy his name, and to chastise his name
and his magic."[138] This recalls the statement from the daily morning
liturgy, "Behold, I am sent to look upon the face of the god."[139] It was
a priestly commission. It carried an official sanction. By "official"
we do not imply simply the proper bureaucratic permission. It was
a royal commission for it was ultimately pharaoh who had major
but not exclusive responsibility for upholding *Ma'at* and defeating
isfet. It was also up to each individual to **do** *Ma'at* in his or her
daily life.

As Kemetic Reconstructionists today, we each can uphold
Ma'at. We can counter *isfet*. For those who feel a special calling to
serve the *Netjeru* by means of the ancient rituals these texts will
provide an authentic means for emulating those priestly forebears.
The priests who carried the title *Hem Netjer* ("servant of the god")
were involved with the innermost service to the god. For after all,
a priest is fundamentally and primarily a servant, that is, "one who
provides service."

That service today may take a variety of forms, including the
performance of the repertoire of rites that made up the cultic
life in an Egyptian temple. But not every priest or priestess need
serve as a "fighter-priest" (known as *"aha-ou-a"* in Egyptian), that

class of priests whose duties apparently revolved around the daily performance of these and similar execration rites.[140]

The various ritual texts for the overthrowing of Apep present us with a blueprint for spiritual combat. Whether you, the reader, choose to perform these rituals or simply study their contents, in either case you will gain insight into how the ancient priesthood viewed their struggle, and how they sought by means of *heka*-power to protect and defend the Lord of Life and His creation.

San Francisco, 3 December 2004, IV Akhet 30
(day 30 in the month *Hwt-Hrw,* in the season of *Akhet*)
Festival of Ma'at, Festival of Heka
RICHARD J. REIDY

Commentary
for Three Rituals from
The Book of Overthrowing Apep

The Bremner-Rhind Papyrus includes among its texts seven different rituals aimed at the serpent enemy Apep and his confederates. These rituals range in length from one that is little more than a paragraph to several others that take at least half an hour to recite aloud. Other than for that briefest text the remaining six stipulate the fashioning of wax images and the writing of the enemy's name(s) on a sheet of papyrus. In each case the images and papyri are consigned to a fire as part of the rite. In classic ancient Egyptian magical practice an image is "named"–or the name is written on papyrus and thus the papyrus is "named"–and then the object is treated as the priest-magician intends to treat the one being named.

Since these rites were part of official temple ritual the enemies named always include the cosmic enemy Apep, and, second, the "children of revolt" (i.e., the confederates of Apep), as well as the human enemies of the pharaoh. The wording of the text leaves no doubt that the enemies of the pharaoh were among the targets of these rituals. The three rituals contained in the present work omit any reference to the enemies of pharaoh and substitute the phrase "foes of *Ma'at*." Since the central role of the pharaoh was the establishing and maintaining of a good and just order, or *Ma'at*, I have taken the liberty of making this substitution. By doing this the ritual works on the terrestrial level as well as on the cosmic plane.

In the Bremner-Rhind Papyrus the first of the seven rituals aimed at Apep is by far the easiest to use because of the inclusion of titles within the text. These titles, written in red ink in the original, identify the cultic action that should accompany the recitation of the text. Thus the title "The Spell of Spitting on Apep" clearly names for the officiants what ritual act needs to be performed. It is this ritual which in the present work is identified as "Ritual I: The Ritual for the Overthrowing of Apep."

Since many of the texts throughout these seven rituals are lengthy and very repetitive in subject matter as well as style I have selected three rituals to illustrate different aspects of such rites. Ritual I is focused on Apep and requires the greatest number of cultic actions. Ritual II also focuses on Apep but it is primarily a recitation rite with a minimal number of cultic actions. Ritual III is directed against the various foes of Ra, the so called "children of revolt" and "rebels who create warfare and cause tumult." Each of these rituals illustrates a variety of magical techniques for combating the foe.

The main ones include: 1) repeating certain statements four times, with four representing the four directions or totality; 2) fabricating a wax image of the serpent enemy and inscribing its name upon it; 3) spitting and trampling as destructive acts aimed against the enemy; 4) using an implement of iron and a knife with a blade made of flint to pierce and cut the wax image and papyrus; 5) binding with black thread; 6) burning with a natural material having caustic properties; and 7) burial of the cremated remains in a red clay pot.

For a detailed scholarly treatment of these magical techniques the interested reader is referred to Robert Kriech Ritner's *The Mechanics of Ancient Egyptian Magical Practice* (The Oriental Institute of the University of Chicago, 1993). In addition, a highly readable book covering a wide range of topics in magic is Geraldine Pinch's *Magic in Ancient Egypt* (Austin: University of Texas Press, 1995).

It was with good reason that an ancient writer stated, "Ten measures of magic have come into the world. Egypt received nine of these, the rest of the world one measure." (Talmud, b. Qid. 49b) Egyptian magical techniques engage all the senses. They are by no means a cerebral affair devoid of materiality. Rather, they take the material and imbue it with a cosmic potency. A bit of wax becomes the frightful enemy. But now that enemy can be "dealt with." By means of materials from nature–such things as spittle, iron, flint, thread, fire, and clay–the priest-magician can enlist the powers inherent in such substances in order to work his *heka*-spell.

Unlike modern secular man who mistakenly sees materials as void of any meaning, the ancient priests saw mythological associations and symbolic significance in stones and woods and plants, in colors and shapes and numbers. All creation teemed with potency, with meaning, and, therefore, with theological implication. And those priests experienced themselves as capable of using those potent materials of nature to momentous effect.

How really–really–can this be? It is because the ancient Egyptian saw himself as coming from the essence of the creator god. He as with every human came from the tears of Ra. As the *Netjeru* came from the creator's sweat, so humans came from his tears. This is more than a picturesque metaphor for the genesis of humankind. It is a pre-industrial, pre-scientific intuition of humanity's deep connection with deity. Unlike the Hebrew story of their god Yahweh creating the first human from the soil–the soil itself being a created thing separate from the creator–the Egyptians envisioned a more intrinsic, more intimate and organic link with divinity.

The degree of separation was fundamentally and dramatically less than for other cultures. Just as the gods could speak and bring into being through the power of their spoken word and through *heka*-power, so humans were–and are–endowed with these powers. After all, the destiny of humankind is deification. Men and women are to be deified and, in mythic terms, together with the creator god and all the *Netjeru* will embark on the sun boat "Millions of Years" on a cyclic journey through cosmic time. That is the vision of ancient Egypt. Humanity springs from deity and, in turn, each individual is capable of becoming a deity. Humanity can return to its Source, but without melting into or merging with that Source. The creative powers of the Source are in some real sense shared by humanity. And *heka* is one of those creative powers.

We come, though, to a final question: Why enact such rites? Perhaps we only should lead good lives, to do *Ma'at*. Focus on the positive. And certainly this is a valid and vital point of view for many. But some who read this will know in their heart that these rites *are* important. These rituals do matter. *Heka*-power— magic–is our birthright. Not all will choose to practice it. Not all need practice it. But some–those called to be fighter-priests or warrior-priests–will resurrect those ancient rituals and resume the old magical struggle against the chaos-serpent. It is not a task for the occasional magician, nor for anyone not able and willing to study and reflect carefully on the profound spiritual legacy of ancient Egypt. But we today are only beginning to recover and reclaim our full heritage from Egypt.

Surely the ancients did not have greater or more ferocious enemies than we. Surely societies have not achieved the longed for peace with justice that we and all humankind long for. Such rites as revealed in the Book of the Overthrowing of Apep point to the power of *heka* for combating evil. A gift to us from the creator, *heka* enables us to call into service that divine strength within each of us. May these three rituals inspire you and guide you so that you can repeat the ancient priestly assertion, "I have overthrown Apep the rebel . . . and the children of revolt from all their seats in every place where they are" (Ritual III).

Prologue

The texts for the following three rituals come from the Bremner-Rhind Papyrus (British Museum, no. 10188) as translated by Robert O. Faulkner and published serially in four successive volumes of the *Journal of Egyptian Archaeology*, Volume XXII (December 1936) through Volume XXIV (June 1938). The following versions for each ritual are based on that portion of the manuscript which contains various ritual scripts together with rubrics for their performance, with the most detailed being "The Book of Overthrowing Apep." This series of execration rituals appears in Volume XXIII (December 1937), page 166 ff., and Volume XXIV (June 1938), page 41 ff. In order to help the reader locate each spell in Faulkner's translation, the volume number and page number where each spell is translated in the *Journal of Egyptian Archaeology* are given after the concluding verse of the spell.

Since the Bremner-Rhind Papyrus contains a number of very similar and lengthy rituals of "the felling of Apep," and in two instances similar versions of the creation story are given, for the sake of economy this present book gives only one of those creation accounts in its entirety, but one which contains an important concluding section that throws light on a basic magical technique widely used in ancient Egyptian magical practice as well as in the surviving morning temple rituals. The priest-magician states, "I am he who has been sent . . ." to do such-and-such. The orders come from a higher authority than the officiant. In the present instance the creator-god Ra describes at length His act of creation, ending with statements regarding the divine origins of these magical rites of felling Apep. A second magical technique that appears throughout these rituals is for the priest-magician to state *as fact* that which is the desired outcome, for example, in addressing Apep the priest announces, "The lance of Sutekh (Set) is thrust into your brow. Ra Himself has destroyed you." [*JEA* 24 (1939), 43]

RITUAL I:
The Ritual for the Overthrowing of Apep

This ritual contains seven distinct divisions–here identified as "chapters"–as they appear in the ancient manuscript. This would have made the step-by-step performance of this rite much easier for the priests. Rubrics, as visual cues, serve as important aids to the ritualist as he or she attempts to coordinate the spoken words with the corresponding cultic act. It was customary for the rubrics themselves to take the form of a title such as "The Spell of Spitting on Apep." They would be written in red ink to serve as a contrast to the black ink used for the recitational text. It was also customary to place at the conclusion of the rite more specific instructions regarding any special materials to be used as well as listing the times and days when the rite is to be performed.

THE CREATION PROLOGUE

The lector-priest and the fighter-priest shall enter the place designated for this rite. They shall bring with them in a box a wax image of the serpent foe and any drawings on papyrus of the foes of *Ma'at* (cosmic order and goodness). The usual rites of purification with water, natron, and incense should be performed. A candle or oil lamp is to be lit while reciting the customary invocation: "Come, come in peace, O glorious Eye of Heru . . . ." The lector-priest shall begin by reciting the Creation Prologue either in its entirety or in the abbreviated version (See APPENDIX A). The following shall be said:

"THE BOOK OF KNOWING THE CREATIONS OF RA
AND OF FELLING APEP."

Thus spoke the Lord of All:
  "When I came into being, 'Being' came into being. I came into being in the form of Khepri who came into being in the First Time. I came into being in the form of Khepri when I came into being, and that is how 'Being' came into being because I

was more primordial than the primordial ones I had made. I was the most primordial of the primordial ones and my name was more primordial than theirs, for I made primordial time and the primordial ones. I did all that I desired in this land and I was all-pervading in it. I knit my hand, being alone, before they had been born, before I had spat out Shu or expectorated Tefnut. I used my own mouth and 'Heka' was my name. It was I who came into being in my own form, having come into being in the form of Khepri. I came into being among the primæval ones, and there came into being a multitude of beings in the beginning, before any being had come into being in this land. I alone achieved all that was made, before there had come into being any other who could act with me in this place.

"I made the beings therein with this, my *Ba* [soul]; I created some of them in Nun as an Inert One when I could as yet find no place where I could stand. I considered in my heart; I surveyed with my sight, and I alone achieved all that was made. I planned in my heart and I created another being; and manifold were the forms of Khepri. Their children came into being in the forms of their children.

"It was I who spat out Shu and expectorated Tefnut. When I had come into being as sole *Netjer* [god], there were three *Netjeru* [gods] in addition to myself, and two *Netjeru* came into being in this land: Shu and Tefnut rejoiced in Nun, in which they were. It was my Eye which brought them to me after a long age when they were far from me. I united my members, and they issued from me myself. After I had made excitation with my fist, my desire came into my hand, and seed fell from my mouth. I spat out Shu and expectorated Tefnut, and my father Nun brought them up and my Eye followed after them .... When I wept with tears .... [? *a lacuna in the manuscript*] .... That is how humans came into being. I replaced it with the Glorious One, and it was enraged with me when it returned, another [Eye] having grown in its place. But its anger died away when I made replacement with it, and it was soothed. I promoted it in my face and it exercised governance over the entire land.

164

"Shu and Tefnut gave birth to Geb and Nut. Geb and Nut gave birth to Ausir [Osiris], Heru Mekhenty-er-irty (*mḫnty r ir.ty* 'He who has no eyes'), Sutekh [Set], Aset [Isis] and Nebet Het [Nephthys], and they gave birth to and created many beings in this land, namely, the forms of children and the forms of their children.

"They made conjuration in my name so that they might fell their foes. They created the magic spells for felling Apep. He is imprisoned in the arms of Aker. He has neither arms nor legs, and he is confined in one place, according as Ra obstructs him, for he has commanded that he be felled on account of his evil character. His face is cut away because of what he has done, and he suffers on account of his evil character. Children fell him and sever his *ba* [soul] from his body and his *khaibit* [shadow]; and the wise ones who are in the barque (of Ra) and the tears of my Eye desire to attack them.

"He shall be rendered impotent, and there shall be made no portion for him in this land. He is despoiled and his *ba* is despoiled. Those who are in the south fell him. Those who are in the north fell him. Those who are in the west fell him. And those who are in the east fell him.

"O you wise ones who are in this land, and you Nine *Netjeru* who came into being from my flesh, be vigilant in felling Apep! Exorcise him and destroy his name. May your arms fell him. May you not permit his name to be spread abroad. His children shall not exist. His seat shall not exist. And he shall have neither *ba* [soul] nor body nor *ka* [spirit], for he is consigned to the Eye of Ra and it has power over him. It devours him.

"I am he who has been sent to fell him, to destroy his name, and to chastise his name and his *heka*-power. I have committed him to the flame. I have allotted him to the heat. I have given him to the Eye of Ra, and the Glorious Eye has parched him. It has consumed his *ba*, his *ka*, his body, his *khaibit*, and his magic, and he shall neither copulate nor become erect for ever and ever."

165

"Here begins the book of the felling of Apep, the Foe of Ra, which is performed daily in the temple of Amun-Ra, Lord of the Thrones of the Two Lands, who dwells in Ipet Sut."

THE FIRST CEREMONY
The Spell of Spitting on Apep

After removing the wax image and papyrus images from the box, the fighter-priest places them on a table. He then spits four times upon the images as the following is said:

"Be spat upon, O Apep–*(four times)*–this is done for Ra and His *Ka*, this is done for me and my *Ka*. Ra has come in power; Ra has come in victory; Ra has come exalted; Ra has come prepared; Ra has come in joy; Ra has come in happiness; Ra has come in rejoicing; Ra has come in triumph.

"Come to me that You may crush all foes of the ones upholding Ma'at even as I fell Apep for You; even as I cut up the Ill-Disposed One for You; even as I give praise to Your might; even as I extol You in all Your manifestations in which You shine for me; even as I fell all Your foes for You daily." [*JEA*, Vol. XXIII, 167]

THE SECOND CEREMONY
The Spell of Trampling Apep with the Left Foot

The priest places on the ground the pieces of papyrus having images of the serpent drawn on them and inscribed with the name(s) of the enemy of Ra. He then proceeds to step on them four times with his left foot as the following is said:

"Rise up, O Ra, and crush Your foes. Shine forth, O Ra, for Your foes are fallen. Behold, I crush all Your foes for You; O Ra, crush for me all foes of the ones upholding Ma'at, dead or alive."

The priest lights the fire beneath the copper brazier, adding the appropriate baneful herbs as the following is said:

"Behold, Ra has power over you, O Apep; his flame rages against you; it has power over you; its fiery blast is sharp against you; and its fire falls on all the foes of Ra–*(four times)***–may its fire fall on all foes of the ones upholding Ma'at.**

"Be mighty, O Ra, against Your foe; go to and fro, O Ra, in Your horizon; may those who are in the Night-barque adore You. May the crew of Your barque serve You with joy. May You reappear rejoicing within the Day-barque. Praise to You, O Ra-Horakhty." *(four times)* [*JEA*, Vol. XXIII, 167]

THE THIRD CEREMONY
The Spell of Taking the Spear to Smite Apep

The priest uses an iron knife or sharp implement of iron and ritually strikes the head of the wax image and also strikes each image on papyrus as the following is said:

"Heru has taken his spear of iron; he has battered the heads of the foes of Ra. Heru has taken his spear of iron; he has battered the heads of the foes of the ones upholding Ma'at. See, Heru has taken his spear of iron; he has smitten the heads of the rebels in front of his barque.

"Rise up, O Ra. Chastise him who rebels against You and cut Apep to pieces so that the confederacy of the Ill-Disposed One may fall. I rise up and I chastise him who rebels against the ones upholding Ma'at, and I cut to pieces the foe of the ones upholding Ma'at, so that his confederacy may fall. Come, O Ra, in Your splendor, that those who are in their shrines may serve You and that they may adore You in Your beauty. Arise and shine forth, for Your foe is not–Your magic power being a protection for Your body."

The fighter-priest pierces the wax image and each image with the iron implement. He then picks up a lighted taper and makes a series of four passes under and around the images. The following is said:

"I adore Ra, and I thrust my spear into Apep. I take a flaming brand and I set fire to him; I chastise the body of Your foe.

"O foes of the ones upholding Ma'at, fire is upon you. Its flame is in you, fire is in you, and it shall devour you. Rise up, O Ra, and chastise him who rebels against You, and set fire to Apep; he is bitten in the middle of his back. Fire is in Apep, but Ra sails with a fair breeze, and His crew are possessed with joy; those who are in the horizon exult at the sight of Him, for He has felled the rebels.

"The fire has power over Apep, the Roarer, the Ill-Disposed One, and they have no peace, no peace. O Ra-Horakhty, turn Your fair countenance to me, that You may crush all foes of the ones upholding Ma'at for me, so that I may adore Ra in very deed.

"Ra is triumphant over Apep–*(four times)* I am triumphant over the foes of Ra." *(four times)* [*JEA*, Vol. XXIII, 167-68].

THE FOURTH CEREMONY
The Spell of Binding Apep

Using a black thread, the priest winds it around the wax image seven times and each time ties a knot for a total of seven knots. The following is said:

"They who should be bound are bound. Apep, that foe of Ra, is bound. May you not know what is done to you, O Apep. Turn yourself back–there is testimony against you. Even were you to flee in your time, you injure your own self. Even were your throat to be released, you injure your own self. You are bound! You are bound by Heru; you are fettered by Ra. You shall not become erect; you shall not copulate. You shall not escape His grasp. You are condemned by Ra; you are fettered by Heru Mekhenty-er-irty (*mhnty r ir.ty*, 'He who has no eyes')." [*JEA*, Vol. XXIII, 168]

THE FIFTH CEREMONY
The Spell of Taking the Knife to Smite Apep

The priest uses a blade of flint to cut off the wax serpent's head. The following shall be said:

"Seize, seize, O butcher; fell the foe of Ra with your knife. Seize, seize, O butcher, fell the foes of Ma'at with your knife. These are your heads, you rebels; this is that head of yours, O Apep, which are cut off by the fighter-priest with his knife."

The priest cuts up the wax image into seven sections, including the head.

"Be sharp, O Sopdet, O flame of Asbyt who has authority over fire: fell the Ill-Disposed One with your knives; cut up 'Wenty' with your knives. Be cut to pieces because of your evil; be cut up because of what you have done–there being testimony against you. Be dealt with according to the evil you have committed. Ra is triumphant over you, and Heru dismembers you." [*JEA*, Vol. XXIII, 168]

THE SIXTH CEREMONY
The Spell of Setting Fire to Apep

The priest places the wax image and the piece(s) of papyrus into the copper brazier while the following is said:

"Fire be in you, O Apep, you foe of Ra. May the Eye of Heru have power over the *ba* and the *khaibit* [shadow] of Apep. May the flame of the Eye of Heru devour that foe of Ra. May the flame of the Eye of Heru devour all foes of the ones upholding Ma'at, dead or alive." [*JEA*, Vol. XXIII, 168]

THE SEVENTH CEREMONY
The Magic Spell to be Uttered
When Putting Apep on the Fire

The priest spits upon the wax image four times and again four times as it melts while the following is said:

"Be utterly spat upon, O Apep. Get back, foe of Ra. Fall, creep away, take yourself off! I have turned you back; I have cut you up, and Ra is triumphant over you, O Apep. *(four times)* **Be spat upon, O Apep.** *(four times)* **Get back, rebel; be annihilated! Truly I have burned you; truly I have destroyed you. I have condemned you to all that is ill so that you may be annihilated, so that you may be utterly spat upon, so that you may be utterly non-existent. May you be annihilated! Be annihilated! May you be utterly spat upon! I have destroyed Apep, the foe of Ra."**

    "Ra is triumphant over you, O Apep." *(four times)*

    "And I am triumphant over the foes of Ra." *(four times)*

The priest empties the ashes and any other residue onto the ground and enacts the following rubric:

"Now afterward you are to trample on Apep four times with your left foot, and then, with your arms bent . . . , you shall say before Ra:

"Ra is triumphant over you, O Apep." *(four times)*
"In truth Ra triumphs over you, Apep. Be destroyed, O Apep!"

The following rubric appears at this point in the manuscript:

"This spell is to be spoken over a figure of Apep drawn on a new sheet of papyrus in green ink, and there shall be made an image of Apep with waxen body with his name inscribed on it in green ink, to be put into a fire so that he may burn before Ra when he manifests in the morning, at noon, and also in the evening when Ra sets in the

*West . . . at the festival of the new moon, at the day of the monthly
festival, at the sixth-day festival, at the fifteenth day festival, and
likewise every day . . . He is to be burnt in a fire of bryony* and his
remains placed in a pot of urine and pounded up into one mass . . .
It will be well with whoever does this upon earth, and it will be well
with him in the realm of the dead. Strength shall be given to that
person to attain a superior office, and it truly will be his safekeeping
from all evil and harmful things." [JEA, Vol. XXIII, 168-69]*

* Bryony is a vine or climbing plant with acrid juice having
emetic and purgative properties; hence, it is an appropriate wood
for "purging" the cosmos of something evil and poisonous, (i.e.,
Apep). In lieu of bryony the ritualist may wish to substitute the
appropriate herb after consulting a book on the magical use of
herbs.

The priest should place the ashes and all that remains in a red clay
pot, fill any remaining space with sand**, and seal the top.

** The manuscript's call for the use of urine–destructively
acidic–may not agree with modern sensibilities so at the very least
the burned remains should be subjected to burial in sand thereby
"encircling" the enemy inside a red pot, a traditional method for
dealing magically with images of the enemy. See Ritner for details
(153-56, and 175-76).

CONCLUDING UTTERANCE
Address to Ra, Lord of Life

Both priests stand with arms raised in the invocation/*nis* position
while the lector-priest says the following:

**"O my father, lord of the *Netjeru*, greatest of the Great Ennead,
first primeval one of the *Netjeru*, who created humans, after
whose coming into being all beings came into being; I am truly
the son of Your heart. Divine is this heart which issued from
Your shrine; praises come into being with You, magic making**

Your protection. How beautiful is that which comes forth from my mouth, for I am one excellent of counsels!

"Come, O Ra. Look upon me with Your eyes; may You praise what I have done. I fell Apep in his moment on Your behalf. I destroy him within his hell, while Heru-merti (Heru of the Two Eyes) with his staff cuts off the heads of Your foes. The Butcher with his great knife cuts to pieces the heads of those who rebel against You; and the Devouring Flame, the fiery one, her fire burns up his *ba* at his execution-block. But Your *ba* is joyful, joyful; it has sailed across the sky with a fair breeze.

"Come, look with Your eye upon what I have done to the body of Apep. His house is destroyed, his wall ruined, his body destroyed. But Your heavens are established, Your cities firmly established. Be enduring! Be flourishing! Be hale! Be youthful, youthful! Rise, rise, shine, shine, every day! May You appear in the Barque, Your heart being glad. May You trust in Your children. But Apep, that enemy, the fierce-faced, he has thought that You were far from him, and he has planned evil at his execution-block. Turn him back with his own evil upon him! You who ascend from the horizon! The Two Lands are in joy, and Your heart, O Ra, is glad every day, for Apep is fallen into the fire, Neki is taken to the fire, and glad is the heart of Amun-Ra, Lord of the Thrones of the Two Lands who dwells in Ipet Sut, for His foe is fallen under Him.

"Ra is triumphant over Apep–*(four times)*–Amun-Ra is triumphant over His foe–*(four times)*–Atum is triumphant over His foe–*(four times)*–Djehuty, the efficacious of magic, lord of letters, is triumphant over His foe." *(four times)* [*JEA*, Vol. XXIV, 53]

The fighter-priest shall pick up the red clay pot and carry it away for burial in a remote place, away from the temple or any holy place. An alternate method for dealing with the charred remains is to dispose of them by flushing down a drain. This would be in keeping with the ritual instructions found in the temple at Esna for another rite directed against demonic enemies of the cosmos. (See Ritner, 209, note 969.)

A concluding rite of purification with water, natron, and incense should be performed. The candle or oil lamp is to be extinguished while the customary invocation is recited:

"This is the Eye of Heru by which you have become great, by which You live, and by which You have power, O Amun-Ra. This is the Eye of Heru which you consume and through which you enchant your body. The *Wedjat* Eye now enters the West, into Manu, but it shall return. Truly, the Eye of Heru returns in peace!"

In silence the priests retire from the "furnace of the coppersmiths," that is, the site, identified in the text, which is used for these particular execration rites. Symbolically this identification of the site with the "furnace of the coppersmiths" magically names the location as an archetypal 'place of destruction' by fire. Utilizing the *heka*-power of the name itself, the priest-magician thus transforms a mundane locale into the site of the cosmic overthrowal of the enemy.

RITUAL II:
The First Book of Felling Apep, The Foe of Ra

The following rite is primarily a recitation ritual with only two identifiable magical actions, burning the papyrus sheet bearing the name of the serpent enemy and a fourfold spitting that comes at the conclusion of the rite.

As indicated for Ritual I, the usual rites of purification with water, natron, and incense should be performed prior to this ritual. A candle or oil lamp is to be lit while reciting the customary invocation, "Come, come in peace, O glorious Eye of Heru . . . ."

The lector-priest shall begin by reading the abbreviated version of the Creation Prologue. (See APPENDIX A.) The priest then shall read the following:

"Fall on your face, O Apep, you foe of Ra. Get back, enemy, rebel who has neither arms nor legs . . . . You are fallen and felled, for Ra-Horakhty has felled you; he has crushed you; he has condemned you; the Eye of his body chastises you, and you are fallen into the fire which issues from it, the flame which issues from its fiery blast which come forth in its moment; its fiery blast is upon you!

"Your raging is dispelled by Aset through the spells of her utterance. Your *Ba* is cut up; your vertebrae are severed. Heru has made you impotent. The Children of Heru break you up, for you are destroyed in their moment (of action).

"Back! Get back! Begone! Take yourself away! You are fallen, you are driven off, you are turned back, O Apep. The Great Ennead which is in Iunu [Heliopolis] drives you off. Heru has repelled your rage. Sutekh has rendered your moment impotent. Aset repels you; Nebet Het cuts you up; the Great Ennead which is in the prow of the bark of Ra drives you off. Sutekh has stabbed at your neck; the Children of Heru set their spears into you. Those *Netjeru* who guard the doors of the mysterious portals repel you—their fiery blast goes forth against you in fire. Take yourself away at the blast of flame issuing from their mouths. Fall down, and creep away, O Apep.

"Take yourself off, you foe of Ra, for you are fallen at this his moment, and they who are in his barque fell you. Get back, for you are exorcised, crushed, and repelled in your moment. Fall down! You are turned back; your *Ba* is turned back; your flesh is taken away, and You are made impotent. Your execution and your dismemberment are achieved. Your rage is crushed. Your power of movement is taken away. Your flesh is beaten from your body, your *Ba* is parted from your shade. Your name is destroyed. Your magic is crushed, and you are destroyed.

"Fall down for you are felled! You shall never again come forth from this your place of punishment. You are made impotent. Once again you are bound, for you have been broken by those who break up ills. Your moment is averted. Your rage is turned back. Your power of movement is taken away. You are ousted from this your place. Fall down, for you have been driven off and condemned to evil. He who should be broken is truly broken, and his deeds shall not succeed. Your *Ba* is annihilated; your shade is destroyed, for you are allotted to the fiery Eye of Heru. It shall have power over you; it shall devour you utterly. Be annihilated, O Apep! The Eye of Heru has pierced you; it has turned you back; it has destroyed you; it has annihilated you."

The priest takes a taper and ignites it from the "Eye of Heru" candle or oil lamp. With this lighted taper he lights a fire in the copper brazier. The following shall be said:

"Fall upon Your face, O Apep, you foe of Ra. The fire which issues from the Eye of Heru comes forth against you. The great flame which issues from the Eye of Heru comes forth against you; it presses on you with a blast of flame; the fire comes forth against you, and fierce is its flame against your *Ka*, your *Ba*, your *heka*, your body and your shadow; the Mistress of Burning has power over you; her fiery blast chastises your *Ka*; she annihilates your shape; she punishes your form, and you are fallen to the Eye of Heru which is enraged against its foe.

"Wepes the Great parches you; the Eye of Ra has power over you; the devouring flame consumes you, and no remnant of you remains to fall.

"Get back! You are cut up; your *Ba* is despoiled; your name is obliterated. May your name be unheard; may your name fall! Be forgotten! Be driven back so that you may be forgotten! Retreat! Turn yourself back for you are cut up and far removed from those who are in his shrine. Be utterly destroyed. Be annihilated, O Apep, you foe of Ra. You shall not exist. Your *Ka* shall not exist in you, for the Eye of Ra shall have power over you and it shall consume you every day, even as Ra commanded should be done to you, O Apep."

The papyrus sheet is placed upon the fire. The following shall be said:

"You are fallen to the flame of fire, and the furnace shall consume you. You are condemned to the devouring flame of the Eye of Heru, and the fiery one has parched you–it consumes your *Ka* and your *Ba*, your body and your shadow, and you shall not become erect nor copulate for ever and ever.

Ra is triumphant over you, O Apep *(four times)*

Heru is triumphant over his foes *(four times)*

The ones upholding Ma'at are triumphant over their foes *(four times)*.

Retire, turn yourself back at this magic which issues from my mouth on behalf of the ones upholding Ma'at for ever . . . ."

The priest then spits four times upon the images as the following is said:

"Apep, you foe of Ra, be spat upon, you enemy, you rebel!"-*(four times)*

At this point in the manuscript the following rubric appears. It refers to the rite just presented. Throughout the Bremner-Rhind Papyrus rubrics appear *after* the text to which they apply, contrary to the modern practice of placing rubrics at the start. In keeping with ancient Egyptian custom the first words of all such rubrics were written in red ink, thus permitting the priest to quickly identify them within the text. (See Faulkner's remarks, *JEA*, Vol. XXIII, 166-67.)

"To be recited by a man who is pure and clean. You shall depict the name of Apep, it being written on a new sheet of papyrus, and it shall be put into the fire when Ra manifests himself, when Ra is at noon-tide, when Ra sets in the West, by night, by day, at every hour of every day, at the monthly festival, at the sixth-day festival, at the fifteenth-day festival, and likewise every day when the foes of Ra-Horakhty are felled." [*JEA*, Vol. XXIII, 169-70]

A concluding rite of purification with water, natron, and incense should be performed. The candle or oil lamp is to be extinguished while the customary invocation is recited:

"This is the Eye of Heru by which you have become great, by which You live, and by which You have power, O Amun-Ra. This is the Eye of Heru which you consume and through which you enchant your body. The *Wedjat* Eye now enters the West, into Manu, but it shall return. Truly, the Eye of Heru returns in peace!"

RITUAL III:
A Rite for Overthrowing the Foes of Ra

In contrast to the previous two, this ritual focuses on the various foes of Ra and only toward the conclusion is the name of Apep pronounced. This is in keeping with the rubrics for this rite–again located immediately after the actual ritual text–which give instructions for fabricating wax images of all Ra's enemies.

In the Bremner-Rhind Papyrus this ritual–unlike Ritual I–does not provide any periodic rubrics that specify exactly what is to be enacted at any given point in the recitation. It is only at the conclusion of the rite that some general rubrics indicate that certain specific actions are to be performed: *"They are to be spat upon, and they are to be trampled with the left foot, felled with the spear and knife, and cast on the fire."* [*JEA*, Vol. XXIII, 170]

I have taken the liberty of inserting rubrics at those points in the text that may plausibly correspond to these cultic acts. This is intended solely as an aid to the contemporary ritualist.

"Fall upon your faces, you foes of Ra, all you rebels, foes and children of revolt, you contrary ones and nameless rebels, doomed ones whose hell is prepared, for it has been commanded to make a slaughter of the rebellious, the foes, and the rebels who create warfare and cause tumult. Fall! All of you, fall at this, the moment of Ra! He will annihilate you; he will cut you down; he will make fall your heads. On your faces! He will destroy you, making a slaughter of you.

The priest pierces each wax image with the iron spear. The following is said:

"O you who deserve annihilation, be annihilated! Be destroyed! O you who have nothing, you shall possess nothing, you shall not exist, you shall not be! Your heads shall be removed; your necks shall be hewn asunder; your vertebrae shall be severed; you shall be made impotent; you shall be slaughtered.

"You shall fall to the Eye of Heru, for its flame is sharp against you, its fiery blast shall have power over you; the Eye of Ra shall appear against you, his might shall have power over you; his Eye shall have power over you; it shall consume you and chastise you in this its name of 'Devouring Flame'; it shall have power over you in this its name of Sekhmet. You shall fall to its blast, and fierce is the flame of fire which comes forth from its blast. It shall destroy you, O you who are doomed to destruction!"

The priest first takes a taper and lights it from the "Eye of Heru" candle. Then he lights a fire in the copper brazier. The following is said:

"The fire comes forth against you, you foes of Ra, you who rebel against Heru, and against your own *Bas*, your bodies, and your *Khaibitu* [shadows]. The fire comes forth; it cooks you, its glow bakes you, its burning burns you. Wepes the great divides you, she devours you, she parches you, she destroys your *Bas*, her fiery blast makes chastisement in your *Khaibitu*."

The priest places on the ground the wax images or pieces of papyrus inscribed with the name(s) of the enemy of Ra. He then proceeds to step on them four times with his left foot as the following is said:

"O you who deserve annihilation, be annihilated! You are crushed, crushed! You shall be burned; you shall be cut down; you shall be slaughtered; you shall be condemned to the great furnace of fire, the mistress of heat, and its glow shall consume your *Bas*; its blast shall make chastisement in your bodies; it shall press on you with its great flame. It shall cut you with its knife; it shall rage against you with its wrath; it shall consume you with its flame; it shall shrivel you with its fire; it shall blast you with its blaze, scorch you with its heat, burn you with its burning. It shall break you in this its name of 'fire.' It shall divide you in this its name of Wepes the Great. You shall fall to its flame, for sharp is the great flame which is in its blast, and its glow shall devour your *Bas*."

The priest uses a blade of flint to cut off the head of each wax image. The following shall be said:

"O you who ought to fall, fall! Fall! You are fallen and felled. Fall to Ra! Fall to the rage of his moment. Be annihilated for him. Be annihilated! He shall destroy you, fell you, cut you up. He shall condemn you, execute you, obliterate your names and cut up your *Bas*. He shall imprison you, destroy you, crush you, chastise you, fell you. You shall fall to the devouring flame, and it shall destroy you. May you not exist! O you who ought to be annihilated, be annihilated, annihilated! Be annihilated, be annihilated, your *Bas* are annihilated. Be annihilated, your bodies are annihilated. Be annihilated, your *Khaibitu* [shadows] are annihilated. You are annihilated! You shall not be, and your *Bas* shall not be. You shall not be, and your bodies shall not be. You shall not be, and your shadows shall not be. You shall not be, and your lives shall not be. You shall not be, and your generative power shall not be. Your heads shall not be knit to your bodies.

"Get back because of Ra. Retreat, rebels! May you not exist; may Djehuty make conjuration against you with his magic. The great *Netjer* is mighty against you. He has crushed you; he has caused men to hate you."

The priest places the wax images with the pieces of papyrus into the copper brazier while the following is said:

"The fire which is on his mouth comes forth against you, so burn, rebels! May you cease to exist. May Djehuty make conjuration against you with his magic. May he fell you, cut you up, destroy you, condemn you to the fiery glance of Heru which comes forth from the Eye of Heru. It shall consume you utterly. It shall destroy you through the greatness of its heat, and it shall not be repelled in the moment of its heart's desire in that its name of Meret-goddess. Be annihilated because of it. Turn back because of it. Turn back because of it. Turn yourself back because of it. Get back because of it. O all you foes of Ra and all you foes of Heru. It shall pierce you. It shall turn you back; it shall destroy you. Be annihilated because of it. Be destroyed because of it. May you neither become erect nor copulate for ever and ever." [*JEA*, Vol. XXIII, 170-71]

The priest spits four times upon the wax image as it melts.* The following is said:

* See Ritner, 87: "It is significant that ritual spitting often occurs while the image of the victim is on fire. . . . This is to reinforce the burning, not extinguish it ..."

"Ra triumphs, and justice is upon you, O Apep and you children of revolt, you greatly rebellious ones! Ra is triumphant over his foes–*four times*– Heru is triumphant over his foes–*four times*–Ausir, First of the Westerners, is triumphant over his foes –*four times*–The ones upholding Ma'at are triumphant over their foes"–*four times*.

"I have overthrown Apep, the rebel, the tortoise, the Ill-Disposed One, and the children of revolt from all their seats in every place where they are. I have over-thrown all the foes of Ra from all their seats in every place where they are; I have overthrown all the foes of Heru from all their seats in every place where they are.

"I have overthrown all the foes of Amun-Ra, Lord of the thrones of the Two Lands who dwells in Ipet Sut, from all their seats in every place where they are; I have overthrown all foes of the ones upholding Ma'at from all their seats in every place where they are."

"To be recited by a man who is pure and clean. You shall depict every foe of Ra and every foe of Ma'at, whether dead or alive, every one of them having been drawn in green ink on a new sheet of papyrus, their names written on their breasts, these having been made of wax, and also bound with bonds of black thread. They are to be spat upon, and they are to be trampled with the left foot, *felled with the spear and knife, and cast on the fire in the melting furnace of the coppersmiths. Afterwards, the name of Apep is to be burnt in a fire of bryony when Ra manifests Himself, when Ra is at noontime, and when Ra sets in the West; in the first hour of the day and of the night . . . at the festival of the New Moon, at the sixth-day festival, at the fifteenth-day festival, and likewise at the monthly festival, felling the foe of Ra . . . . It will be well with the man who makes conjuration for himself from this book in the presence of this august Netjer . . . ."* [JEA, XXIII, 171]

Any charred remains should be disposed of according to ancient custom. (See the concluding remarks for Ritual I.) As with every ritual, a concluding rite of purification with water, natron, and incense should be performed. The candle or oil lamp is to be extinguished while the customary invocation is recited:

"This is the Eye of Heru by which you have become great, by which You live, and by which You have power, O Amun-Ra. This is the Eye of Heru which you consume and through which You enchant your body. The *Wedjat* Eye now enters the West, into Manu, but it shall return. Truly, the Eye of Heru returns in peace!"

APPENDIX G

The Creation Prologue (Abbreviated Version)

"THE BOOK OF KNOWING THE CREATIONS OF RA AND OF FELLING APEP." Thus spoke the Lord of All:

"When I came into being, 'Being' came into being. I came into being in the form of Khepri who came into being in the First Time. . . . I considered in my heart; I surveyed with my sight, and I alone achieved all that was made. I planned in my heart and I created another being; and manifold were the forms of Khepri. Their children came into being in the forms of their children.

"It was I who spat out Shu and expectorated Tefnut. . . . Shu and Tefnut gave birth to Geb and Nut. Geb and Nut gave birth to Ausir [Osiris], Heru Mekhantenirti, Sutekh [Set], Aset [Isis] and Nebet Het [Nephthys], and they gave birth to and created many beings in this land, namely, the forms of children and the forms of their children.

"They made conjuration in my name so that they might fell their foes. They created the magic spells for felling Apep. . . .

"O you wise ones who are in this land, and you Nine *Netjeru* who came into being from my flesh, be vigilant in felling Apep! Exorcise him and destroy his name. May your arms fell him. May you not permit his name to be spread abroad. His children shall not exist. His seat shall not exist. And he shall have neither *Ba* [soul] nor body nor *Ka* [spirit], for he is consigned to the Eye of Ra and it has power over him. It devours him.

"I am he who has been sent to fell him, to destroy his name, and to chastise his name and his *heka*-power. I have committed him to the flame. I have allotted him to the heat. I have given him to the Eye of Ra, and the Glorious Eye has parched him. It has consumed his *Ba*, his *Ka*, his body, his *khaibit* [shadow], and his magic, and he shall neither copulate nor become erect for ever and ever." [*JEA*, XXIV, 41-42]

APPENDIX H

Items Needed for Conducting Rituals for the Overthrowing of Apep

The following articles are needed for Rituals I and III:

- the usual items of water, natron, and incense for the customary opening rites
- a candle or oil lamp
- an image of the serpent-enemy made from beeswax*
- new sheets of papyrus with names written in green ink
- a copper brazier or copper pan, with wood or charcoal
- one or more herbs for exorcism such as agrimony, clove, cypress, dragon's blood, fern, nettle, myrrh, tamarisk, vetiver, or yarrow (These herbs are suggested as possible substitutes for the bryony called for in the text. In general they are regarded as useful for exorcism, banishing, and binding. Be sure not to use anything with poisonous vapors.)
- an iron knife or an iron nail**
- black thread
- a blade of flint (a flint arrowhead may be substituted)
- a red clay pot, sand, and a lid or means for sealing the clay pot

* For the symbolic notions connected with beeswax see Maarrten J. Raven's article "Wax in Egyptian Magic and Symbolism," *Oudheid Kundige Mede Delingen,* Volume 64 (1983), 7-47.

** For information on other materials specified for use in execration rites see Robert Kriech Ritner's *The Mechanics of Ancient Egyptian Magical Practice* (Chicago: The Oriental Institute of the University of Chicago, 1993).

PART TWO:

Rituals from the Temple of Ra

Aegyptus
deorum in terras suae religionis merito
sola deductio,
sanctitatis et pietatis magistra

Egypt,
the only land that by the strength of its religion
brought the gods down to earth,
teacher of holiness and piety
Asclepius 25

Introduction

Esoteric orders as diverse as the Hermetic Order of the Golden Dawn, the Rosicrucians and Freemasons, the Temple of Set, the Fellowship of Isis, the OTO, practitioners of Western Ceremonial Magick, and a whole host of present-day neo-pagan groups, find inspiration in the rich spiritual vision and magical practices of ancient Egypt. Borrowing bits and pieces according to their individual bent, each group incorporates what it deems important or useful into its own ritual or theoretical framework. Under certain circumstances this can be an effective strategy for enriching and deepening a group's spiritual landscape and magical technologies. But, by so doing, a certain danger arises that the elements selected may be taken out of anything resembling their original context and thereby loose much of their original meaning, or even suffer a substantial distortion in the process. A new and even incompatible interpretation may be given to that which has been borrowed. This, of course, is always a risk when members of one culture attempt to incorporate elements from a different cultural tradition into their own spiritual worldview. One example of this is found in the work of the originator of Thelemic magick, Aleister Crowley, who is reported to have misheard a museum's Arabic curator's pronunciation of "Behadit" (a specific form of the god Horus) as "Hadit." Crowley then proceeded to fabricate a mythology around his newly minted deity "Hadit," with the implicit message that it somehow and in some sense reflected elements of genuine Egyptian mythology. It does so in only the most superficial way.[141]

Equally problematic is the use of terms and values of one culture in order to explain elements from another culture. A notorious example of this is Plutarch's work *De Iside et Osiride* ("On Isis and Osiris"), which sought to explain Egyptian religion to a Greek audience and in so doing ended up distorting a whole host of Egyptian spiritual concepts by using distinctly ill-fitting Greek philosophical categories and superficial correspondences.

Likewise, when one takes elements from one cultural tradition and attempts to incorporate them into another, the resulting pastiche may resemble nothing so much as a jumble that in the end does not and cannot long satisfy the yearnings of the human spirit. Deep inconsistencies, shallow resemblances, and poorly thought-out theologies do not have staying power, the absolutely essential quality for a school of spirituality to survive and thrive.

What then can be done when we find our dominant culture's spiritual offerings unsatisfying or troubling or even outright false? This question will be answered in a variety of ways, depending on what speaks to the seeker's heart and mind. The remarkable growth of nature-based religions such as Wicca, Goddess spirituality, Asatru, Native American shamanism, and many others clearly demonstrates the appeal such life-affirming paths have for a growing number of seekers. These include the many different Reconstructionist groups that work to reclaim ancient spiritualities long suppressed by the dominant monotheist religious establishments. Among these are Greek and Roman Reconstructionists, Celtic, Druidic, and Kemetic (after Kemet, the name the ancient Egyptians gave their land).

It was to this last named tradition that I was drawn in the 1990s. Raised as a Christian, I attended a well-respected graduate school of theology as a fulltime student in the late 1970s, and after three years of study I received a Master of Divinity degree. As an elected executive of my denomination, I spent well over seven years working on a number of committees within the National Council of Churches. As time passed, I became increasingly dissatisfied with the tenets of Christianity. After several years investigating various nature-based paths–reading extensively, speaking with members of different groups, and participating in public rituals–I found myself turning again and again to the teachings of ancient Egypt.

As a postgraduate student, I had learned how to locate and use scholarly materials not easily available to the general public. Through the good offices of the interlibrary loan department of my local library, I was able to access literally hundreds of books and articles on aspects of ancient Egyptian religion, spirituality, and magic. I also had the great good fortune to come across an online Kemetic Reconstructionist group dedicated to the great goddess Hathor, officially known as Akhet Hwt-Hrw ("the Resplendent Horizon of Hathor"). The chief priest and moderator, Kerry Wisner, proved to be an exceptionally gifted and erudite guide for those drawn to ancient Egyptian spirituality. A man of deep insight, Kerry Wisner gently but firmly guided the online community to an ever deeper appreciation of Kemetic religion, ritual, and magic. By means of individualized courses of instruction, he was able to guide members, including myself, in real spiritual growth and development. Three of his books are, in my estimation, among the finest, most reliable texts bringing together all the key concepts of the ancient Egyptian path, as well as providing a wide variety of workable rituals based on the ancient texts.[142]

After experiencing the lively, informative online discussions that Kerry moderated, and having completed a course of studies under his supervision, I grew determined to dedicate my own efforts to researching and reclaiming as many of the ancient rites as possible. It was at this time that I met a number of persons interested in forming a Kemetic group for worship, fellowship, and magical practice. In 1998 the Temple of Ra was born. Eleven years have passed, new members have joined, and most of the original members still actively participate in the temple's monthly rites.

The challenge for any Reconstructionist–of whatever ancient tradition–lies first in locating reliable sources of information for the ritual practices and beliefs of that tradition. In the case of ancient Egypt we enjoy the twin benefits of climate and the availability of actual ancient ritual texts. The arid climate of Egypt has helped preserve significant quantities of texts on papyrus in tombs and in other archeological sites where ancient manuscripts have been found. In addition, the walls of many temples are covered with detailed inscriptions of the actual words to be recited or hymns to be sung for each action in the temple's various liturgies. These "words to be spoken [aloud]" (in Egyptian *djed medu*) are accompanied by extensive graphics that visually record the progression of cultic events, for example, offering incense, pouring a libation, consecrating and offering a variety of food offerings, as well as other specific actions making up a particular rite. By correlating gestures, body postures, and recitational text, Egyptologists have been able to reconstruct more than a few important rites from beginning to end. In addition, by analyzing the recitational texts we gain insight into the theological vision informing those rites.

The ancient Egyptian priesthood did not leave us books of systematic theology such as we would find in seminaries today. But they did leave us many detailed ritual texts revealing their understanding of divinity, humanity, our mutual interdependence, the nature of good and evil, and all the great religious themes that are important for a rich, balanced spiritual life.

The Latin saying *"lex orandi, lex credendi"* translates as "the law [or rule] of praying is the law of belief." In other words, the way people pray will tell us what they believe. By studying the prayers, rituals, songs, and festivals of a people we gain insight into what they believe. The professional theologians, clergy, or official spokespersons for a group may or may not actually convey accurately the true beliefs of a religion. They may be overly influenced by societal or theoretical considerations, personal likes and dislikes, or even by a certain theological agenda that ends up distorting and thus misrepresenting the beliefs of their particular tradition. Theologians and clergy come and go. But students of religion recognize that the prayers, rites, mythic stories, and songs remain remarkably stable over the course of centuries. In the case of ancient Egypt we are fortunate to have literally thousands of recitational texts, hymns, and prayers to guide us in our efforts to understand that great spiritual tradition which spanned some five thousand years.

Why, though, should men and women of our own era look to such an ancient culture as that of Egypt in order to find spiritual guidance and fulfillment? Why bother resurrecting rites and rituals from a bygone age? Why not simply invent our own rituals? These are important questions and deserve a reasoned response. Anthropology attests to the staying power of religious rites. Across the globe, in vastly different cultures, the patterns of religious ritual tend to endure essentially unchanged and constant in spite of alterations in the political or social landscape. In the case of ancient Egypt religious texts that date to the age of the great pyramids endure essentially unchanged for several thousand more years, only ceasing because of the oppressive measures of the new monotheist religion of a Christianizing Roman Empire.

Rituals that were performed in temples across Egypt for over thirty centuries have built up a great reservoir of energy and power that endures to this day. In reviving those rites and reciting those "words of power" we can tap into that ancient grid of spiritual energy. Many modern day visitors to Egypt remark about the very unusual and mystical feelings they experienced at some ancient temple or pyramid. Those holy sites still retain a certain ineffable power that can be felt even by persons unfamiliar with the theology of ancient Egypt. It has been reported by Egyptologists and anthropologists that even today local Moslems continue to visit certain ancient sites for blessings of fertility and healing.[143] This aura of sacred power that continues to emanate from those sites is also accessible to us through the words and rites of the ancient priesthood. For after all, it was by means of centuries of ritual enactment that these centers of mystical power were built up. It is my experience and the experience of members of the Temple of Ra that these ancient rituals assist us in accessing the powerful, loving energies of the great gods and goddesses of ancient Egypt.

Both classical Greece and imperial Rome looked upon Egypt with admiration and awe, not only for its great monuments and advanced civilization but also for its spiritual wisdom and deeply religious vision. It was not at all uncommon for educated Greeks and Romans to have spent time visiting and even studying in Egypt.[144] Such luminaries of the Greek world as Plato, Pythagoras, Solon, Thales, Lycurgus, Eudoxus, and Demokritos of Abdera were reputed to have studied with Egyptian priests.[145]

In the Hermetic treatise *Asclepius* Egypt is referred to as "the image of heaven . . . the temple of the whole world." (*Ascl.* 24)[146] It was precisely the piety and devoutness of the Egyptian people that so impressed visitors. But unlike the puritanical and somber upstart religion coming from the Roman province of Judea, it was a joyful piety that celebrated the pleasures of the created world and saw in this world the active, immanent presence of divine powers. The gods and goddesses of ancient Egypt were very much present and approachable. The natural world was a palette upon which the invisible gods made manifest their presence, their power, and their love for humankind. A Hymn of Praise to the first among the gods illustrates the Egyptians' attitude toward their deities:

"Hail, Amun-Ra!
Every face says, 'We belong to You,'
Strong and weak alike,
Rich and poor from one mouth,
All things equally.
Your loveliness fills their hearts,
No body is devoid of Your beauty.
Do not the widows say, 'You are our husband,'
While others say, 'Our father and our mother'?
The rich boast of Your beauty,
The poor turn their faces to You.
Prisoners turn to You,
The sick call upon You.
Your name is an amulet for the lonely,
Prosperity and health for those on the water,
A saviour from the crocodile.
To think of whom is good in times of distress,
Who rescues from the mouth of the hot-blooded.
Everyone turns to You to implore You,
Your ears are open to hear them and fulfill their wishes.
[You are] our Ptah, who loves His handiwork,
Our shepherd, who loves His flock.
His reward is a 'beautiful burial'
For a heart that is satisfied with *ma'at* (righteousness)."[147]

We at the Temple of Ra have worked to recover and reestablish the ancient rites of Egypt. We are under no illusion about the limits of our endeavor. We do not have the substantial resources of a state-supported temple, and neither do we have a full time priesthood capable of celebrating the many daily temple liturgies as would have been done in ancient times. But what we are able to do is celebrate authentic rituals that would in fact be recognized by members of the Egyptian priesthood.

As Reconstructionists our goal is to model our ritual acts in so far as we can on the sacred rites of Egypt without, however, rigidly restricting our every action to only those documented in the ancient texts. We do not espouse a sterile "theology of repetition." But neither do we advocate innovation simply for the sake of doing something new and different. Other traditions have beautiful and meaningful aspects and practices that are to be admired. But while we may admire them, we do not incorporate them into our own rituals.

Just as Egypt did not exist in a vacuum, but interacted with and was enriched by contact with neighboring cultures, so, too, we Kemetic Reconstructionists can benefit from our experience as members of contemporary society. But in matters of ritual practice, the ancient priesthood was particularly dedicated to maintaining its own time-tested rituals and celebrations. The efforts of an early Greek ruler of Egypt, Ptolemy I, (305-285 BC) to introduce the worship of the syncretistic deity Serapis and other hybrid deities such as Hermanubis met with polite but firm disinterest from the native Egyptian populace and priesthood.[148]

The Egyptian religious vision is whole and complete. It neither needs nor seeks elements from other traditions. That is not to cast aspersions on the practices of other traditions. Unlike the various sects of Christianity–which borrowed heavily from a wide number of pagan practices, festivals, and beliefs–the spiritual vision of ancient Egypt is complete and adequate to itself. This really should come as no surprise for a pagan culture that was able to endure and thrive and develop for five millennia. In America we have a national culture that is barely two and a half centuries in the making. Egypt had one twenty times that long.

If then we are not simply engaging in a "theology of repetition," blindly duplicating cultic acts of a bygone era, what exactly are we advocating? As Kemetic Reconstructionists we encourage research into the ancient rites so as to arrive at a true understanding of their constituent elements and, ultimately, their spiritual meaning. We are aided by nearly two centuries of research by archaeologists, papyrologists, and Egyptologists from many nations. Ever since the French linguist Champollion made his inspired breakthrough in the decoding of hieroglyphs in the 1820s, teams of scholars have been occupied with recording and translating the ancient texts. Scholars of religion continue to examine and debate fine points of the Egyptian religious vision. We are the beneficiaries of their labors.

As ritualists we attempt to be "creative conservators" of traditional rituals, using expert knowledge to modify the rites *when truly necessary* but always working to preserve their underlying ideologies. When we innovate, we do so within standard patterns from *within* the tradition. Any modifications are modifications of established rituals, enacted with very specific purposes in sight. As "creative conservators" of this ancient tradition, we regard it as incumbent upon ourselves to revive and restore the beautiful and rich liturgies of Egypt in such a way that they can be understood and enacted by our contemporaries. And, finally, as practitioners of Egyptian *heka* (magic), we work in traditional Egyptian methods with the gods and goddesses to establish *ma'at* (Goodness and Right Order) for individuals in need and for society.

It needs to be said that innovation in ritual practice is not a sign of disloyalty to the tradition. There are a variety of practical, moral, and social considerations that we as Reconstructionists will make regarding the rituals and religious practices of our spiritual ancestors. First, are they genuinely relevant to present day circumstances? The ceremony for crowning a pharaoh is no longer applicable. But asking the gods to bless and guide our elected leaders makes good sense. Second, do we have the material resources and time necessary to perform a specific rite or ritual action? A fulltime priesthood obviously was able to maintain a full cycle of daily and seasonal services to honor the gods. But since our communities meet only occasionally we will need to select carefully from among the wealth of rites available. Are the ancient texts silent about something we consider important? We have no indication how marriage was celebrated–if at all–from a religious standpoint. But we do know that the married couple was often portrayed sitting side by side for all eternity, with arms wrapped lovingly around each other's waist. Thus we see that the union of husband and wife was regarded as important–and enduring. Would it not be good, then, to design a rite of union using traditional elements as well as creating ceremony that reflects modern sensibilities? Or, in the opposite case where we have a great deal of textual evidence for intricate and lengthy rituals, for a funeral rite the ancient practice involved the ritual embalmment of the deceased, an all-night vigil with hourly recitations, followed by a variety of rites on the actual day of burial. Currently no group that I am aware of has thoroughly researched all the ancient rites and come up with meaningful and authentic alternatives. Finally, we have moral considerations. Is there any practice whose omission would be disrespectful to the gods and goddesses? In ancient Egypt ritual purity or cleanliness was vital for the priesthood. Likewise priests and priestesses were enjoined to avoid wearing clothing made from any animal products in the temple–specifically leather and wool. There also exists a detailed moral code that priests were expected to adhere to. Every morning the officiating priest affirms before the doors of the temple, "I have not shown partiality in judgment. I have not consorted with the strong. I have not reproached the lowly. . . . I have not disturbed the Balance." Modern day servants of the god can do no less.

Like the ancient Egyptians, the Temple of Ra is polytheistic, honoring many gods and goddesses. These divine powers are perceived and experienced as living entities, not as creations or projections of the human mind. Like the ancient Egyptians, the Temple of Ra values continued contact with the *akhu*, the shining spirits of the departed, and sees our relationship with them as mutually beneficial. Like the ancient Egyptians, the Temple of Ra regards *heka* (magic) as a gift of Ra to humankind. In a famous example of instructional literature dating to 2060 BCE, a pharaoh advises his son, "Shepherd the people, the cattle of God, for it is for their sake that He created heaven and earth. . . . He has ordained for them magic *(heka)* as weapons to fend off the impact of what may come to pass."[149]

In this section we offer rituals intended for personal use as well as general rituals that can accommodate groups. We include three rituals for the great deities Sekhmet, Djehuty, and Sutekh. In addition, we present the important ceremony known as "Opening the Mouth," whereby a statue of a god or goddess is enlivened and becomes an abode of divinity.

Each text reflects the current practice of the Temple of Ra in San Francisco. Nothing has been borrowed from other traditions. Each prayer and each action reflect ancient practice as best as can be determined through current research. It is our hope that you the reader will be inspired to adopt these rites as part of your own service to the gods and goddesses. It is our belief that your efforts will be rewarded for these great divine beings will not be outdone in generosity. The gods of ancient Egypt call to us today to once again pronounce "words of power" capable of restoring the Balance and reestablishing *ma'at,* that is, the harmony of truth and peace and joy.

Rising With the Sun

With the rising of the sun comes both light and renewed life. Throughout Egypt's long history the experience of the sun as source of light and life continued to shape its theology and served in a variety of ways as a metaphor for a great array of key theological concepts: birth and rebirth, renewal and transformation, victory over the forces of chaos, the nature of cyclical time, and the very rhythm of creation.

Sunrise was seen as a liminal time, crossing from night into the day, from deathlike sleep to conscious wakefulness. It was at this time that in imitation of his divine father, the sun god Ra, the pharaoh participated in the first ritual act of the day, a bathing ceremony. The two recitational texts that are presented here reflect passages from the Pyramid Texts, the Litany of Ra, Chapter 42 from the Book of Coming Forth into the Day, and inscriptions from the Temple of Seti I. Their purpose is the individual's magical–and spiritual–transformation.

The first of these texts employs a classic Egyptian magical technique involving the identification of the reciter with one or more *Netjeru* (deities). A related strategy has the reciter identify the parts of his or her body with a whole host of individual *Netjeru*. These methods stem ultimately from two basic insights. The first has to do with the origin of humanity as well as the origin of the gods. The second flows from the first and concerns the effective power of speech.

Many texts assert that humans are created from the tears of the creator god Ra, with the *Netjeru* themselves being the sweat of Ra. This graphic description comes from a culture that, unlike that of the Greeks, used very sensible, physical images to describe deeply abstract ideas. The important point here is that mankind comes from and is an intrinsic part of deity. Unlike the Hebrew creation accounts that have their god create man from dirt and woman from a rib of man–which points to the fundamental gulf between creator and the created–the Egyptian account asserts an intimate, even organic link. The creator and his creation, both gods and humans, are intrinsically related. Like members of one family, they share in a common nature. In line with this perception all the ancient funeral rituals clearly show that the destiny of humankind is deification–each human can become divine. Just as humanity springs from deity, so the destiny of the individual is to become a deity. To put it in more Western philosophical terms, humanity's essence derives from the divine essence, and its destiny is ultimately to be transfigured into fully divinized beings, participants in the divine nature but all the while remaining unique and individual.

The second insight concerns the effective, creative power of the spoken word. For the ancient Egyptians speech held a potency that could create or destroy. Just as the divine powers can speak things into existence, so humans, sharing in a divine nature, also possess what Egyptologist Geraldine Pinch describes as "the power of creative utterance."[150]

In the Morning Rite for Bathing the reciter identifies him or herself with Ra and makes reference to a mythic event in the Lake of Rushes. Egyptian magic regularly invokes the mythic *Zep Tepi*, the "First Occasion," the time before time, what the noted historian of religions Mircea Eliade refers to as *in illo tempore*, paraphrased as "in those days." A present situation is transported into the Eternal Present and thus "penetrated by the gigantic forces that, *in illo tempore*, made the Creation possible."[151] It is not only the creation stories but all mythic narratives that in Egypt might supply material for the priestly magician. This is a form of ritual speech referred to as the "magical antecedent." An event that occurred in prehistoric times, and which now possesses a mythical eternity and typicalness, is *by the power of the formula* rendered present in the literal sense and made actual and fruitful.[152]

By a narrative that cites events occurring in cosmogonic or mythic time, the reciter draws those powers into the human present. The human dimension is conjoined to a mythic dimension. Through ritual recitation of the story the reciter taps into the power of the entire mythic event, making that power present and effective. In healing spells it may refer to Aset (Isis) healing her son Heru (Horus). As the goddess healed him, so she heals the patient who is identified with him. In the Morning Rite for Bathing the First Time is evoked, the reciter identifies as Ra, and the earthly act of bathing becomes iconic of divine restoration. The earthly situation is transposed into a heavenly reality. Earth is united to heaven. There are several variations on this basic technique employed by the ancient priesthood, but each one employs a mythic narrative to effect change in this world.

The reciter then refers to the ibis-headed Djehuty (in Greek called Thoth) who functions as Tongue of Ra, that is, spokesperson for the creator. As preeminent lord of magic Djehuty is the archetype of the Great Magician., "whose words are truly effective."

Notice how the speaker addresses the water itself. The ancient Egyptians regarded creation as brimming with divine life and divine energy. Therefore, in addressing water or some other inanimate object the speaker acknowledges a living, divine presence in material objects. They are not themselves divine but they are imbued with and penetrated by the creative energy of divinity.

Finally, note that a veritable constellation of *Netjeru* (deities) is invoked to participate in this mythic act. The text of this spell is based on the morning ritual of the pharaoh. It also has parallels in a number of lustration spells in the Pyramid Texts.[153]

Morning Rite for Bathing

In accordance with ancient tradition begin by cleansing your mouth with Natron, an important ingredient in ritual bathing. Natron is a naturally occurring substance made of sodium bicarbonate (baking soda) and sodium chloride (salt). It is not found in nature outside of certain areas in Egypt, but it can be closely approximated by using the following recipe:

> Take equal parts of sea salt and baking soda, and spread the mixture in a large pan. Carefully pour the water on top of the mixture, making certain to cover the mixture by at least one inch. Place the pan on the stove and bring to a gentle boil while stirring frequently. When the mixture attains the thickness of oatmeal, remove it from the heat. Spread it on a cookie sheet and place in the oven on low heat. This will speed the drying time. When the Natron is

hard to the touch, remove and cool. It can be broken into small pieces once it has cooled.[154]

It has been conventional practice among European and American scholars to use the Greek names from antiquity for the gods and goddesses of Egypt. As Reconstructionists we want to restore usage of the original Egyptian names. However, in order to facilitate recognition of the deity we have enclosed in parentheses the common Greek name; e.g., Hwt-Hrw (Hathor). Hwt-Hrw is pronounced "Hut-Hru" or "Hut-Heru."

After chewing Natron and rinsing the mouth with water, the reciter enters the water and says aloud:

"I, [*insert reciter's name*], am a child of Ra.
I am a child of the Lord of Life, Lord to the Limit.
I am created from the tears of the Eye of Ra.
As Ra bathes in the waters of the Lake of Rushes,
so now do I bathe in the waters of the Lake of Rushes.
As Ra I am purified and cleansed.
As Ra I am renewed and rejuvenated.

"And now with words of effective power, with words of the *Netjer* Djehuty [Thoth], Tongue of Ra, whose words are truly effective, I say and I proclaim,

"O water, may you remove all evil,
As Ra who bathes in the Lake of Rushes,
May Heru [Horus] wash my flesh,
May Djehuty cleanse my feet,
May Shu lift me up and Nut take my hand.
May Sutekh [Set] be my strength, and may Sekhmet be my healing.
May Wadjet be my protection,
May Anpu [Anubis] be my guide,
May Wepwawet open the way before me in safety and in peace;
May Heru grant me victory,

May Heru bring me victory;
May Amun-Ra grant me life and may He prosper me daily.
May Amun-Ra be my life and may He prosper me greatly!"

The Apotheosis Rite for Bodily Members: Divine Identifications of the Parts of the Human Body

This Utterance can be used in conjunction with the preceding ritual bath recitation or it can stand alone. There are over half a dozen ancient texts quite similar to this. There is no single recognized alignment between specific *Netjeru* and the different parts of the body. It would seem, therefore, that individual preference may have played a part in identifying one or another part of the body with a particular *Netjer*. You may want to include the names of other *Netjeru* or identify them with different parts of the body than recorded here. In either case, though, it is important to recite the Utterance aloud and with thoughtful intent.

Divine Identifications of the Body
(based on Chapter 42 in The Book of Going Forth by Day)

"My hair is the hair of Nun, the Primordial One;
my face is the face of Ra, Lord of Life;
my eyes are the eyes of Hwt-Hrw (Hathor), Lady of Jubilation;
my ears are the ears of Wepwawet, Opener of the Way;
my nostrils are the nostrils of Amun, the Hidden One;
my lips and tongue are the lips and tongue of Heka, Eldest Magician;
my teeth are the teeth of Khepera, the Becoming One;
my blood is the blood of Min, Lord of Fertility;
my neck is the neck of Aset (Isis), Great of Magic;
my hands are the hands of Khnum, He who shapes and forms the Ka;
my fingers and leg-bones are the fingers and leg-bones of the living uraei, gracious protectresses;

my shoulders are the shoulders of Wadjet, the Rising One, Protectress;

my forearms are the forearms of Neith, Lady of Sais, the Veiled One;

my backbone is the backbone of Sutekh (Set), Slayer of the serpent, the Chosen One of Ra;

my phallus is the phallus of Ausir (Osiris), Lord of those who are 'true of voice'; [alternately: my vulva is the vulva of Bast, lady of love, lady of joy]

my flesh is the flesh of Anpu (Anubis), Seer of Hearts, wise guide and counselor;

my muscles and my back are the muscles and back of Sekhmet, the Great One of Healing;

my buttocks are the buttocks of the Eye of Heru (Horus), the Complete One, the Perfected One;

my hips and my thighs are the hips and thighs of Nut, the Azure One;

my feet are the feet of Ptah, He Who Hears Prayers;

my toes are living falcons, carrying me where I would go in safety and in peace.[155]

There is no member of my body which is not the member of a *Netjer*;

and Djehuty (Thoth) is the protection of all my flesh.

"My members are *Netjeru* (gods); I am a *Netjer* (god) completely. There is not a member in me without a *Netjer*; the *Netjeru* have become my members.[156]

"I am like unto Ra every day. None shall seize me by my arms; none shall drag me away by my hand. And there shall do me harm neither men, nor women, nor *Netjeru*, nor blessed dead, nor they who have perished, nor anyone of those of former times, nor any mortal, nor any human being. I am like unto Ra. I am like unto Ra.[157] May all protection, life, stability, and dominion, joy, bravery and strength be around me, like Ra.[158] "I am like unto Ra. I am like unto Ra."

General Rituals for the *Netjeru*

In Part One a morning (sunrise) ritual honoring Amun-Ra was presented based upon various ancient texts reflecting the standard morning liturgies of three great religious centers–Karnak, Abydos, and Thebes. Therefore, the present section does not include a complete morning rite as such. However, the Temple of Ra–like the temples of antiquity–does include worship of and service to other deities. And since many of those who will be using this book will be holding ritual at times other than early morning, it seems useful to offer examples of a general ritual honoring various *Netjeru*. We include rituals for the great *Netjeret* Sekhmet, Eye of Ra, for Djehuty (Thoth), Lord of Wisdom, and for Sutekh (Set), Defender of the Barque of Ra, "Millions-of-Years."

The standard sunrise ritual in use throughout Egypt is comprised of two major sections: the first deals with the opening of the shrine and the preparatory toilette of the *Netjer*, and the second deals with the divine banquet of offerings. The cultic prototype of this liturgy came from the temple of the chief *Netjer*, the great creator god, Amun-Ra. Other temples throughout the land emulated this ritual, making appropriate changes according to the particular *Netjer* or *Netjeret* of the temple.

Egyptian temples also had a relatively brief midday service and a longer evening service. All three services shared certain features in common: purifications, censings, and libations. The morning and evening services also included food offerings of some type. Therefore, the general rituals developed by the Temple of Ra incorporate these and other important elements that appear in the three ancient morning/sunrise rites. The Utterances, prayers, and ritual actions of these liturgies are each based upon authentic texts preserved for us either in the Karnak, Abydos, or Theban liturgies, the Berlin papyrus (No. 3055), or from inscriptions on temple walls or papyri. They have not been "modernized" to suit current tastes or sentiments. They are timeless rites that are forever young, meaningful and life-giving. Although at first some of the images may sound strange to our ears, with patience, study, and reflection they will reveal their lasting beauty to the willing student.

The daily rituals of the Egyptian temple were not designed for a congregation or audience. They are not intended as inspirational or educational pageants for laypersons. They are magical technologies performed by a skilled and educated priesthood. These sacred rites are aimed at the maintenance of the entire cosmos–affecting both the world of the *Netjeru* and the world of humankind. In fact, the entire Temple cult can best be understood as humanity's contribution to the maintenance of divine presence in our world. This subject would carry us well beyond the scope of the present book, but the interested reader is encouraged to read *Image of the World and Symbol of the Creator: On the Cosmological and Iconological Values of the Temple of Edfu* by Egyptologist Ragnhild Bjerre Finnestad (Wiesbaden: Otto Harrassowitz, 1985).

It is not the intention of this writer to substitute the general rituals presented here for the traditional morning/sunrise rite. These general rituals are a necessary accomodation aimed at facilitating a revival of traditional service to the *Netjeru* in our own era. The sunrise ritual was *the* single most important rite of the day for through its cultic actions the sacred image of the *Netjer* or *Netjeret* was once again endowed with divine life. The precise timing of that ritual was considered critical. It occured at sunrise and was not transferable to other times due to the very real connection between solar time and the reanimation or awakening of the divine image. The first hours of daylight had been an essential condition for this rite. As the sun rises, bringing light and awakening life for the new day, so the sunrise ritual "awakens" the *Netjer* to life on the earthly plain.

Today this may seem like a condition impossible to fulfill but if we intend to restore and revitalize the ancient practices we can try to perform even a very brief ritual each morning. It can consist of four simple elements: 1) the call to "Awake in peace"; 2) the embrace of life; 3) the offering of water; 4) and, last, the offering of bread and "of all things good and pure." This also gives us an opportunity to ask the *Netjer*'s blessing on us as we move through our day.

1) We begin a brief morning service with the call to "awake in peace," followed by the name of the *Netjer* and the recitation

of those epithets of that *Netjer* we intend to invoke. Here is an example:

"**Awake in peace, O Sekhmet, may you awake in peace.**
Awake in peace, O Lady of Life, may you awake in peace.
Awake in peace, O Great One of Healing, may you awake in peace.
Awake in peace, O Beautiful Sekhmet, may you awake in peace."[159]

The doors of the *Kar-shrine* are opened and we bow before the image.

2) We extend our right hand and touch the left shoulder of the sacred image. With our left hand we touch the *Netjer*'s right wrist. Doing so we say:

"**Djehuty has come to you. Awake when you hear his words. I have come as the envoy of Atum. My two arms are upon you like those of Heru. My two hands are upon you like those of Djehuty. My fingers are upon you like those of Anpu. Homage be to you. I am a living servant of (*name of deity*).**"[160]

This ritual embrace is a vehicle for transferring life force (*Ka*) into the sacred image. The priest or priestess is the conduit for the life renewing and life creating energy of the primordial creator Atum. The Liturgist functions as envoy of Atum and, as a consequence, the words of this Utterance coupled with the ritual actions effectively reanimate the sacred image.

3) The third action for this brief morning rite is the offering of a water libation. Water is the universal symbol of a life sustaining and life invigorating power. With the pouring of water the Liturgist repeats the following Utterance identifying the libation water with Nile water coming from the great river's mythical source at Elephantine (known as *Abu* in Egyptian).

"I bring to you these libations which have come forth from Abu, from 'Place-of-Refreshment' (*Kebhu*, the region of the First Cataract). **Nun satisfies you. I have brought to you these libations so that your heart may be refreshed."**[161]

4) The morning rite concludes with the offering of bread and of "all things good and pure." For the Egyptians bread epitomized the "staff of life." Made from grain grown from seed, and then through human industry ground into flour, mixed with life-giving water and, finally, baked to become the food staple for every level of society, bread represents the collaborative effort of the *Netjeru*, nature and humankind. What better gift to present to *Netjer*?

"O (name of *Netjer*), **come to this your bread. Come to this your bread which I give to you. All life is with you, all stability is with you, all health is with you, all joy is with you."**[162]

The rite concludes with the classic *"Peret er kheru"* offering formula:

"May offerings of every kind come forth in abundance, like the things which come forth from the mouth of the god (goddess)."

Peret er kheru mee pereret em reh en netjer (netjeret). (4 times)[163]

For more on this offering formula please see Section 15 below.

At this point you may want to speak with deity in your own words, presenting petitions or offering thanksgiving and asking for guidance for the upcoming day.

Unlike some modern pagan groups the ancient Egyptians did not invoke deity into a sacred image only to dismiss or bid farewell to that divine energy at the conclusion of ritual. The continuous beneficent presence of *Netjer* was a major objective for the Egyptian cult. The living presence of deity in this world was the purpose of the daily rites in the temples. In the Egyptian tradition the god or goddess is not experienced as a lord/lady in absentia, or as one who upon occasion visits this world, but rather as a numinous and powerfully *present* divine reality. This is the reason why a morning/ sunrise ritual is important. Every day is experienced as a new creation, as an awakening to new life. Every day is a miracle of divine immanence that invites us to be co-creators and co-participants in the cosmic drama. Through sacred ritual we enter into and make present that "Time before time" and in so doing we reveal the world to be holy and noble and a manifestation of overflowing love.

General Rituals from the Temple of Ra

Each General Ritual used by members of the Temple of Ra follows a standard format whose elements derive from ancient ritual texts:

1. Utterance (recitation) outside the Temple Chamber
2. Recitations for Opening the doors of the Temple Chamber and the *Kar*-Shrine
3. Presentation of water and natron
4. Purification of the Temple Chamber
5. Lighting the candle or oil lamp
6. Offering incense
7. Address to the *Netjer* or *Netjeret*
8. Offering incense
9. The Henu Rite–Embracing the Earth, the Fourfold Salute
10. Offering Ma'at
11. A Water Libation
12. The Sand Rite
13. Offering Wine
14. Offering Food
15. The *"Peret er kheru"* recitation
16. Presentation of the *Ankh* (life)
17. Presentation of the *Ib* (heart)
18. Meditation and/or Magical Action
19. "Removing the foot" ceremony
20. Reversion of Offerings

1. Utterance (recitation) outside the Temple Chamber

The priest or priestess addresses the assembled deities of the temple and asserts his/her innocence. As will occur repeatedly in the rite, the ritualist identifies with one or another *Netjer*. This is a strategy found throughout Egyptian ritual and magic. The ritualist's claim to be a specific *Netjer* (god) or *Netjeret* (goddess) puts him/her within a divine context, an otherworldly milieu that enables him/her to interact with deity on an equal footing. At the same time the priest/ess remains human, asserting his/her ritual and moral purity. There is no contradiction between being fully human and fully divine. This insight is central to the Kemetic religious vision.

In the mytho-theological vision of the Egyptians humankind came from the tears of the creator-god Ra. The gods came from his sweat. Therefore, both humans and *Netjeru* emanate in a fundamental way from the *same* Source of Life. They–humans and *Netjeru*–are intrinsically related. They share a common origin. In both instances the place of origin is *within* the creator. This is a radically different vision of creation theology from the Hebrew notion of men manufactured from earth and women from the rib of man. The Hebraic admonition, "Thou art dust, and unto dust shalt thou return," is utterly alien to the vision of Egypt in which humanity can aspire to divinity precisely because its source is divine.

The image of tears holds a certain ambiguity: they may represent equally tears of joy or tears of sorrow. Humanity experiences both, and, we may say, can cause both in the Creator, depending on the "rightness" of our actions–upholding *ma'at* or injuring that sacred moral order. The imagining of the *Netjeru* as the sweat of the creator-god is related to the belief that the presence of divinity was always accompanied by a sweet, pleasant odor, regularly compared to the fragrance of incense. This odor emanated from and surrounded the *Netjeru*, announcing as it were the divine Presence. The grains of incense themselves are exudations of trees or various plants, akin to sap that hardens in the air after seeping from the living plant. Metaphorically the *Netjeru* are exudations of the creator-god and incense is an exudation of a living organism. This graphic image presses home the belief in the deep, intimate relation between the creator-god and all the *Netjeru* who originate from him, who is called the Great He-She, the one containing both male and female.

For the modern mind, accustomed to very abstract, non-material notions about divinity, the Egyptian view may seem too physical, too material in nature. Rather, that ancient view represents a wonderfully visceral approach to creation theology. This view can serve as a corrective to the overly abstract, colorless concepts we have inherited from Western philosophical and theological thought. Both humans and gods come from a common Source and as a result share in a common ground of divine nature. Tears and sweat are visual metaphors revealing an underlying unity–*both* are composed of salt and water which likewise form important elements in sacred ritual as Natron, a naturally occurring salt, and water, the source of life and regeneration.

2. Recitations for Entering the Temple Chamber and Opening the *Kar-shrine*

As the priest/ess opens the doors of the Temple Chamber he/she addresses all the *Ba*-souls of the assembly of *Netjeru* in this temple. Every temple was residence for a number of deities, not solely the principle *Netjer* or *Netjeret*. The *Netjeru* always appear in groups or constellations of relationships.[164] The priest/ess plays a vital role in that divine constellation as he proclaims, "If you are strong, I am strong. If your *Ka*-spirits are strong, my *Ka*-spirit is strong at the head of the living." This announcement is clearly a means of identifying with the *Netjeru*. The reciter then soon announces, "I am Heru in the height of heaven, the beautiful one of awe . . . ." Egyptologist Jan Assmann explains that the most distinctive characteristic of the Egyptian cult is that ritual *"was not conceived of as a communication between the human and the divine, but rather as an interaction between deities."* [Italics are his.][165] With this and similar proclamations identifying the ritualist with a *Netjer* cultic actions are transposed into the divine realm. They *become* divine actions.

At this point the priest/ess solemnly opens the double doors of the *Kar*-shrine housing the divine image. Beginning with the acclamation, "The Doors of the Sky are opened; the Doors of the Earth are unlocked," we see that this ritual is not simply a mundane affair. It is a cosmic event with cosmic implications. The priest/ess verbally acknowledges that the temple is the dwelling place of divinity. The temple doors, or the doors of the god's shrine house (Egyptian *"Kar,"* Greek *"Naos"*) are a cosmic gateway to divinity. In a classic Egyptian manner the polarities of Earth and Sky are alluded to, and the mythic role of the god Shu, who lifts up and separates Geb and Nut, that is, Earth and Sky, is brought into play. Remember that in the opening Utterance the Liturgist exclaims, "I am Shu." The Liturgist assumes the role of the god and opens up the space between earth and heaven.

3. Presentation of water and natron

Spiritual traditions throughout the world regard water as purificatory and life sustaining. Ancient Egypt also used water for cleansing as well as for restoring and sustaining life. Natron, or its chemical equivalent (see above, Morning Rite for Bathing) is a form of salt that was used for cleansing and purification. Notice that in each case the recitation removes the speaker from the mundane by ritually identifying the action with its mythic counterpart. Water is referred to a divine event (i.e., Ra in the Lake of Rushes), and Natron is related to four *Netjeru*: Heru, Sutekh, Djehuty, and Geb. Heru represents lawful order; Sutekh embodies physical force and strength; Djehuty stands for intellect, and Geb as earth god is emblem of the material world. The priest/ess claims this fourfold purity as his/her own–order, strength, intellect, and materiality. The *Netjeru* must only be approached in an absolute state of purity, both physical and moral.

4. Purification of the Temple Chamber

Even though every Egyptian temple was formally consecrated at its founding and reconsecrated at the start of every New Year, there still were rites of purification conducted each day within the temple proper. Today few of us have the luxury of a separate room that we can dedicate exclusively for use as a temple. Therefore we find ourselves in the very modern situation of having to create "sacred space" for ritual. But as "creative conservators" we can use traditional Egyptian elements and apply them to our present situation.

As recorded in the Temple of Heru at Edfu, prior to the Morning Service two priests drew water from a well within the temple and took it into the Chamber of the Nile where it was consecrated. The water then was used to replenish libation vessels throughout the temple.[166] Offerings typically had water sprinkled or poured over them prior to being presented to the *Netjer*. Words recited while such aspersions were conducted indicate that the intent was to cleanse and purify. Many different types of ritual dating as far back as the time of the Pyramid Texts also used natron for purifications.

For the Egyptians ritual purification with water has a twofold effect. First, it removes anything "evil," that is, lacking in goodness. This is the negative meaning. But, unlike their Israelite neighbors, this was not the primary meaning of purification for the ancient Egyptians. Rather, it was fundamentally a positive power, the power of conveying life. When Ra "purifies" himself in the primeval water of the Lake of Rushes before his rising, he transfers its inherent life force to himself and thus, using created matter, he is enabled to rise and ascend the hill of creation. As W. Brede Kristensen remarks

> To become purified means here the same as to be born to new life, *viz.* resurrection. A convincing proof of this is that the water of purification is sometimes drawn as thin streams, consisting of a series of "life" signs (*ankhs*); the king is sprinkled with this life water, before he performs the holy temple ceremonies. It could hardly have been more clearly expressed, that purification has a positive result; it gives that spontaneous life which the water of life (creation water/waters of birth) possesses.[167]

Through the sprinkling of water and natron the priest/ess purifies the space serving as the temple, imbuing it with the radiant energy of life. He/she turns to face each of four directions–in the classic Kemetic order of south, north, west, and finally east–then returns to face the altar and image of the *Netjer*. There is no circle casting as in some Western magical traditions.

The two directional pairings–south and north, then west and east–reflect the twofold balancing of opposites. The balancing of dualities is a very important concept in Kemetic spirituality, one that recurs in a variety of combinations: the fertile land and the desert land, darkness and light, Heru and Sutekh. Neither one cancels out its opposite, but harmony is achieved through balance and equilibrium.

An issue related to the directions is the orientation of the altar table. According to the extensive research of Sir Norman Lockyer, the founder of archeoastronomy, the temples of Egypt were positioned on the landscape to achieve two goals, one solar and the other stellar.[168] Certain temples in Upper Egypt were oriented to either sunrise or sunset at the winter solstice, resulting in an east-west orientation, while other temples in Lower Egypt were oriented to the equinoxes, giving a north-south alignment. Other temples throughout the land were oriented to particular stars or star groups associated with the chief *Netjer* of the temple. Lockyer showed that the oldest and largest temples were aligned to stars of the northern sky, in particular the Pole Stars which held great significance for Egypt. These stars remained visible throughout the night, unlike most stars that have a limited period of visibility. It is the practice of the Temple of Ra to use a northern orientation for the altar table, but certain practical considerations may require use of a different orientation.

5. Lighting the candle or oil lamp

The mundane act of lighting the candle/oil lamp becomes an event of cosmic importance when the priest/ess names and thus transforms the lighted candle or lamp into the radiant Eye of Heru. With the lighting of the fire the darkness is pushed back and so the Eye of Heru defeats the enemies of life and light. The Eye of Heru became the symbol *par excellence* for the defeat of the hostile powers of darkness.

The ancient priesthood understood this act–and other ritual acts–as more than mere imitations of spiritual realities. In a deep and genuinely mystical sense those actions *become* divine actions. The lighted candle or lamp is not just *like* the radiant Eye of Heru; it *is* that victorious power. As the late antique Hermetic text, the Emerald Tablet, states,

> What is below is like that which is above, and what is above is like that which is below. They work to accomplish the wonders of the One Thing.[169]

The power of the effective word, coupled with ritual action, brings about the transformation of the mundane into the celestial. Magic, understood as the means whereby mundane acts become heavenly acts of cosmic significance, permeates the entire corpus of cultic activities. This is the fundamental reason why the human ritualist identifies with one or another deity as the one performing the ritual action.

Notice that the flame is not brought from outside. The priest "strikes the fire," that is, he brings forth new fire. It is the very light of creation emerging from the primordial darkness and thus it is addressed as "the Eye of Heru," which "shines like Ra in the double horizon." The light springs forth from the darkness; the new day is a new creation. The world awakens to life!

6. Offering incense

The offering of incense is both purificatory and restorative. A typical Utterance recited for the offering of incense states, ". . . It cleanses you (i.e., the *Netjer*), it adorns you, it takes its place upon your two hands."[170] And in the Ritual of Amun [XII, 10] we read: "It (the incense) is the Eye of Heru. If it lives, the people live, your flesh lives, your members flourish." In a mortuary text in an address to the deceased the priest says, "Her head is fumigated with incense. This N. is vigorous by means of incense. The *Netjer's* dew [approaches] towards your flesh."[171] Incense is identified with the sweat or exudation of the *Netjer*, and consequently both purifies and rejuvenates the recipient. Incense as the Eye of Heru purifies and brings life and health to the recipient. It is both exudation of the *Netjer* as well as being the Eye of Heru. This doubling or even tripling of identifcations is a frequent method of asserting the multi-aspected reality of divinity.

Remember the Daily Ritual, like mortuary rites, are series of *reciprocal* actions. Gifts–libations, incense, food offerings–are given to sustain the god/dess residing in the sacred image, and the deity in return extends material and spiritual blessings upon the giver. The deity in his/her earthly manifestation in the sacred image relies upon the services of humans. This may be a difficult concept for modern minds to appreciate; the gods and goddesses depend upon us to facilitate their physical presence among us.This does not in any sense diminish their status as *Netjer*, but it does point to the fundamental interdependence between the divine beings and humanity. In the study of religious traditions throughout the world the concept referred to by the Latin phrase *"Do ut des"* ("I give so that you give") is an important aspect of worship.

7. Address to the *Netjer* or *Netjeret*

The literary style of ancient Egyptian addresses to deity typically consists of an enumeration of that deity's epithets along with references to mythological events involving that particular *Netjer*. Knowledge of the deity's names or epithets is an essential aspect of invoking a deity. For it was by knowing the names of the *Netjer* that the ancient priesthood exhibited its knowledge of that *Netjer*. Both in temple literature as well as funerary spells the Liturgist will assert, "I know your name," and again,"I know your secret forms (*kheperu*)," thus establishing a living link with the *Netjer* and a claim on the right to be heard. Remember that the names by which we know the *Netjeru* are quite often simply descriptive of their nature. For example, Aset (Greek Isis) literally means "throne," Nebet Het (Greek Nepthys) means "Mistress of the Household,"

Hwt-Hrw (Greek Hathor) "House of Heru (Horus)," and Amun "the Hidden One." We are not able to discern the etymology (if any) for every divine name, but we can study the epithets for they, too, are a classic Egyptian way of "naming" the deity. The epithets of a deity form a unique kaleidoscope of the god's emanations or aspects, and as they are pronounced we draw down that divine presence. The ancient Egyptian priesthood was keenly aware of the importance of the name as an aspect of the person's or god's essence. To know the name, therefore, is to gain insight into the essence of the person or deity.

Often the address includes specific requests for assistance or guidance of one type or another, but these requests refer in some manner to an attribute or facet of that particular deity. Thus, if we call upon Djehuty (Greek Thoth) by pronouncing his epithet as Lord of Wisdom, we are invoking that particular aspect of the *Netjer.*

8. Offering incense and the *Ka*

As incense is offered the priest/ess makes reference to the *Ka* of the *Netjer.* The *Ka* is sometimes explained as the person's or *Netjer's* spiritual "double." It is the universal–as opposed to individual–vital force that both surrounds and penetrates the person of the *Netjer* or individual. It is pictured as being a duplicate of but separate from the person, hence the references to the arms and legs of the *Ka.* Since the *Ka* shares in and, indeed, is a part of the universal life force, it provides a natural protective as well as energizing function. The *Ka* is one aspect of the *Netjer* that inhabits or descends upon the sacred image of the *Netjer.* Incense for the *Netjer* and for his/her *Ka* forms a linkage between these two worlds. Recall that incense both purifies and revitalizes the recipient. The recitation concludes with the optative statement, "May your face be filled as this essence spreads itself over you." Here filling has the meaning of re-energizing or revitalizing. The reference to the *Netjer's* face is a literary technique naming a part for the whole, as if to say, "May you yourself be revitalized through this offering of incense."

9. The Henu Rite–Embracing the Earth, the Fourfold Salute

Embracing the Earth: The celebrants kneel on both knees, raise both hands to shoulder height with palms facing outward–referred to as the *dua* or adoration gesture–then bring head and hands down to touch the ground. Remain with forehead touching the ground for a few moments and then perform the Fourfold Salute.

The Fourfold Salute: Keep the right knee on the ground with the right foot under the buttocks. Bring the left foot forward and flat on the ground, left leg bent and pointing up. Bend the right arm at the elbow with the hand at the level of the head. Rotate the raised arm to the right so it is parallel to the body. The fist should be clenched. With the fist of the left hand tap the chest just above the breast. Then bring both hands up, palms facing outward, in the adoration/*dua* position. This series of gestures is repeated four times. Finally, repeat the Embracing the Earth gesture, then conclude by reciting the Utterance "Homage to . . . ."

The word *henu* contains at the same time the twin concepts of "praise" and "rejoice." The hieroglyph for *henu* shows a worshipper kneeling on one knee, extending an arm with hand held open while holding the other arm with closed fist touching the chest. The actual performance of the *henu* gesture transforms the worshippers into living hieroglyphs.

The Fourfold Salute is depicted in scenes showing the *Ba*-souls of Pe and Nekhen. These are two groups of divine ancestors from Pe (Buto) in Lower Egypt and Nekhen (Hierakonpolis) in Upper Egypt. The former are shown with the heads of falcons, and the latter with those of jackals. In both instances they represent deceased ancestor-kings of important predynastic settlements. This pairing of divine royal ancestors from both Upper and Lower Egypt illustrates the ancient priesthood's consistent habit of acknowledging the duality that made up the unity of Egypt.

When the Fourfold Salute is performed, it represents a reaching back into archaic times and, therefore, the gesture is a sign and token of a temporal "oneness" and continuity of praise, worship, and rejoicing. Every *Netjer* and *Netjeret* is perceived as benevolent lord and divine ruler of his/her temple realm, and, therefore, the natural subject for this act of praise. Even though a deity may have been local to one particular vicinity in Egypt it was not unusual for the worship of that deity to have spread throughout the country. The power of *Netjer* is *never* restricted geographically. A *Netjer* may often have had a specific geographic cult center, but worship of that *Netjer* in other locales was quite common because the *power* of that *Netjer* was experienced as present and efficacious. Persons immigrating from one place to another may have been responsible for introducing a *Netjer* to a new locale, but only the dynamic presence of that *Netjer* as experienced by the local inhabitants can explain the longevity of a cult over several millennia.

10. Offering Ma'at

This is *the* perfect offering. Ma'at is more than an intellectual construct. She is the living divine hypostasis of goodness, truth, beauty, balance, and perfection. The ritualist addresses the *Netjer*, "I have come to you as Djehuty." This act is a divine act. It occurs on earth and in the divine realm. In the Morning Ritual in the Temple of Amun-Ra, the expanded version of this recitation states, "You exist, for Ma'at exists. Ma'at exists, and you exist. . . . An offering of Ma'at has been made to you to give satisfaction to your heart, and your heart shall live in her, and your *Ba*-soul shall live, O Amun-Ra. You are at peace and you flourish through her. . . ." The state of ma'at is a collaborative effort of gods and humans.

11. A Water Libation

The significance of the ritual pouring of water before the sacred image is graphically illustrated in a number of temple carvings that show pharaoh having water poured over him by Heru and Sutekh or Heru and Djehuty. The images show a stream of ankh ("life") hieroglyphs pouring out of the vessels. The message is clear: water brings life. Water renews life. An additional meaning is revealed within the recitation; "I present to you that which flows forth from you, so that your heart shall continue to beat." Life comes from *Netjer* to us, and we in turn present it to *Netjer's* earthly vessel, the sacred image.

The recitation concludes with the statement, "For it is with you [the *Netjer*] that all comes forth at the sound of the voice." In Egyptian spirituality the voice, that is, the spoken word, is capable of *heka*-power–the creative magical capacity to bring things into existence. This concluding statement is a recognition of the inherent creative power of every *Netjer*.

12. The Sand Rite

As Egyptologist Robert Ritner explains

> By virtue of its early appearance from the receding flood waters [of the Nile], sand was intimately associated with the creation of the Egyptian cosmos, and hence with all creative acts. As a purifying substance, sand is thus used in the foundations (and foundation deposits) of temples and sanctuaries, is ritually strewn during processions of the gods and private magical rites, is offered to deities, and even serves in the composition of divine figures and as a platform for magical images . . . .[172]

In the ancient daily temple liturgies the sprinkling of sand is identified with the restoration of the Eye of Heru, the great archetype of that which has been injured but is now restored whole and complete. In a comparable text from Abydos there occurs a helpful expansion in the recitation: *"Qu'il (l'oeil) fasse le don de vie, stabilite, force, sante, comme le soleil, a jamais."* "Which (i.e., the Eye) makes the gift of life, stability, power, health, like the sun, forever."[173] The restored Eye of Heru is seen as the divine conduit from which flow all of these blessings. This is, in a sense, an *emanationist* theology. The divine originator or source is the creator god. This great *Netjer* is depicted with two eyes, sometimes described as the sun and moon, the two great orbs of the heavens. The Eye of Heru is envisioned as both moon and the restored Eye of the *Netjer* Heru. From this restored, now perfect Eye there emanates to humanity the manifold blessings of the creator *Netjer*.

At this point more needs to be said about the metaphysics informing the ancient Egyptian concept of an emanationist universe. This is crucial for understanding the role of ritual. The universe is arranged hierarchically: from the creator *Netjer* there emanates a radiance that forms a multi-leveled created order. Just as the light of the sun is not dissipated by being given off, so, too, emanation takes place but the source–*Netjer*–is not diminished in any way. All varieties of creation are seen as having a real connection, in their very being, with the divine Source. Humanity has the capacity to trace back up the chain of emanation and strive toward the divine source. This Source is *Netjer*. Through ritual humans can transform the mundane into a divine reality. This is the whole point of theurgy–sacred ritual opens the way to uniting earth with heaven. In the Egyptian view of things contemplation is not sufficient to elevate humans to the divine state. Rituals–theurgic rites–have the capacity to change the mundane into the divine–not as *escape from* this world as we find in the religions of "salvation," but as a religion of transformation and sanctification. This world is experienced as essentially *good*, as an emanation of divinity. Humans are emanated beings, and as such, we have a natural inclination to strive to return to our Source. And, indeed, we humans *can* ascend to the realm of the gods, that is to say, we can return to the divine Source, not to be absorbed, but to take our individual places in the divine barque "Millions of Years."

The ritualist creates just like the cosmos unfolds, only backwards. A physical symbol such as the lighted candle/torch, or incense or a food offering is raised through the power of the spoken word coupled with cultic action to a higher metaphysical level–"from earth to heaven." This is a process of transfiguration. There is a profound ontological connection between the realities of the divine realm and those of this earthly realm. Through ritual acts we humans take part in those divine realities.

13. Offering Wine

In *Wine and Wine Offering in the Religion of Ancient Egypt* Mu-Chou Poo offers a structural analysis of the many different wine offering liturgies preserved on temple walls. He shows conclusively that while there are numerous variations of expression in the liturgies themselves there are clear types of texts or "formulae" associated with the offering of wine. Wine carries a certain significance in the context of Egyptian religious beliefs. The offering liturgy alludes to

> . . . various aspects of myths as well as theological and symbolic meanings associated with wine. When wine was offered to the deity, it was not merely an offering of divine drink, but an offering of the creative and rejuvenating power–an act that contributed to the restoration or maintenance of cosmic order.[174]

In some offering texts wine is identified with the Eye of Heru, the Green Eye of Heru, or even the sweat of Ra. "Green"–*w3dt* in Egyptian (pronounced "wadjet")–is written with the papyrus plant. The symbolic association of the papyrus is freshness and prosperity.

The word *w3d*, . . . is phonetically very close to *wd3*–prosperous. Thus, a pun on *wd3* was probably implied in *w3d*, because the two words shared the common meaning "prosperity." [therefore] when wine was designated as "Green Horus Eye," it also implied rejuvenating powers that creates prosperity.[175]

In many texts, though, it is not so identified with a divine counterpart. Instead, the statement is made, "I fill the Eye of Heru for you with wine."[176] In this statement we see that wine has the capacity to "fill," rejuvenate or heal the Eye of Heru. Many texts conclude with some sort of optative statement. Several often recurring wishes addressed to the divine recipient include "May your mouth be opened with wine"; "may you be powerful through it"; "may you drink and be powerful therein"; "may your heart be happy by means of it"; and "may anger be removed from your heart." The idea that wine could "open the mouth" points to its having a rejuvenating power. The ritual of Opening the Mouth was *the* ritual par excellence for restoring vitality to the deceased.

14. Offering Food

The word *hu* means "word of command" or "creative word." It also is the word for victuals, that is, food and drink. A *Netjer* by the same name accompanies the sun god in the solar barque. So we see *Hu*, the lord of the creative word, is also lord of victuals/ sustenance, and he is at times depicted in the form of the Nile god Hapy who is pictured bearing an abundance of foodstuffs for the *Netjeru*. We must ask why victuals are so closely identified with the creative word. The scholar W. Brede Kristensen explains

> . . . food and drink represent the word of creation in a special way. . . .Victuals are the staff and stay of life. Eating and drinking which give mankind fresh bodily and spiritual powers, must participate to a special degree in the mysterious energy or magical power which is the essence of life. Therefore food characterizes more than anything else which has been created, the nature of the word of creation. . . . The idea was that in and through food the mystery of life is materialized.[177]

Food brings us and the *Netjeru* into contact with the mysterious, creative powers of life. The offering of food, therefore, represents far more than a lovely gesture of generosity toward the *Netjeru*. It represents in a material way the renewal of life.

Many different kinds of food offerings are depicted both in temple and tomb. A rich variety of foods were typically presented as at a banquet: breads of different types, vegetables, meats, and fruits, as well as wine, beer, milk, and honey. In examining the recitation texts that accompany each food offering we repeatedly encounter what Egyptologists call "wordplay," but is more accurately named "word-links," that is, associations between words sounding very similar or sharing the same consonants. As Egyptologist Stephen Quirke explains

> The word-links ... violate our dearly held philological faith in etymology. In our sciences of language, we construct family trees for words, and derive meanings from their history. Against this, the ancient Egyptians linked words not because they shared origins, but because they shared consonants, or structure. The interest is not in the past behind each word, but in a present perceived as immutable and god-given. Words correspond to the created matter of creation.[178]

The following recitational examples come from what is referred to as the "Menu (*dbht-htp*) for the Festival of Amun, Lord of Opet, and Amun-Ra, Lord of the Thrones of the Two Lands." Please note that the transliterations of the hieroglyphs do not fully convey the linguistic correspondences, but give an approximation only.

> O Amun, take to thyself the sound teeth of Horus with which his mouth is equipped (*htm*), onion bulbs (*hdw*), 4 vessels.

> O Amun, take to thyself the breast of Isis of which the gods taste (*dp*), figs (*db*), 2 vessels.

> O Amun, take to thyself the Eye of Horus which he has tasted (*dpt*), *dpt*-bread, 1 vessel.

> O Amun, take to thyself the fluid (*hnk*) which comes from Osiris, beer (*hnk*), 2 jars.

> O Amun, take to thyself those who rebel against thee, grasp (*ndr*) them for thyself, side of beef (*drww*), 1 vessel.

> O Amun, take to thyself the flesh (*swtt*) of the Eye of Horus, *swt*-joints, 1 vessel.[179]

For the ancient Egyptian priesthood there existed a real and profound link between sound and symbol (hieroglyph) and object. We, however, come from a cultural tradition that is blind and deaf to such associations and, therefore, we may have difficulty appreciating the value of such word-links. We also must contend with the fact that we are neither speaking not reading Middle Egyptian, that form of the Egyptian language which at a certain point in history became the canonical tongue for religious rites. But even this form underwent expansion and elaboration of the hieroglyphs so thousands of new hieroglyphs were eventually added to the original Middle Egyptian corpus. As with the hieroglyphs, so also the pronunciation of Egyptian changed over the course of the millennia. And today scholars are still working at refining our knowledge of the various stages of the ancient Egyptian language.

In spite of all this, we can learn something about the great importance of the language we use when addressing the *Netjeru*. Our own language is a beautiful language, and we can use the literary and poetic power of it to create new and powerful offering formulae. Certainly our gods and goddesses hear us when we pray. We should not erect stumbling blocks for ourselves or others by insisting on using a language other than our own. So although we can derive great benefit from studying the original texts, we can rest secure that the *Netjeru* hear us in our own language and accept our offerings as they once accepted those of the Egyptian people.

Another important component to the offering formulae is the multitude of references to mythic realities, the most frequent of which is the Eye of Heru. Others include the Testicles of Sutekh, exudations from the body of Ausir, the nourishing milk from the breasts of Aset, and the identification of the meat offering with either the pairing of the Eye of Heru and the Testicles of Sutekh, or with the bodies of defeated enemies. The Eye of Heru is that eye once injured but now restored and more perfect than before. The Testicles of Sutekh likewise were injured but now are restored and perfect. The Eye represents intellect and its logical operations, and the Testicles represent active physical energy including sexual activity. Through struggle they were injured, but through the *heka*-magic of Djehuty, who is both Heart and Tongue of the creator god, they are healed and indeed strengthened, and the warring Powers are reconciled and again in balance. On one level these are mythic archetypes–but simultaneously they also are *real*, that is, individual, unique beings with whom we can and do interact.

When the priest/ess identifies the offering with a divine counterpart, the *heka*-power of the spoken word both transforms that offering and reveals it to be what it truly is–a divine reality. In *naming* the offering a veil is lifted, a transformation takes place. An action on earth becomes an otherworldly or heavenly act. These rites are not just pious exercises intended to provoke a "religious" feeling in the participants. Nor are they solely acts of worship. They are actions that enable us to participate in a great, eternal cosmic drama–"as above, so below." When we approach liturgy with this in mind, we begin to sense the awesomeness of what we do.

15. The *"Peret er kheru"* recitation

Having completed the offering of individual items, all present stretch forth their hand over the offerings and repeat four times the ancient *"Peret er kheru"* formula: "May offerings of every kind come forth in abundance, like the things that come forth from the mouth of the *Netjer/Netjeret* (god/goddess)." This reflects classic creation theology. When the creator made the world, he uttered the names of things and they came into being. This ancient formula refers to that creative word. The ancient Egyptian would pronounce these words in order to bring offerings into existence for the blessed dead. Being an eminently practical people, the Egyptians were well aware that actual material offerings for their beloved dead were likely to cease at some point in time. But they also believed in the genuinely creative power of the spoken word. Almost every funerary monument of ancient Egypt contains this or a similar request that the passerby simply recite the offering formula for the *Ka* of the departed. In this way the blessed dead would continue to be nourished by the living.

In the daily liturgy we, the servants of the *Netjer*, may be able to offer only a modest array of actual food offerings. This power-filled formula enables us to present the gods with a true abundance of offerings. As we pronounce the words–here in the original language–we reach across time and join the men and women of ancient Egypt in service to the *Netjeru*. These creative "words of power" are repeated four times, with four being the sign of the four directions or totality. At many points in the ancient liturgies we read the instructions that some phrase or statement is to be recited four times. Purely on the psychological level this fourfold repetition helps us focus and intensify our intention. On the magical level it facilitates the raising of power to affect the desired outcome, namely, offerings for the *Netjeru*.[180]

16. Presentation of the Ankh (life)

The three words, *"Ankh neheh djet,"* "Live for all time and for eternity," sum up the ancient Egyptian conception of the two aspects of time. *Neheh* is the time of eternal return, the cycle of the year as we experience the seasons and the daily cycle of the sun which is renewed and repeated throughout linear time. The sun god Ra epitomizes *neheh* time in his recurring journey of rising and setting and rising again. On the other hand *djet* time represents the durability and perfected state of eternal and imperishable completeness, epitomized by Ausir (Osiris). As Egyptologist Jan Assmann explains

> Ra and Osiris . . . formed a constellation. They were what they were only in relation to one another. Only the two together yielded reality, and it was only their combined effect that gave rise to the complex of *neheh* and *djet* that humankind experienced as "time": a periodically consummated union of the two aspects, change and completion, from which reality proceeded as a sort of continuity of the life of the cosmos. The Egyptians thus conceived of time as a combination of "solar time" and "osirian time" that had its origin in the active, combined effectiveness of the two gods.[181]

In numerous texts describing the nightly journey of Ra through the *Duat* (underworld), the Lord of Life encounters and unites with the Lord of the Blessed Dead in a mystical union that benefits both Lords and guarantees the continued dual aspects of reality, that is, *neheh* cyclic time and *djet* eternal time.

When the Liturgist extends the *ankh* symbol to the *Netjer* and pronounces the optative words, "Live for all time and for eternity," we encounter one of the deepest mysteries in Kemetic ritual. We, the human person, present life to the divine person. Going back to the final words of the opening Utterance Before the Closed Doors of the Temple, we read, "I present his [i.e., the god's] offerings . . . *that I may endow his image with life.*" The human priest/ess gives life to the god. It is by means of the ritual actions that the god's earthly image, the statue, continues each day to be the abode of deity. The Liturgist acts as a *Netjer*. The actions of the liturgy are *both* human actions and divine actions. In the morning liturgy the human priest/ess exclaims, "I am Shu" (Opening Utterance); "I am Heru in the height of heaven," (Fifth Ceremony); "I am Djehuty who journeyed at the two seasons to seek for the Eye of its Lord," (Eleventh Ceremony); "I am Djehuty, and my two hands are joined under *ma'at*" (Fourteenth Ceremony); "I am Djehuty, who reconciles the *Netjeru*" (Thirty-second Ceremony).[182] Every god and goddess is capable of giving life. The human becomes the vehicle, as it were, for divinity, just as the statue becomes the abode of divinity. And yet the human is still fully a human being, and the statue is still fully a material statue. Both in the temple liturgies and in magical ceremonies we will hear the statement often repeated, "I am . . . ." The earthly event becomes an otherworldly event by means of such "words of power" that transfigure the mundane into the heavenly, or as the Hermetic text observes,

> Ascend from earth to heaven
> and descend again from heaven to earth,
> and unite together the power
> of things superior and inferior.[183]

The god's servant–priest or priestess–is both representative of humanity and of divinity at one and the same time. He or she acts not on his or her own accord as a private individual but as "one sent" on behalf of humanity for as the Liturgist states when first standing before the divine image, "Behold, *I am sent* to look upon the *Netjer*" (Seventh Ceremony). Simultaneously the god's servant performs, that is, brings into reality the acts of one or another god. Ultimately in a very real sense this is both a human as well as a divine drama. The Liturgist who can keep in his/her consciousness the magnitude of what is happening is well on the way to opening this ancient gateway for mystical communion with the divine.

The idea of approaching deity as "one sent" stems originally from the priest being "sent" by pharaoh who delegated many cultic duties to the priesthood. Today an individual who serves as a "god's servant," that is, as a priest or priestess, does so because of an inner calling by the god. So in a real sense that individual is indeed "sent" by something greater than himself. The individual often feels drawn to a particular god or goddess and begins a spiritual relationship that may lead to true priestly service.

17. Presentation of the *Ib* (heart)

The offering of the heart is attested in the daily morning ritual at Karnak and Abydos as well as other important religious centers throughout Egypt. This cultic act has its origin in the funeral rite. As Alexandre Moret explains

> *Rappelons-nous que le dieu, au debut du service sacre, est semblable a uncorps sans vie et sans ame. . . . Le chap. XVI [de donner le coeur] nous en indique un autre [des moyens], par la restitution au dieu de son coeur, symbole de l'ame.*[184]

> Let us recall that the god, at the beginning of the sacred service, is like a body without life and without soul. . . . Chapter 16 [i.e., "Giving the heart"] shows us one other

[means or way] for the restoration to the god of his heart,
symbol of the soul.

In the original funeral liturgy, during the Opening of the Mouth
ceremony, the heart and thigh of a sacrificed bull were presented
to the deceased and ritually touched to the lips of the mummy.
The intent was to transfer the life force from the animal to the
deceased. The heart was regarded as the seat of all vital powers. It
(i.e., the heart) was regarded as the spiritual center of a person, the
place where a person would come closest to his or her *Ka* (or vital
spirit), which was associated with the heart: "Follow the heart as
long as you live. . . . Don't lessen the time of following the heart,
for this offends the *Ka*." . . . . In the Book of the Dead, Ani says
of his heart: "You are my *Ka* within my body which forms and
strengthens my limbs."[185]

The heart was regarded as the seat of memory and intention. In
Chapter 30b of the Book of the Dead the speaker addresses his
heart:

O my heart which I had from my mother!
O my heart which I had from my mother!
O my heart of my different ages!
. . . .
For you are my *Ka* which was in my body,
the protector who made my members hale.[186]

Recall that the statue, that is, the abode of the deity, is awakened and
revivified each morning as if dead or "*Ka*-less," and the presenting
of the heart signifies the return of vital power to the sacred image.
The lengthy ceremony of the Opening of the Mouth was simplified
and condensed in the daily Temple rite so that it sufficed, as Moret
explains, to present a heart fabricated from stone or metal in
place of the heart of a sacrificed animal. The shape of this heart
is a three dimensional representation of the hieroglyph for heart,
resembling a vase or vessel with top and two handles. The word

for heart is *ib* (pronounced "eeb"). The presentation of the *ib*-heart to the *Netjer* is the ritual restoration of that vital center.

In addition to this allusion to the funerary rite, the presentation of the heart recalls certain mythic events involving Heru, his mother, Aset, as well as Djehuty and the goddess referred to as *Nesert*, that is, "the flaming one," Sekhmet. The Liturgist proclaims:

> I bring to you your heart to set it in its place; just as Aset (Isis) brought his heart to her son, Heru, and set it in its place; just as her son Heru brought her heart to Aset and set it in its place; just as Djehuty brought her heart to the Flaming One; just as this goddess was reconciled by Djehuty.

In typical Egyptian fashion an act in earthly time is referred to a divine act occuring in otherworldly time. The present situation is made to refer to a parallel mythical situation. This text like so many of our ritual texts "aims at conveying to the present situation its primeval, universal, real significance,"[187] and by so doing makes an earthly action conform with its mythological antecedents, and at the same time it receives its power from those divine events.

In the words of this Utterance the present action is equated to the divine actions of Aset, Heru, and Djehuty, effectively drawing upon the inherent power of those divine prototypes to raise up and transform the mundane act into those divine counterparts. The Utterance acts as an "efficacious statement" thus tapping into the power of the original event. The verbal recitation in which truly "the word is made flesh" has the power to effect the hermetic maxim "as above, so below."

In one more elaborate text for the presentation of the *Ib*-heart, the priest adds the words, "Come, let me draw near to you with your heart, that you may have pleasure through me, and that by means of me you may have power over your body."[188] In this we see the intent or purpose of this priestly act. It effectively enables the *Netjer* to once again have a vital presence in the sacred image.

It is most striking that *Netjer*'s presence is facilitated by human intervention. Each day is a new opportunity to bring divinity into the human sphere. Without the service of the Temple cult the presence of deity would be diminished, and, in turn, the world would be impoverished as a result.

18. Meditation and/or Magical Action

This is the point in the ritual when participants may quietly commune with the *Netjer*. It is the time for presenting requests for divine aid. Among the members of the Temple of Ra many are comfortable addressing aloud their requests or concerns. The vocalization of one's requests is an important means of placing into the material universe the desires of the heart. This may be done so that others may hear, or spoken very quietly so only *Netjer* hears. Requests may also be written down and presented at this time. This may be appropriate when dealing with highly personal or sensitive matters. Participants may also use this time to offer aloud thanks for blessings received.

This time may also be used to effect change through ritual magic. A great deal of psychic energy has been raised up to this point and it can be put to good use through the performance of *heka*-magic. Later in this book we will provide examples of such rituals as practiced in the Temple of Ra. Such rites will likely be most effective if all participants have been previously notified of the nature and form of the magical action so each person can familiarize him or her self with the words and actions of the spell. Details for performing the spell should be prepared beforehand so nothing is left to chance. *Heka*-magic is power-filled magic and deserves to be treated with genuine respect, not in a haphazard or off-handed way.

The priest-magicians are dealing with divine realities and ought to be zealous in carrying out such rites with forethought and precision.

19. "Removing the foot" ceremony (Ancient Egyptian *int rd*)

The ancient Egyptian term *int rd* means "removing" or "withdrawing the foot"; in other words, walking out of or exiting the place of offering or Temple room. As Egyptologist Patrick Boylan explains

> Part of the "withdrawal" consisted in sweeping the floor of the shrine with a besom consisting of a bundle of shrubs, or something similar. This besom was the *hdn*, and because it was supposed to remove uncleanness and other hostile influences from the shrine of the god, it was invested with magical qualities and entrusted to the care of Thoth [Djehuty], who thus became *nb hdn* [Lord of the *heden*].[189]

There are at least fifteen surviving temple reliefs that show this act as part of the daily temple ritual.[190] The key to understanding the significance of this act lay in the words of the accompanying Utterance which are inscribed at Abydos: "Thoth comes, he has rescued the Eye of Horus from his enemies, and no enemy, male or female, enters into this sanctuary." In sweeping the floor–recall that sand had been strewn liberally in front of the shrine, the priest/ess obliterates his/her own footprints and thus returns the temple room to its pristine condition. Also, in the actual morning rite the statue of the god is placed on a pile or small hill of sand in imitation of the first hill of creation that emerges from the void. Sweeping, therefore, first of all returns the area to its previous unmarked state. A second purpose of the act is to "sweep" the area free from any negative influences that might have accompanied the participants–"no enemy, male or female, enters into this sanctuary." The Liturgist impersonating Djehuty, Lord of *Heka-*Magic, "whose words are truly effective," establishes and affirms the continued pristine purity of the Temple Chamber.

In Rainer Hannig's monumental work *Ägyptisches Wörterbuch* the *hdn* plant is identified by the scientific name "Bupleurum." In Erman-Grapow's *Wörterbuch der Ägyptischen Sprache*, Bd II,

506, the *hdn* plant is further identified as a plant imported from Nubia.[191] Seeds for the variety "Bupleurum rotundifolium" can be ordered from major seed suppliers. We may well choose to grow and cultivate the Bupleurum as a very physical link with the ancient usage for this plant. Or, as "creative conservators" we may choose to adopt an alternative for the *hdn* plant. In some Western traditions birch is used in making the sweep of a magician's broom, with birch regarded as having both a protective and a purifying power, specifically against evil entities.[192] In any event the modern ritualist may prefer to choose an individually crafted broom or assemble his/her own using branches that are locally available. The important point is that the broom or bundle of branches, like all items employed in the ancient rites, be dedicated for use exclusively in sacred ritual. And, as with the case of amulets, the branch bundle or broom should be washed in pure water, passed through the purifying smoke of myrhh incense, and finally dedicated for sacred use through anointing with frankincense oil.

After all participants have backed out of the Temple Chamber, the doors are solemnly closed. The Utterance accompanying this penultimate action is a declaration that the lord of sacred ritual, Djehuty, has in fact restored the Balance–he has filled the Eye of Heru and restored the Testicles of Sutekh. As the spell for "Removing the Foot" had just proclaimed, "all the *Netjeru* are in harmony." The whole intent and purpose of the divine service has been to restore the Balance. Every action in the sacred ritual is designed to renew and restore and maintain the equilibrium of human and divine life.

20. Reversion of Offerings

One final ceremonial act remains: the removal of the food offerings and their reversion for distribution and consumption by the servants of the *Netjer*. One priest/ess and as many assistants as are needed enter the Temple Chamber a final time. The bread offering is the single food item that should remain. All other food offerings are lifted up before the shrine (*Kar* mansion or Naos) housing the statue of the *Netjer* and the appropriate Utternace is recited.

It has been speculated that bread was the single food stuff that could remain fresh and not spoil for a day, whereas other foods were prone to loose their freshness rather quickly in the hot Egyptian climate.[193] There is, however, a deeper meaning. Ausir (Osiris) is called *Ba tau*, "soul of loaves." As lord of resurrection he is lord of that spontaneous life that emerges out of death. Just as the wheat grows from the soil, is harvested, and from the grain bread is formed and renews the lives of humankind, so bread becomes iconic of the renewal of life. Among all foods it is bread which epitomizes the renewal of life, and the continual renewal of life is, in the Egyptian view, the essence of eternal life. Eternal life is not a static state, but rather continually renews itself both in this terrestrial world and in the divine world.

When a meat offering is to be removed, the Liturgist exclaims, "O (name of *Netjer*), your enemy withdraws for you." Meat offerings bore a dual meaning–as a food offering and also as a symbol of the defeated enemy. In Egypt we find no ritual whatever for the sacrificial slaughter of animals. Animals were not slaughtered anywhere near the *Netjer*'s altar. Unlike Israelite practice, there is no animal holocaust or burnt offering. Meat was offered solely as an item of the divine banquet. But because of the necessary slaying of the animal and the shedding of its blood there is associated with every meat offering a connection with the slaying and defeat of the cosmic enemies, Apep and his brood.

Every type of food was then and is still now capable of carrying a significance that goes beyond its physical form. Even in our secular culture certain foods are associated with specific holidays. The ancient Egyptians saw very many foods as pointing to spiritual realities. They were less materialistic than modern people who see food simply as belonging to the natural world. This ancient people saw that every meal and every food brings us into contact with the creative powers of life. Therefore, every food most assuredly has significance beyond itself. These connections reveal themselves in symbolic associations that enable us to see through the veil of materiality to an eternal prototype.

The priesthood, then, should not exhibit a parsimonious attitude in selecting or preparing food offerings. The *Netjeru* are generous with us. Can we be less than generous with them? Let your offering tray be well laden and beautiful to behold–bread, meat, fruits and vegetables, wine, beer, milk, honey, and whatever you yourself would place before an honored guest in your home.

Conclusion: Sustaining a Sense of the Sacred

The central point for the following rituals is service to the *Netjer* or *Netjeret*. The ancient Egyptian title for a person appointed to conduct sacred rites within the Temple is *hem Netjer*, "servant of the god." As servant of the sacred the "god's servant," the priest or priestess, unites earth with heaven, and through sacred liturgy makes possible the presence of deity in the divine image. This presence in the divine statue serves as a tangible point of contact between the two worlds, the divine and human. The sacred image is housed in a shrine (*Kar* mansion or naos) that as we mentioned previously serves as a gateway between the worlds: "The doors of the sky are opened; the doors of the earth are unlocked. . . . The double doors of heaven open, the Company of the *Netjeru* send forth light."[194]

These words for the opening of the doors of the shrine point to two great mysteries: the shrine house is that liminal place "between the worlds" from which divinity erupts into our world, and, second, it is from deity that mankind receives the gift of illumination, spiritual as well as material. The light coming forth from the gods removes darkness and delusion and reveals the world to be what it truly is, creation imbued with radiant holiness. The world is radically and fundamentally good and the *Netjeru* actively *desire* to be present in that world. This divine presence is facilitated, maintained, and protected by "servants of the god."

In ancient Egypt these rites were not open to the public. In fact, only the highest grades of "servant of the god" were permitted entry to the Temple Chamber housing the divine image. On festival days ordinary people did have access to the outer courts of the temple building and participated in hymns as well as elaborate processions when the sacred image was carried out of the innermost Chamber. But even at those times the image itself was concealed from view. The statue would be housed in a naos-like cabin and placed on a portable boat that would be carried on the shoulders of a cadre of priests. Depictions on temple walls most often indicate that the statue itself was not visible. In a few instances the sides of the cabin appear to be waist high and, therefore, the upper portion of the divine image might have been open to view. This, though, is uncertain. Why, we might ask, were such measures taken to keep people from seeing the sacred image? Certainly many large statues of the *Netjeru* were openly displayed along processional routes and private individuals owned statues for their home shrines.

The answer lies in the Egyptian's realization of the utterly awesome and unique presence of divinity in the cult image and the subsequent sacredness of the innermost Temple Chamber. Modern persons often have difficulty understanding this. The world has become banal and de-sacralized, and for modern man a statue is little more than a reminder of something absent. For the Egyptians it was a *presence* rather than an absence. The innermost Chamber *literally*, not figuratively, housed a god. We will revisit this subject of the indwelling divine presence of the cult statue when, in a later chapter, we treat the important ritual known as Opening the Mouth.

The Kemetic Reconstructionist who wishes to enact the following rites should obtain a statue of the *Netjer* or *Netjeret* whom he/she is to serve. If a statue is not available, then a picture will suffice. In either case once the image is consecrated through the Opening of the Mouth ritual it should be treated with genuine reverence for then it is the material abode of a divine presence. Also a *Kar* or sacred shrine house for the image can be constructed. It is rectangular in shape with two hinged doors in the front. It need only be large enough to accommodate the sacred image. It can be of very simple but beautiful design.

Traditionally the doors of the *Kar*-shrine are kept closed except during the daily ritual. This is not only to safeguard the image from incomprehending eyes, but it serves as a material re-creation of the *Zep Tepi*, the First Occasion of existence as the creator *Netjer* emerged from a lightless primeval flood, the Nun. Since every god and goddess originates from that earliest creator *Netjer*, Atum, the deep meaning is that every god and goddess was in fact already present *in potentiality* at that First Occasion. This is substantiated in the Morning Ritual, when in imitation of the first moment of creation the doors of the *Kar*-shrine are opened, the first light is struck, the sacred image is brought out and immediately placed on a small hill of sand. The sand represents the Primeval Mound which first emerged from the undifferentiated darkness of the Nun. The dark interior of the *Kar* represents that primeval darkness, filled with the potential for all life. Atum is called "the One Who Made Himself into Millions" and "He Who Made Himself into Millions of Gods."[195] The *Kar*-shrine, then, is much more than simply an enclosure for a statue. It is an essential element for connecting the human with the divine realm through sacred ritual.

The following General Rites are not intended for public enactment. All participants should be genuinely and deeply familiar with the spiritual significance of the various cultic actions. Casual observers or the merely curious are not only a distraction for the servants of the god, but bring a profane energy to what is fundamentally the sacred act of uniting earth to heaven.

The servants of the *Netjer* need to be completely focused on the words and actions of the ritual. Their own physical and moral purity should be understood as essential before they participate in these divine rites. The following inscription from the Temple of Heru at Edfu can serve as a meditation for those of us who are called to be servants of the god:

O ye prophets, senior *wab* priests, chiefs of the mysteries, purifiers of the god, all who enter into the gods . . . . Do not initiate wrongfully; do not enter when unclean; do not utter falsehood in his house; do not covet the property (of his temple); do not tell lies; do not receive bribes; do not discriminate between a poor man and a great; do not add to the weight or the measuring-cord, but (rather) reduce them; do not tamper with the corn-measure; do not harm the requirements of the Eye of Ra; do not reveal what you have seen in all the mysteries of the temples .... Beware, moreover, of harboring an ungrateful wish in the heart, for one lives on the bounty of the gods. . . .[196]

In another inscription at Edfu we read:

Beware of entering in impurity, for the god loves purity more than millions of offerings, more than hundreds of thousands of electrum; he sates himself with Truth (*Ma'at*), he is satisfied therewith, and his heart is satisfied with great purity.[197]

In addition to physical cleanliness it is apparent from these and similar texts that moral and ethical uprightness or purity is also required in servants of the god. It is a high standard of conduct but one that prepares us for the fruitful and effective performance of the sacred rites. When the priest/ess holds in his/her hands the image of Ma'at as the ultimate offering, his or her own hands and heart must be pure, that is, free from acts that compromise or hinder the triumphal rule of Ma'at for Ma'at represents goodness, peace, truth, harmony, and cosmic equilibrium–the order of the universe as created by deity on the First Occasion.

General Rituals: Three Examples

The following daily rituals are three from among numerous daily rites used in the Temple of Ra. The great *Netjeret* Sekhmet, like all the *Netjeru*, is a multi-aspected and multi-dimensional deity. As you read through the various texts of this rite you will begin to see some of the many aspects this goddess manifests. In this age when so many are in need of healing and protection and strength it seems appropriate to share with you these texts relating to this most beneficent *Netjeret*.

For those readers interested in researching the ancient texts upon which these General Rites are based the Notes section at the conclusion of this book will provide a valuable guide for further reading and study. Each of these three General Rites follows an identical model. Each, however, is tailored to honor a specific *Netjer/Netjeret*. All such "tailorings"–including divine epithets and specific references to myths involving the deity–follow the example set in temple inscriptions throughout Egypt. Whether we examine the ritual inscriptions at Edfu, Dendera, Kom Ombo, or Philae, we find the same general model originating in the great temple of Amun-Ra at Karnak.

All divine epithets and mythic referents in the following three General Rites come from equally authentic ancient sources. Any one of the three can serve as a general model for reconstructing an appropriate liturgy honoring a specific deity. This method conforms to ancient practice in which the daily liturgy in the temple of Amun-Ra at Karnak became the standard form for all daily liturgies throughout Egypt.

The second General Rite celebrates the powerful *Netjer* Sutekh (Set). This great *Netjer* is often misunderstood and feared as the embodiment of evil. This contradicts Sutekh's ancient and long lasting role as Defender of the Barque of Ra and Slayer of the Serpent Foe. It was only in the declining era of Egyptian history that this god was excluded from worship and honor. A number of temple reliefs and inscriptions spanning the millenia show Sutekh paired with Heru as co-protectors of pharaoh. He is also honored as the one *Netjer* powerful enough to defeat the serpent foe Apep. He, together with Aset (Isis), shares in the task of magically disabling that cosmic enemy. It is our conviction in the Temple of Ra that when Sutekh was no longer revered by the ancient Egyptians, they in effect deprived themselves of a mighty Defender. The original Balance the priesthood had sought to maintain was no longer attainable and the culture, including the cultic life of the temples, suffered an impoverishment opening them to distortion and decline.

The third General Rite honors Djehuty (Thoth), Lord of Sacred Rites, Great Lord of the Balance. In our modern world we often have need of balance, wisdom, and compassion. One of my favorite ancient titles for Djehuty is Lord of Kindliness, a quality that can ennoble each of us. As Lord of *Heka*-magic we in the Temple of Ra seek to emulate in our own magical practice Djehuty's wisdom and service to Ma'at.

General Rite Honoring Sekhmet

Like members of the ancient priesthood, participants should be clothed in white linen. No items made of animal products such as leather or wool are to be worn. Linen represents a pristine product of the earth whereas leather and wool come from humankind's domination of the animals, a domination that becomes part of the "natural order" only *after* the First Time when the *Netjeru* and humans and animals lived in peace and harmony. Just as the Morning Ritual harkens back to that First Time (*Zep Tepi*), so every temple rite re-presents mythic prototypes that occurred "in the beginning," that is, in that time before time. Even the sandals worn by the god's servants were made of white papyrus. This avoidance of animal products by the priesthood fits well with the fact that the priest/ess acts as a *Netjer* and verbally asserts that he or she is a *Netjer.*

As with all Egyptian rituals, begin with your purification–washing of hands and cleansing of mouth with Natron.

Participants assemble outside the Temple Chamber and begin by softly rattling sistra. This time–several minutes or more–is used to focus minds and intention so that distracting thoughts are left behind. The sound of the sistra dispels negative energy, purifying the atmosphere in preparation for encountering divinity.

Standing before the closed doors, the Liturgist recites the entrance spell:

UTTERANCE BEFORE THE CLOSED DOORS OF THE
TEMPLE

The priest/ess raises his/her hands in adoration (*dua* position–arms stretched out in front of the body and raised up to face level, with palms facing outward). The following shall be said:

"O you *Netjeru* of this Temple, you guardians of the great portal, great *Netjeru* of mysterious abode, who sanctify the goddess in her shrine, who consecrate her oblation, who receive the offerings in her presence in the Hall of the Ennead: I have made my way and I enter into your presence. I am one of you. I am Shu, the eldest son of his father, the senior *wab* servant-priest of Sekhmet. Do not repulse me on the goddess's path. My feet are not impeded. I am not turned back from the court of the great portal so that I may conduct the divine service, that I may present offerings to her that made them, that I may give bread to Sekhmet. I have come on the way of the goddess. I have not shown partiality in judgment. I have not consorted with the strong. I have not reproached the lowly. I have not stolen things. I have not diminished the constituents of the Eye of Ra. I have not disturbed the Balance. I have not tampered with the requirements of the Sacred Eye. O Council of the Great *Netjeret* in this Temple, behold, I have come to you to offer Ma'at to the Lady of Ma'at, to content the Sound Eye for its mistress. I am Shu; I flood her offering table. I present her offerings, this great goddess consorting with me, that I may adore Sekhmet at her festivals, that I may kiss the earth so great is her majesty, that I may endow her image with life. I am pure. I am purified."[198]

At this point the priest/ess opens the doors to the Temple Chamber, or, if there are no doors, makes a gesture of opening unseen doors, and steps forward as if crossing over a threshold. The following is said:

"O you *ba*-souls of Mennefer (i.e., Memphis*), if you are strong, I am strong. If I am strong, you are strong. If your *Ka*-spirits are strong, my *Ka*-spirit is strong at the head of the living. As they are living so shall I live. . . . Sekhmet, the great *Netjeret*, beloved of Ptah, has given to me life, stability, and serenity round about my members, which Djehuty has gathered together for life. I am Heru in the height of heaven, the beautiful one of awe, Lord of Victory, mighty one of awe, exalted one of the two plumes, great one in Abdju (Abydos). I am pure."[199]

Mennefer (Greek, Memphis) is the cult center for Ptah and his consort Sekhmet.

Entering in, close the double doors and proceed to stand in front of the *Kar*-shrine and altar. All bow, touching their hands to their knees.

The priest/ess slowly opens the two doors of the *Kar*-shrine housing the sacred image. All others bow, touching their hands to their knees. The following is said:

"The doors of the sky are open, the doors of the earth are unlocked. This House is open for its Mistress. Let me come forth as she shall come forth. Let me enter in as she shall enter in. Sekhmet, Daughter of the Limitless One, Beloved of Ptah, is exalted upon her Great Seat. The Great Company of the *Netjeru* are exalted upon their seat."[200]

The Liturgist holds up the **bowl of water** in which he/she will be mixing the Natron. The following is said:

"O water may you remove all evil,
As Ra who bathes in the Lake of Rushes,
May Heru wash my flesh,
May Djehuty cleanse my feet,
May Shu lift me up and Nut take my hand!
May Set be my strength, and may Sekhmet be my healing!
And may Amun-Ra be my life and my prospering!"[201]

The bowl of water is set aside and the container of **Natron** is lifted up. The following is said:

"It is pure, it is pure.
My Natron is the Natron of Heru and the Natron of Heru is my Natron.

My Natron is the Natron of Sutekh and the Natron of Sutekh is my Natron.
My Natron is the Natron of Djehuty, and the Natron of Djehuty is my Natron.
My Natron is the Natron of Geb and the Natron of Geb is my Natron.

My mouth is the mouth of a milking calf on the day that I was born."[202]

Four pinches of Natron are mixed into the water as this Utterance is recited:

"I give you essential water, a tide in your time.
I bring the flood waters to purify your sanctuary.
I bring you the flood waters to purify your Temple and your statue in its place, the primordial water that purifies as in the First Time!"[203]

The Liturgist places an **index finger** into the water and moves it in a circular, clockwise direction four times as the following is said:

"Sekhmet, the Daughter of Ra, does purify this water;
Sekhmet, the Beloved of Ptah, does cleanse this water;
Sekhmet, Sweet One of Heru and Sutekh, does sanctify this water;
Sekhmet Herself does endow this water with power and with life."

The **Bowl of Natron-infused water** is then taken up and the Liturgist sprinkles this lightly in front of the statue of the goddess as the Utterance is recited:

"I come close to You, O Pure One, Lady of the Waters of Life.
I bring the water of rejuvenation that flows from the Two Caverns. I sprinkle the water, purifying your image and your Temple from all impurity!"[204]

The Liturgist picks up the bowl of **Natron** and sprinkles a small amount in each of the four directions as the following is recited:

"**The goddess Sekhmet herself does cleanse and purify this, her Temple to the South.**
The goddess Sekhmet herself does cleanse and purify this, her Temple to the North.
The goddess Sekhmet herself does cleanse and purify this, her Temple to the West.
The goddess Sekhmet herself does cleanse and purify this, her Temple to the East."

Replacing the Natron on the altar, the Liturgist takes up the bowl of **water**, sprinkling a small amount in each of the four directions. The following Utterance is recited:

"**The goddess Sekhmet herself does sanctify and consecrate this, her Temple to the South.**
The goddess Sekhmet herself does sanctify and consecrate this, her Temple to the North.
The goddess Sekhmet herself does sanctify and consecrate this, her Temple to the West.
The goddess Sekhmet herself does sanctify and consecrate this, her Temple to the East.
The Temple of the goddess Sekhmet is established. It is established for millions of years."[205]

The Liturgist returns to the altar and lights the **candle** or **oil lamp** while the following is said:

"**Come, come in peace, O glorious Eye of Heru.**
Be strong and renew your youth in peace,
for the flame shines like Ra on the double horizon.
I am pure, I am pure, I am pure, I am pure."[206]

The Liturgist places **incense** on the burner and censes each sacred image beginning with the statue of the goddess while the following is recited:

"The fire is laid, the fire shines;
The incense is laid on the fire, the incense shines.
    Your perfume comes to me, O Incense;
    May my perfume come to you, O Incense.
Your perfume comes to me, you *Netjeru*;
May my perfume come to you, You *Netjeru*.
    May I be with you, you *Netjeru*;
    May you be with me, you *Netjeru*.
May I live with you, you *Netjeru*;
May you live with me, you *Netjeru*.
    I love you, you *Netjeru*;
    May you love me, you *Netjeru*."[207]

Standing in front of the image of Sekhmet the Liturgist **offers the burning incense** and says:

"Take the incense,
Its essence is for you.
Its smoke permeates your shrine, bringing life!
Take the incense,
Its essence is for you.
Your Majesty is appeased with the incense.
This Eye of Heru,
This essence of the Eye of Heru comes to you."[208]

At this point the following is said:

"Homage to you, O Sekhmet, Daughter of Ra, mistress of the *Netjeru*, bearer of wings, lady of the red apparel, queen of the crowns of the South and North, Only One, sovereign of her Father, superior to whom the *Netjeru* cannot be, mighty one of enchantments in the Boat-of-Millions-of-Years, you who are preeminent, you who rise in the Seat of Silence, mother of the god Nefertum, smiter of the enemies of Ra, mistress and lady of the tomb, Mother in the horizon of heaven, gracious one, beloved, destroyer of rebellion, offerings are in your grasp–offerings are in your grasp–and you are standing in the boat of your divine Father to overthrow the fiend Qetu.

"You have placed Ma'at in the bows of His boat. You are the fire goddess Ammi-seshet, whose opportunity escapes her not . . . Praise be to you, O Lady, who are mightier than the *Netjeru*. Words of adoration rise up to you from the Eight *Netjeru* of Khemenu (Hermopolis).

"The living *ba*-souls who are in their hidden places praise the mystery of you, O you who are their mother; you the Source from which they sprang, who make for them a place in the hidden Underworld, who make sound their bones and preserve them from every terror, you who make them strong in the Abode-of-Everlastingness, who preserve them from the evil Chamber of the souls of HES'-HER, you who are among the company of the *Netjeru*. Your name is *zfy pr m Hs Hr hApu Dt.f* (pronounced "seh-fee per em Hes' Her h'poo jet-ef").* Your name is "Lady-of-life."[209]

* *This epithet translates as "Child Who comes of/from 'Fierce-of-Face,' mysterious of His forms." "Fierce-of-Face" may refer to the scorching heat of the sun and thus to the god Ra, or it may refer to a netherworld deity called "Fierce of Face." In either case this epithet may be regarded as a "name of power" for invoking this Netjeret in her capacity as powerful Protectress of those in the Duat (Netherworld or Afterlife Realm). This entire paragraph refers specifically to those "in the hidden Underworld."*

The Liturgist places **more incense** on the charcoal and again and again **slowly raises and lowers the incense cup** as the following is recited:

"O Sekhmet, May you advance with your Ka.
O Luminous One, the arm of your Ka is before you,
The arm of your Ka is behind you.
O Lady of Heaven, the foot of your Ka is before you,

The foot of your Ka is behind you.
O Beautiful Sekhmet, this incense is offered to you,
May your face be filled as this essence spreads itself over
you."[210]

All present perform the **Henu Rite**–Embrace the Earth, the
Fourfold Salute to the Goddess, Embrace the Earth–and then the
following is said:

"Homage to Sekhmet, Eye of Ra, Great of Flame,
who is established on the Great Seat!
I have placed myself on the floor in awe of you.
I embrace the earth before you as before the Lady of All
Powers.
I have come that I might kiss the earth,
that I might worship my Mistress,
For I have seen her Beauty;
I give praise to Sekhmet,
For I have seen her Power.
Her form is more distinguished than the *Netjeru*;
Her arm is more powerful than the *Netjeru*.
I am pure, I am pure, I am pure, I am pure!"[211]

Everyone stands up. The Liturgist holds in the palm of one hand
the image of Ma'at and with the other hand open and raised over
the image as if sheltering it, repeats the following:

"I have come to you as Djehuty, whose two hands are joined
together under Ma'at. She comes to be with you, for she is
everywhere. You are provided with Ma'at. You move in Ma'at,
you live in Ma'at. She fills your body, she rests in your head,
she makes her seat upon your brow; the breath of your body is
of Ma'at, your heart does live in Ma'at. All that you eat, all that
you drink, all that you breathe is of Ma'at. Djehuty presents
Ma'at to you, his two hands are upon her beauty before your
face."[212]

The Liturgist places the image of Ma'at near the divine statue. Then he/she holds up before the image of Sekhmet **a pitcher of water** and pours the water slowly into an offering bowl as the following Utterance is recited:

"**This libation is for you, O Sparkling One.
This libation is for you, O Sekhmet.
I have brought to you this offering of water,
that your heart may be refreshed.
I have brought to you this Eye of Heru,
placing this at your feet.
I present to you that which flows forth from you,
that your heart shall continue to beat.
For it is with you
that all comes forth at the sound of the voice.**"[213]

The offering bowl is placed on the altar. At this point the Liturgist lightly **sprinkles sand** on the floor in front of the altar as the following is recited:

"**O Sekhmet, who resides in Mennefer***, [**The Egyptian name for the ancient city of Memphis*]
**Take to yourself the Eye of Heru.
You have rescued it, O Protectress of the Divine Order.
You have sprinkled with sand your Eye.**"[214]

Lifting the **wine offering** before the sacred image, the Liturgist repeats the following:

[*mn n.k irp irt Hr w3dt* pronounced *"men nek eeu-rep ee-ret Hoor wadjet"*]

"*Take to Yourself wine, the green Eye of Heru,* **which I offer to your Ka.** **
**O Ruler, how beautiful is your beauty!
May you drink it; may your heart rejoice;
may anger be removed from your face.**

It is pure." [*iw.w w'b* pronounced *"ee-oo oo oo-ab"*][215]

Slowly elevating the **food offerings** four times before the image of the goddess, the Liturgist repeats the following:

**"I offer to Sekhmet, O Powerful One.
All life emanates from you,
All health emanates from you,
All stability emanates from you,
All good fortune emanates from you,
O Great One of Heka-u, Sekhmet, forever."**[216]

The Liturgist places the **food offering** before the divine image, and then all present extend one hand, palm down, over the offerings and recite the following:

"May offerings of every kind come forth in abundance, like the things which come forth from the mouth of the goddess."

Peret er kheru mee pereret em reh en netjeret. (4 times)

"May offerings of every kind come forth in abundance, like the things that come forth from the mouth of the goddess."[217]

Holding the **Ankh** before the Goddess, the Liturgist says:

"Live, O Sekhmet, Eye of Ra, live for all time and for eternity!"

Ankh neheh djet.

The **Ankh** is placed next to the Goddess.

Holding the *Ib* (**the golden heart**) before the Goddess, the Liturgist says:

"Hail to you, O Sekhmet, Mistress of Awe. I have brought to you your heart to set it in its place. Let me draw near to you with your heart, so that you may have pleasure through me, and so that by means of me you may have power over your body. Ascend, O Solar Feminine Disk, radiant, rejuvenating, equipped as a goddess. Live, O Eye of Ra, live forever and ever!"[218]

After placing the *Ib* near the sacred image, everyone sings or chants the hymn to Sekhmet. Participants may wish to alternate the singing of verses.

"I praise the Gleaming One, I worship her majesty. I exalt the Daughter of Ra. Adoration to Sekhmet, praise be to my mistress! O Golden One, breath of my life, Lady of All Powers who enfolds me! All hail, jubilation to you, the mistress of all!

"O Golden One, sole ruler, Eye of Ra! Bountiful One who gives birth to divine entities, forms the animals, models them as she pleases, who fashions humanity. O Mother! Luminous One who thrusts back the darkness, illuminating every human being with her light!

"I revere you, Sekhmet, Enrapturing One, Enlightener! O Mother of the *Netjeru*, from sky, from earth, from south, from north, from west, from east, from each land, from each place, where your majesty shines forth! See what is in my heart, what is in my inmost; my heart is blameless, my inmost open, no darkness is in my breast!

"I adore you, O Queen of the *Netjeru*! O Golden One! Lady of Intoxications, Lady of Jubilation, Adorable One! It is the Gold of the divine entities who comes forth. Heaven exalts, the earth is full of gladness, Sekhmet the Great rejoices!"[219]

At this point perform the **meditation or magical action** or, if it is a special feast, add the appropriate prayers.

Afterwards all present back out of the Temple Chamber with heads slightly bowed while the Liturgist performs the **"removing the foot."**

With the **broom** the Liturgist, as the last person to exit, ritually sweeps the area beginning at the altar. (This is known as "removing the foot.") While performing this action the Liturgist recites the following:

"The distress that causes confusion has been driven away, and all the *Netjeru* are in harmony. I have given Heru his Eye; I have placed the *Wedjat*-Eye in the correct position. I have given Sutekh his Testicles, so that the two lords are content through the work of my hands."

"I know the sky, I know the earth;
I know Heru, I know Sutekh.
Heru is appeased with his eyes;
Sutekh is appeased with his Testicles.
I am Djehuty, who reconciles the *Netjeru*,
who makes offerings in their correct form."[220]

The double doors are solemnly closed as the ritualist says the following:

"Djehuty has come.
He has filled the Eye of Heru;
He has restored the Testicles of Sutekh.
No evil shall enter this Temple.
Ptah has closed the door,
Djehuty has set it fast.
The door is closed, the door is set fast with the bolt."[221]

All bow, touching the palms of their hands to their knees.

THE REVERSION OF OFFERINGS

One priest or priestess and as many assistants as necessary enter the Temple Chamber a final time. While he/she and any assistants lift up the offerings before the sacred image the priest/ess shall say:

"O Sekhmet, your enemy withdraws for you. Heru has turned himself to his Eye in its name of 'Reversion-of-Offerings.' I am Djehuty. I come to perform this rite for Sekhmet, queen of the *Netjeru*. These, your divine offerings revert, they revert to your servants for life, for stability, for health and for joy! O that the Eye of Heru may flourish for you eternally!"[222]

Everyone withdraws, carrying away all food offerings except the bread offering which is to remain on the altar table until evening.

It is important to consume the food offerings after the ceremony. Water used should either be drunk or poured onto the earth.

General Rite Honoring Sutekh

Like members of the ancient priesthood participants should be clothed in white linen. No items made of animal products such as leather or wool are to be worn. As with all Egyptian rituals begin with your purification–washing of hands and cleansing of mouth with Natron.

Participants assemble outside the Temple Chamber and begin by softly rattling sistra. This time–several minutes or more–is used to focus minds and intention so that distracting thoughts are left behind. The sound of the sistra dispels negative energy, purifying the atmosphere in preparation for encountering divinity.

Standing before the closed doors, the Liturgist recites the entrance spell:

UTTERANCE BEFORE THE CLOSED DOORS OF THE TEMPLE

The priest/ess raises his/her hands in adoration (*dua* position–arms stretched out in front of the body and raised up to face level, with palms facing outward). The following shall be said:

"O you *Netjeru* of this Temple, you guardians of the great portal, great *Netjeru* of mysterious abode, who sanctify the god in his shrine, who consecrate his oblation, who receive the offerings in his presence in the Hall of the Ennead: I have made my way and I enter into your presence. I am one of you. I am Shu, the eldest son of his father, the senior *wab* servant-priest of Sutekh. Do not repulse me on the god's path. My feet are not impeded. I am not turned back from the court of the great portal so that I may conduct the divine service, that I may present offerings to him that made them, that I may give bread to Sutekh. I have come on the way of the god. I have not shown partiality in judgement. I have not consorted with

the strong. I have not reproached the lowly. I have not stolen things. I have not diminished the constituents of the Eye of Ra. I have not disturbed the balance. I have not tampered with the requirements of the Sacred Eye. O Council of the Great Netjer in this Temple, behold, I have come to you to offer Ma'at to the Chosen One of Ra, to content the Sound Eye for its lord. I am Shu; I flood his offering table. I present his offerings, Sekhmet consorting with me, that I may adore Sutekh at his festivals, that I may kiss the earth so great is his majesty, that I may endow his image with life. I am pure. I am purified."

At this point the priest/ess opens the doors to the Temple Chamber, or, if there are no doors, makes a gesture of opening unseen doors, and steps forward as if crossing over a threshold. The following is said:

"O you *ba*-souls of Nubt (i.e., in Greek "Ombos," Set's principle city), if you are strong, I am strong. If I am strong, you are strong. If your *Ka*-spirits are strong, my *Ka*-spirit is strong at the head of the living. As they are living so shall I live . . . . Sekhmet, the great *Netjeret*, beloved of Ptah, has given to me life, stability, and serenity round about my members, which Djehuty has gathered together for life. I am Heru in the height of heaven, the beautiful one of awe, Lord of Victory, mighty one of awe, exalted one of the two plumes, great one in Abdju (Abydos) I am pure."

Entering in, close the double doors and proceed to stand in front of the *Kar*-shrine and altar. All bow, touching their hands to their knees.

The priest/ess slowly opens the two doors of the *Kar*-shrine housing the sacred image. All others bow, touching their hands to their knees. The following is said:

"The Doors of the Sky are open; the Doors of the Earth are unlocked. The House of Reconciliation* is open for its Lord.

Let me come forth as He shall come forth. Let me enter in as He shall enter in. Sutekh, Lord of the Seven Stars, the Dark One, is exalted upon His great seat. The Great Company of the *Netjeru* are exalted upon their seat."

---

* *"House of Reconciliation" is the ceremonial name for the capital of the 10th nome in Upper Egypt, an important cult center for Sutekh. The Greek name for the city was Antaeopolis, "the city of Antywey." Antywey is Heru and Sutekh "united and reconciled in one god" according to Herman te Velde, 68-70.*

Entering in, **close the double doors** and proceed to stand in front of the altar. All bow, touching their hands to their knees.

The Liturgist holds up the **bowl of water** in which he/she will be mixing the Natron. The following is said:

"O water may you remove all evil,
As Ra who bathes in the Lake of Rushes,
May Heru wash my flesh,
May Djehuty cleanse my feet,
May Shu lift me up and Nut take my hand!
May Sutekh be my strength, and may Sekhmet be my healing!
And may Amun-Ra be my life and my prospering!"

The bowl of water is set aside and the container of **Natron** is lifted up. The following is said:

"It is pure, it is pure. My Natron is the Natron of Heru and the Natron of Heru is my Natron.
My Natron is the Natron of Sutekh and the Natron of Sutekh is my Natron.
My Natron is the Natron of Djehuty, and the Natron of Djehuty is my Natron.
My Natron is the Natron of Geb and the Natron of Geb is my Natron.

My mouth is the mouth of a milking calf on the day that I was born."

Four pinches of Natron are mixed into the water as this Utterance is recited:

"I give you essential water, a tide in your time.
I bring the flood waters to purify your sanctuary.
I bring you the flood waters to purify your Temple and your statue in its place;
the primordial water that purifies as in the First Time!"

The Liturgist places an **index finger** into the water and moves it in a circular, clockwise direction four times as the following is said:

"Sutekh, the son of Geb, does purify this water;
Sutekh, the son of Nut, does cleanse this water;
Sutekh, the Chosen One of Ra, does sanctify this water;
Sutekh Himself does endow this water with power and life."

The **Bowl of Natron-infused water** is then taken up and the Liturgist sprinkles this lightly in front of the statue of the god as the Utterance is recited:

"I come close to You, O Powerful One, Dread Initiator into new forms of existence. I bring the water of rejuvenation that flows from the Two Caverns. I sprinkle the water, purifying your image and your Temple from all impurity!"

The Liturgist picks up the bowl of **Natron** and sprinkles a small amount in each of the four directions as the following is recited:

"The god Sutekh himself does cleanse and purify this, his Temple to the South.
The god Sutekh himself does cleanse and purify this, his Temple to the North.
The god Sutekh himself does cleanse and purify this, his Temple to the West.

The god Sutekh himself does cleanse and purify this, his Temple to the East."

Replacing the Natron on the altar, the Liturgist does the same with the **water**, sprinkling a small amount in each of the four directions. The following Utterance is recited:

"The god Sutekh himself does sanctify and consecrate this, his Temple to the South.
The god Sutekh himself does sanctify and consecrate this, his Temple to the North.
The god Sutekh himself does sanctify and consecrate this, his Temple to the West.
The god Sutekh himself does sanctify and consecrate this, his Temple to the East.
The Temple of the god Sutekh is established. It is established for millions of years."

The Liturgist returns to the altar and then lights the **candle** or **oil lamp** while the following is said:

"Come, come in peace, O glorious Eye of Ra.
Be strong and renew your youth in peace,
for the flame shines like Ra on the double horizon.
I am pure, I am pure, I am pure, I am pure."

The Liturgist places **incense** on the burner and censes each sacred image beginning with the statue of the god while the following is recited:

"The fire is laid, the fire shines;
The incense is laid on the fire, the incense shines.
    Your perfume comes to me, O Incense;
    May my perfume come to you, O Incense.
Your perfume comes to me, you *Netjeru*;
May my perfume come to you, you *Netjeru*.
    May I be with you, you *Netjeru*;

May you be with me, you *Netjeru*.
May I live with you, you *Netjeru*;
May you live with me, you *Netjeru*.
    I love you, you *Netjeru*;
    May you love me, you *Netjeru*."

Standing in front of the image of Sutekh the Liturgist **offers the burning incense** and says:

"Take the incense,
Its essence is for you.
Its smoke permeates your shrine, bringing life!
Take the incense,
Its essence is for you.
Your Majesty is appeased with the incense.
This Eye of Ra,
This essence of the Eye of Ra comes to you."

At this point repeat the following:

"Homage be to Sutekh, Lord of the the Northern Sky, Sutekh, who resides beyond the Imperishable Stars. O Powerful-of-Forefoot, may you stretch forth your arm to let Apep fall! Your Foreleg brings swift destruction to the enemy, the snake. Your lance is thrust into his brow; you break his vertebrae, you severe his neck, you stab him with your strong lance.

"You have rendered his moment impotent. The bark of Ra is enabled to sail in peace. O Strong Bull, the people rejoice in Your Might. Every living being, and every Netjer is in awe of you when you thunder in the sky, for you are conceived as the One whose name is 'He-before-whom-the-sky-shakes.' All do dance, and all do sing, 'Setekh, Setesh, Sutekh, He who protects the Company of the *Netjeru*.'

"Advance, O far-striding Master of the Seven Stars. May your powerful face be gracious to me. May you establish a crown upon my head even like the Disk upon the head of Amun-Ra, and give to me all life, and strength, and health."

The Liturgist places **more incense** on the charcoal and again and again **slowly raises and lowers the incense cup** as the following is recited:

"O Sutekh, May you advance with your Ka.
O Chosen of Ra, the arm of your Ka is before you,
the arm of Your Ka is behind you.
O Lord of Darkness, the foot of Your Ka is before you,
the foot of Your Ka is behind you.
O Powerful Sutekh, this incense is offered to you.
May your face be filled as this essence spreads itself over you."

All present perform the **Henu Rite**–Embrace the Earth, the Fourfold Salute to the God, Embrace the Earth–and then the following is said:

"Homage to Sutekh, Great Wild Bull,
who is established on the Great Seat in the House of Reconciliation.
I have placed myself on the floor in awe of you.
I embrace the earth before you as before the Lord of Life.
I have come that I might kiss the earth,
that I might worship my Master,
For I have seen His Strength;
I give praise to Sutekh,
For I have seen His Power.
His form is more distinguished than the *Netjeru*;
His arm is more powerful than the *Netjeru*.
I am pure, I am pure, I am pure, I am pure!"

Everyone stands up. The Liturgist holds in the palm of one hand **the image of Ma'at** and with the other hand open and raised over the image as if sheltering it, repeats the following:

"I have come to you as Djehuty, whose two hands are joined together under Ma'at. She comes to be with you, for she is everywhere. You are provided with Ma'at. You move in Ma'at, you live in Ma'at. She fills your body, she rests in your head, she makes her seat upon your brow; the breath of your body is of Ma'at, your heart does live in Ma'at. All that you eat, all that you drink, all that you breathe is of Ma'at. Djehuty presents Ma'at to you, his two hands are upon her beauty before your face."

The Liturgist places the image of Ma'at near the divine statue. Then he/she holds up before the image of Sutekh **a pitcher of water** and pours the water slowly into an offering bowl as the following Utterance is recited:

"This libation is for you, O Lord of Life, Great in Strength.
This libation is for you, Sutekh, Nubti (He of Gold Town, i.e. "Ombos").
I have brought to you this offering of water,
that your heart may be refreshed.
I have brought to you this your appendage,
placing this at your feet.
I present to you that which flows forth from you,
that your heart shall continue to beat.
For it is with you that all comes forth at the sound of the voice."

Place this libation on the altar near the god. At this point lightly **sprinkle sand** on the floor* in front of the altar as you repeat:

"O Sutekh, Who resides in Nubt (Ombos).
Take to yourself your Testicles.
Djehuty has rescued them,
He has restored them whole and sound.
He has sprinkled with sand your Testicles."

The next three items offered are specific to Sutekh: 1) the Testicles, symbol of virile strength; 2)the *Was* scepter; and 3) the sculptor's Adze.

The ritualist takes in his hands the symbol of the Testicles* and holds it forth before the god's statue. After reciting the following text, the ritualist places the symbol to one side of the sacred image.

"I come as Djehuty. Your Testicles which were injured are restored, whole and intact. I, Djehuty, have healed them. May your Ka be content with this healing of your injury."

The hieroglyph for testicles resembles an inverted Valentine's heart, with tip pointing up and the two rounded halves below. They can easily be crafted from clay and afterwards gilt. I have also seen small heart-shaped stones or paper weights that might serve the purpose.

The ritualist holds in one hand the *Was* scepter and extends his arm as he recites the following:

"The scepter of power is yours, O Sutekh. You conquer every enemy with your might. May you defeat the enemies of Ra with your strong arm. May you pierce them with your lance of iron. I present to you your scepter of power."

The ritualist takes in his hands the Adze and extends his arms toward the god's image as he recites the following:

"I present to you the Adze by which you open the mouths of *Netjeru* and humankind. The *Meshkhetyu* instrument of iron wherewith you make firm the mouth and by which you open the two eyes. It is yours for all time and for eternity."

Lifting the **wine offering** before the sacred image, the Liturgist repeats the following:

[*mn n.k irp fdt ne R'* pronounced *"men nek eeu-rep fedet neh Ra"*]

"Take to Yourself wine, the sweat of Ra, **which I offer to your Ka. ****
O Ruler, how mighty is your strong arm!
May you drink it; may you be powerful through it;
may your mouth be opened by means of it.
It is pure." [*iw.w w'b* pronounced *"ee-oo oo wab"*]

Slowly elevating the **food offerings** four times before the image of the god, the Liturgist repeats the following:

"I offer to Sutekh, Powerful of Forefoot.
All life emanates from you,
All health emanates from you,
All stability emanates from you,
All good fortune emanates from you,
Lord of Life, Great in Strength, Sutekh, forever."

The Liturgist places the food offering before the divine image, and then all present extend one hand, palm down, over the offerings and recite the following:

"May offerings of every kind come forth in abundance, like the things that come forth from the mouth of the god."

Peret er kheru mee pereret em reh en Netjer. (*4 times*)

"May offerings of every kind come forth in abundance, like the things which come forth from the mouth of the god."

Holding the **Ankh** before the god, the Liturgist says:

"Live, O Sutekh, Chosen One of Ra, live for all time and for eternity!"

"Ankh neheh djet."

Holding the *Ib* (**the golden heart**) before the god, the Liturgist says:

"Hail to you, Sutekh, Powerful of Heart, great god of this Temple, lord of Nubt (Ombos)! I have brought to you your heart to set it in its place, even as your sister Aset brought the heart of her son Heru to him and set it in its place, and even as Heru brought the heart of his mother Aset to her and set it in its place.

"Keep silence, you *Netjeru*, and listen, you Ennead. Attend to the good words which I speak to my father Sutekh, so that he thereby might have greatness, glory, and power, that he thereby might be present with me, and that he might be here as Great-in-Strength.

"A way is given to you, O Sutekh, like Ra in his horizons, and You have honor therein even as Ra has honor. A way is given to you like Geb, your father, made for Amun-Ra. A way is given to you like Ra in his horizons.

"You, being in heaven, O Master of the Seven Stars, great Lord of *Meskhet***, come in your glory.

"You, being upon earth, O Lord of Victories, come in your triumph. Come, your mother Nut opens for you the gates of heaven. Come, your father Geb has opened for you the gates of the earth–south, north, west, and east.

Come, let me draw near to you with your heart, that you may have pleasure through me, and that by means of me You may have power over your body.

Ascend, glorious as Ra, powerful and equipped as a god. Live, Powerful-of-Heart***, live forever and ever!"

* Based on a spell in The Ritual of Amenophis I, Chester Beatty Papyrus No. IX,.86 in Hieratic Papyri in the British Museum, Alan H. Gardiner, editor. Vol. I. Text. (London, 1935).

** The constellation of Sutekh is the Bull's Foreleg, the seven stars currently referred to as the Big Dipper, and referred to as the Great Bear (Ursa Major) by the Greeks. This constellation in ancient times was visible throughout the entire night, hence these stars were called the "Imperishable Ones." The Egyptians saw in these stars two patterns: the foreleg of a bull, and also an adze, the important ritual instrument used to "Open the Mouth" of statues and mummies. Meteors appear to fall from the northern sky, the location of this constellation. Hence, meteoric iron–the only type of iron available to the ancient Egyptians–was regarded as the metal of Sutekh. Notice in the following hymn to Sutekh the reference, "Mysterious One who opens the mouths of the Netjeru with the metal that came forth from You." Sutekh as Lord of Meskhet (the Adze) is therefore intimately connected with the central ceremony of Opening the Mouth.

*** This honorific title is based on Djed medu ("Words to be said") on the third epagomenal day of the year, the birthday of Sutekh: "O Sutekh, son of Nut, great in strength . . . Protection is at the hands of your holiness. I am your son. The name of this day is 'Powerful of Heart.'"

After placing the **Ib** near the sacred image, everyone sings or chants the hymn to Sutekh. Participants may wish to alternate the singing of verses.

"I praise the Son of Nut, I worship His majesty, I exalt the Lord of Heaven. Adoration be to Sutekh, praise be to my master! O Powerful One, breath of my life, Lord of the Seven Stars who enfolds me! All hail, jubilation to you, the master of all! Heaven rests upon your hands; the earth is under your feet. What you command, takes place. May you bless me with life and strength and health. O Father, hear me!

"O Dark One, Thunderer, Chosen of Ra! Mysterious One who opens the mouths of the Netjeru with the metal that came forth from you. Strong One who destroys the serpent, thundering in heaven, the Feared One! O Sutekh, powerful of magic in driving away enemies.

"I revere you, Sutekh, Lord of Winds! O Defender of the *Netjeru*, throughout the sky and earth, in the south, the north, the west, the east, in each land, in each place where your powerful voice thunders forth!

"See what is in my heart, what is in my inmost; my heart is blameless, my inmost open, no evil is in my breast! I adore you, O Thunderer! O Dark One! Lord of unbridled forces, Strong Bull of erotic energy, most virile among the Ennead!

"It is the Iron of the divine entities which comes forth from you. With it the mouths of the *Netjeru* were opened; with it the mouths of men are able to speak before the great Ennead.

"Heaven makes merry, the earth is filled with life, Sutekh rejoices!"

(Repeat this final acclamation four times.)

The various epithets for Sutekh can each be found in Herman te Velde's important work, Seth, God of Confusion (Leiden: E. J. Brill, 1977).

At this point perform the **meditation or magical action** or, if it is a special feast, add the appropriate prayers.

Afterwards all present back out of the Temple Chamber with heads slightly bowed while the Liturgist performs the **"removing the foot."**

With the **broom** the Liturgist, as the last person to exit, ritually sweeps the area beginning at the altar. (This is known as **"removing the foot."**) While performing this action the Liturgist recites the following:

"The distress that causes confusion has been driven away and all the *Netjeru* are in harmony. I have given Heru his Eye; I have placed the *Wedjat*-Eye in the correct position. I have given Sutekh his Testicles, so that the two Lords are content through the work of my hands."

"I know the sky, I know the earth;
I know Heru, I know Sutekh.
Heru is appeased with His eyes;
Sutekh is appeased with His Testicles.
I am Djehuty, who reconciles the *Netjeru*, who makes offerings in
their correct form."

The double doors are solemnly closed as the ritualist says the following:

"Djehuty has come.
He has filled the Eye of Heru;
He has restored the Testicles of Sutekh.
No evil shall enter this Temple.
Ptah has closed the door;
Djehuty has set it fast.
The door is closed, the door is set fast with the bolt."

THE REVERSION OF OFFERINGS:

A priest or priestess, and as many assistants as necessary, enter the Temple Chamber a final time. While he/she and any assistants lift up the offerings before the sacred image the priest/ess shall say:

"O Sutekh, your enemy withdraws for you. Sutekh has turned himself to his Testicles in their name 'Reversion-of-Offerings.' The strength of Sutekh is restored whole and complete. I am Djehuty. I come to perform this rite for Sutekh, the Chosen One of Ra. These, your divine offerings revert, they revert to your servants for life, for stability, for health and for joy! O that the Eye of Heru may flourish for you eternally!"

Everyone shall withdraw, carrying away all food offerings.

It is important to consume all the food offerings after the ceremony. Water used should either be drunk or poured onto the earth.

General Rite Honoring Djehuty

Like members of the ancient priesthood participants should be clothed in white linen. No items made of animal products such as leather or wool are to be worn. As with all Egyptian rituals, begin with your purification–washing of hands and cleansing of mouth with Natron.

Participants assemble outside the Temple Chamber and begin by softly rattling sistra. This time–several minutes or more–is used to focus minds and intention so that distracting thoughts are left behind. The sound of the sistra dispels negative energy, purifying the atmosphere in preparation for encountering divinity.

Standing before the closed doors, the Liturgist recites the entrance spell:

UTTERANCE BEFORE THE CLOSED DOORS OF THE TEMPLE

The priest/ess raises his/her hands in adoration (*dua* position–arms stretched out in front of the body and raised up to face level, with palms facing outward). The following shall be said:

"O you *Netjeru* of this temple, you guardians of the great portal, great *Netjeru* of mysterious abode, who sanctify the god in his shrine, who consecrate his oblation, who receive the offerings in his presence in the Hall of the Ennead: I have made my way and I enter into your presence. I am one of you. I am Shu, the eldest son of his father, the senior *wab* servant-priest of Djehuty. Do not repulse me on the god's path. My feet are not impeded. I am not turned back from the court of the great portal so that I may conduct the divine service, that I may present offerings to him that made them, that I may give bread to Djehuty. I have come on the way of the god. I have not shown partiality in judgement. I have not consorted with the strong. I have not reproached the lowly. I have not stolen

things. I have not diminished the constituents of the Eye of Ra. I have not disturbed the balance. I have not tampered with the requirements of the Sacred Eye. O Council of the Great *Netjer* in this temple, behold, I have come to you to offer Ma'at to the Bull of Ma'at, to content the Sound Eye for its lord. I am Shu; I flood his offering table. I present his offerings, Sekhmet consorting with me, that I may adore Djehuty at his festivals, that I may kiss the earth so great is his majesty, that I may endow his image with life. I am pure. I am purified."

At this point the priest/ess opens the doors to the Temple Chamber, or, if there are no doors, makes a gesture of opening unseen doors, and steps forward as if crossing over a threshold. The following is said:

"O you *ba*-souls of Khemenu (i.e., in Greek "Hermopolis," Djehuty's town), if you are strong, I am strong. If I am strong, you are strong. If your *Ka*-spirits are strong, my *Ka*-spirit is strong at the head of the living. As they are living so shall I live . . . . Sekhmet, the great *Netjeret*, beloved of Ptah, has given to me life, stability, and serenity round about my members, which Djehuty has gathered together for life. I am Heru in the height of heaven, the beautiful one of awe, Lord of Victory, mighty one of awe, exalted one of the two plumes, great one in Abdju (Abydos) I am pure."

Entering in, close the double doors and proceed to stand in front of the *Kar*-shrine and altar. All bow, touching their hands to their knees.

The priest/ess slowly opens the two doors of the *Kar*-shrine housing the sacred image. All others bow, touching their hands to their knees. The following is said:

"The Doors of the Sky are open, the Doors of the Earth are unlocked. The House is open for its Lord. Let me come forth as He shall come forth. Let me enter in as He shall enter in. Djehuty, Lord of the Moon, the Luminous One, is exalted upon

His great seat. The Great Company of the *Netjeru* **are exalted upon their seat."**

The Liturgist holds up the **bowl of water** in which he/she will be mixing the Natron. The following is said:

"O water may you remove all evil,
As Ra who bathes in the Lake of Rushes,
May Heru wash my flesh,
May Djehuty cleanse my feet,
May Shu lift me up and Nut take my hand!
May Sutekh be my strength, and may Sekhmet be my healing!
And may Amun-Ra be my life and my prospering!"

The bowl of water is set aside and the container of **Natron** is lifted up. The following is said:

"It is pure, it is pure. My Natron is the Natron of Heru and the Natron of Heru is my Natron.
My Natron is the Natron of Sutekh and the Natron of Sutekh is my Natron.
My Natron is the Natron of Djehuty, and the Natron of Djehuty is my Natron.
My Natron is the Natron of Geb and the Natron of Geb is my Natron.

My mouth is the mouth of a milking calf on the day that I was born."

Four pinches of Natron are mixed into the water as this Utterance is recited:

"I give you essential water, a tide in your time. I bring the flood waters to purify your sanctuary. I bring you the flood waters to purify your Temple and your statue in its place, the primordial water that purifies as in the First Time!"

The Liturgist places an **index finger** into the water and moves it in a circular, clockwise direction four times as the following is said:

**Djehuty, the heart of Ra, does purify this water;
Djehuty, the tongue of Ptah, does cleanse this water;
Djehuty, the throat of Him of the Hidden Name, even Atum, does sanctify this water;
Djehuty, mighty in his words and Lord of *Heka*-power, does endow this water with power and with life."**

The **Bowl of Natron-infused water** is then taken up and the Liturgist sprinkles this lightly in front of the statue of the god as the Utternance is recited:

"I come close to you, O Judge of *ma'at*, who sets all things in their proper places. I bring the water of rejuvenation that flows from the Two Caverns. I sprinkle the water, purifying your image and your Temple from all impurity!"

The Liturgist picks up the bowl of **Natron** and sprinkles a small amount in each of the four directions as the following is recited:

**"The god Djehuty himself does cleanse and purify this, his Temple to the South.
The god Djehuty himself does cleanse and purify this, his Temple to the North.
The god Djehuty himself does cleanse and purify this, his Temple to the West.
The god Djehuty himself does cleanse and purify this, his Temple tothe East."**

Replacing the Natron on the altar, the Liturgist does the same with the **water**, sprinkling a small amount in each of the four directions. The following Utterance is recited:

"The god Djehuty himself does sanctify and consecrate this, his Temple to the South.

The god Djehuty himself does sanctify and consecrate this, his Temple to the North.
The god Djehuty himself does sanctify and consecrate this, his Temple to the West.
The god Djehuty himself does sanctify and consecrate this, his Temple to the East.
The Temple of the god Djehuty is established. It is established for millions of years."

The Liturgist returns to the altar and then lights the **candle** or **oil lamp** while the following is said:

"Come, come in peace, O glorious Eye of Heru.
Be strong and renew your youth in peace,
for the flame shines like Ra on the double horizon.
I am pure, I am pure, I am pure, I am pure."

The Liturgist places **incense** on the burner and censes each sacred image beginning with the statue of the god while the following is recited:

"The fire is laid, the fire shines;
The incense is laid on the fire, the incense shines.
Your perfume comes to me, O Incense;
May my perfume come to you, O Incense.
Your perfume comes to me, you *Netjeru*;
May my perfume come to you, you *Netjeru*.
May I be with you, you *Netjeru*;
May you be with me, you *Netjeru*.
May I live with you, you *Netjeru*;
May you live with me, you *Netjeru*.
I love you, you *Netjeru*;
May you love me, you *Netjeru*."

Standing in front of the image of Djehuty the Liturgist offers **the burning incense** and says:

"Take the incense,
Its essence is for you.
Its smoke permeates your shrine, bringing life!
Take the incense,
Its essence is for you.
Your Majesty is appeased with the incense.
This Eye of Heru,
This essence of the Eye of Heru comes to you."

At this point **repeat** the following:

"Excellent One of Magic, homage be to you! Lord of Divine Words, adoration be to you! O Djehuty, you repeat to us what Ra has declared. You are master of the divine words which put all things in their proper place. You give offerings to the *Netjeru* and to the blessed dead. You are Djehuty who puts *ma'at* in writing for the Ennead. Everything that comes out of your mouth takes on existence as if you were Ra. You are he who cannot be driven from the sky or earth because you know what is concealed in the sky, inaccessible on earth, and hidden in the Primeval Ocean. You are the recorder and preserver of knowledge.

"O Lord of Kindliness, leader of the entire multitude, I give praise to you, O Djehuty, Straight Plummet in the Scales, who repulses evil, who accepts him who leans not on crime; I make rejoicing to you every day.

"You are He who gives breath to the weary-hearted one and vindicates him against his enemies. Vindicate me against my enemies and adversaries. You are the Vizier who settles cases, who changes turmoil to peace, the Scribe of the *ma'at* who keeps the book, who punishes crime, who accepts the submissive, who is sound of arm, wise among the Ennead, who relates what was forgotten. Relate to me the secrets of magic, O God of the Moon! Speak with me the words of power so the magic I enact is your own invincible magic, O Lord of Magic!

"O creator of written language, Lord of the Divine Books, guide my hand in all my magical writings so the words are alive with your own divine power. O Ibis splendid in *heka*, Tongue of Ra and Lord of Divine Words, speak through my mouth the words of power; O Heart of Ra, mighty in his words, empower my words as utterance coming forth from your own heart so they at once take place. Encircle my workings with your protective presence, O Lord of Wisdom. Adoration be to you, O Djehuty!"

The Liturgist places **more incense** on the charcoal and again and again **slowly raises and lowers the incense cup** as the following is recited:

"O Djehuty, May you advance with your Ka.
O Tongue of Ra, the arm of your Ka is before you,
The arm of Your Ka is behind you.
O Lord of Spells, the foot of Your Ka is before you,
The foot of Your Ka is behind you.
O Ibis splendid in *heka*, this incense is offered to you,
May Your face be filled as this essence spreads itself over you."

All present perform the **Henu Rite**–Embrace the Earth, the Fourfold Salute to the God, Embrace the Earth–and then the following is said:

"Homage to Djehuty, Thrice Great of *Heka*-power,
who is established on the Great Seat in the Mansion of the Moon!
I have placed myself on the floor in awe of you.
I embrace the earth before you as before the Bull of Ma'at.
I have come that I might kiss the earth,
that I might worship my Master,
For I have seen his Wisdom;
I give praise to Djehuty,
For I have seen his Power.
His form is more distinguished than the *Netjeru*;
His arm is more powerful than the *Netjeru*.

The spells of this great god are my spells, and my spells are his spells.
I am pure, I am pure, I am pure, I am pure!"

Everyone stands up. The Liturgist holds in the palm of one hand **the image of Ma'at** and with the other hand open and raised over the image as if sheltering and protecting it, repeats the following:

"I have come to you as Amun-Ra, whose two hands are joined together under Ma'at. She comes to be with you, for she is everywhere. You are provided with Ma'at. You move in Ma'at, you live in Ma'at. She fills your body, she rests in your head, she makes her seat upon your brow; the breath of your body is of Ma'at, your heart does live in Ma'at. All that you eat, all that you drink, all that you breathe is of Ma'at. Amun-Ra presents Ma'at to you, his two hands are upon her beauty before your face."

The Liturgist places the image of Ma'at near the divine statue. Then he/she holds up before the image of Djehuty **a pitcher of water** and pours the water slowly into a libation cup as the following Utterance is recited:

"This libation is for you, O Lord of Magic,
This libation is for you, Djehuty, who reconciles the brother-gods.
I have brought to you this offering of water,
that your heart may be refreshed.
I have brought to you this Eye of Heru,
placing this at your feet.
I present to you that which flows forth from you,
that your heart shall continue to beat.
For it is with you that all comes forth at the sound of the voice."

Place the libation cup on the altar in front of the god. At this point lightly **sprinkle sand** on the floor in front of the altar as you repeat:

"O Djehuty, Who resides in Khemenu (Hermopolis),
take to yourself the Eye of Heru.
You have rescued it, O Lord of Triumph and Orderer of Fate.
You have sprinkled with sand your Eye."

Lifting the **wine offering** before the sacred image, the Liturgist repeats the following:

[*mn n.k irp fdt ne R'*, pronounced '*men nek eeu-rep fedet neh Ra'*]

"*Take to Yourself wine, the sweat of Ra,* which I offer to your Ka. **
O Bull of Ma'at, how mighty is your strong arm!
May you drink it; may you be powerful through it;
may Your mouth be opened by means of it.
It is pure." [*iw.w w'b* pronounced "*ee-oo oo wab*"]

** *Refer to pages 92, 93, 99, and105 in Mu-Chou Poo's Wine and Wine Offerings in Ancient Egypt.*

Slowly elevating and lowering the **food offerings** four times before the image of the *Netjer*, the Liturgist repeats the following:

"I offer to Djehuty, Bull of Ma'at.
All life emanates from you,
All health emanates from you,
All stability emanates from you,
All good fortune emanates from you,
Lord of Judging who drives away evil, Djehuty forever."

The Liturgist places the **food offering** before the divine image, and then all present extend one hand, palm down, over the offerings and recite the following:

"May offerings of every kind come forth in abundance like the things that come forth from the mouth of the god."

Peret er kheru mee pereret em reh en Netjer. (four times)

"May offerings of every kind come forth in abundance like the things that come forth from the mouth of the god."

Holding the **Ankh** in his/her outstretched hand before the statue of the *Netjer*, the Liturgist says:

"Live, O Djehuty, Heart of Ra, live for all time and for eternity!"

"Ankh neheh djet."

Holding the *Ib* **(the golden heart)** before the god, the Liturgist says:

"Hail to you, O Djehuty, Lord of the Moon. I have brought to you your heart to set it in its place. Let me draw near to you with your heart, so that you may have pleasure through me, and that by means of me you may have power over your body. Ascend, O Silver Sun, radiant one, who illumine the darkness with your light. Live, O Chief of Nut*, live forever and ever!"

*The epithet "chief of Nut" comes from the Pyramid Text 2150C and refers to the brightness of the moon in the night sky.

After placing the *Ib* near the sacred image, everyone sings or chants the hymn to Djehuty. Participants may wish to alternate the singing of verses.

"I praise Djehuty, thrice great, Lord of Khemenu (Hermopolis), the glorious Ibis, presiding over the Two Lands, sprung from Ra, born at the beginning (1); I worship His majesty, I exalt the Lord of Heaven.

"Adoration to Djehuty, Praise to the Heart of Atum which has fashioned all things! (2) O Djehuty who loves Ma'at, who looks into hearts, the Knowing One who searches out the hidden things of the body! (3)

"All hail, jubilation to You, Djehuty the Great, the *Bau* of Ra, the representative of Atum! (4) You are the god sprung from the sun-god himself, for whom the gates of the horizon opened on the day of his birth. Every god came forth at his command; his word passes into being. You are Khonsu-Djehuty. (5) Heaven rests upon your hands; the earth is under your feet. What you command, takes place. May you bless me with life and strength and health. O Lord of Strength, hear me!

"Hail to you, Djehuty, reckoner of time, who divides seasons, months, and years, who increases time and multiplies years, grant me long life! (6)

"Hail to you, Djehuty, Great in Magic and Lord of Divine formulae, dreaded of demons, the Peaceful One who knows how to repel evil, assist me in speaking the words of power! (7)

"Hail to you, Djehuty, Lord of Terror, strong of arm, who bathes in the blood of the enemies of the god, come to me when I call and be a shield round about me, defending me from every assault. (8) Grant that no evil being, male or female, can enter into my house. (9)

"Hail to you, Djehuty, mighty in his words, Lord of speech, fill my words with your effective power, and grant that I, like you, may be called 'excellent in counsel' and 'mighty in his words.' (10)

"O Beautiful One of the night, O Silver Sun, go forth in your name Ausir-Iooh-Djehuty, that you may illumine the Two Lands, and make full the Eye on the 15th of the month. (11)

"Advance, O Lord of judging; you have made Heru glad; you have appeased the Rivals in the hour of their trouble. . . You have put away every evil thing. (12)

"O Djehuty, Lord of the Balance, Judge of *ma'at*, stretch out your hand from heaven and lead me when I go into the presence of the Lords of Ma'at. (13)

"O Lord of the effective word, Author of the formulae of power (14); when my life here shall have come to its end, may you yourself speak the Divine words that cause me to ascend, even to the stars, to the stars. O Lord of gladness, hear me!

1) *from a Denderah text quoted in Patrick Boylan's Thoth: The Hermes of Egypt (London: Oxford Univ. Press, 1922), 118. 2) 120. 3) 101. 4) 114. 5) 121. 6) 84. 7) 125-128. 8) 131-134. 9) 135. 10) 185, 188, and 214. 11) 65. 12) 40 and 192. 13) 139. 14) 94-95.*

At this point perform the **meditation or magical action** or, if it is a special feast, add the appropriate prayers.

Afterwards all present back out of the Temple Chamber with heads slightly bowed while the Liturgist performs the **"removing the foot."**

With the **broom** the Liturgist, as the last person to exit, ritually sweeps the area beginning at the altar. (This is known as "removing the foot.") While performing this action the Liturgist recites the following:

"The distress that causes confusion has been driven away, and all the *Netjeru* are in harmony. I have given Heru his Eye; I have placed the *Wedjat*-Eye in the correct position. I have given Sutekh his Testicles, so that the two Lords are content through the work of my hands."

"I know the sky, I know the earth;
I know Heru, I know Sutekh.
Heru is appeased with His Eyes,
Sutekh is appeased with His Testicles.
I am Djehuty, who reconciles the *Netjeru*, who makes offerings in

their correct form."

The double doors are solemnly closed as the ritualist says the following:

"Djehuty has come.
He has filled the Eye of Heru;
He has restored the Testicles of Sutekh.
No evil shall enter this Temple.
Ptah has closed the door,
Djehuty has set it fast.
The door is closed, the door is set fast with the bolt."

THE REVERSION OF OFFERINGS

One priest or priestess and as many assistants as necessary enter the Temple Chamber a final time. While he/she and any assistants lift up the offerings before the sacred image the priest/ess shall say:

"O Djehuty, your enemy withdraws for you. Heru has turned himself to his Eye in its name of 'Reversion-of-Offerings.' I am Shu. I come to perform this rite for Djehuty, mighty of *heka*-power. These, your divine offerings revert; they revert to your servants for life, for stability, for health and for joy! O that the Eye of Heru may flourish for you eternally!"

Everyone shall withdraw, carrying away all food offerings.

It is important to consume all the food offerings after the ceremony. Water used should either be drunk or poured onto the earth.

Conclusion: The Renewal of Life

At first these rituals may seem difficult to enact or even to thoroughly understand in terms relevant to our contemporary condition. But with careful repetition you will find yourself becoming increasingly familiar and comfortable with them. As with all great art forms, understanding comes only with effort and perseverance. Some of the symbols such as water and fire are universal tokens found in many different cultures and times. Others are specific to the spiritual universe of ancient Egypt. But taken together they form a deeply meaningful–and beautiful–vision of the divine/human drama.

The words and actions of these rituals revive and renew the sacred rites enacted in the temples of Egypt over the course of millennia. Know that as you stretch forth your hand in offering to *Netjer* you are repeating what occurred daily for thousands of years in temples throughout Egypt. You are joining yourself with the innumerable priests and priestesses who daily served *Netjer*. And just as those sacred servants of *Netjer* worked to renew the life of the world each and every day, know that you are working to restore the Balance, to renew the cosmos, and to establish *ma'at* in your own land and time. Whether you serve *Netjer* as a solitary or with others, have full confidence that you are not alone. The *Netjeru* hear your words and it is their fervent desire to once more have their abode on earth. You can make this a living reality.

APPENDIX I

Items Needed for the General Rituals

- a sacred image of the deity
- an altar table
- a bowl of pure water
- a bowl of natron
- an incense cup and charcoal briquette
- a new candle or lamp with fresh oil
- frankincense
- a statue of the goddess Ma'at
- a pitcher of fresh water
- a broad brimmed bowl to receive the water libation
- a glass of wine
- a round loaf of uncut bread
- a variety of foods and fruit for the offering tray
- an *Ib* or heart, fabricated to resemble the heart hieroglyph
- an *Ankh* symbol
- a ritual broom

The Opening of the Mouth: A Ritual of Transformation

Theology of the Sacred Image

The spiritual vision of ancient Egypt recognizes and affirms the gods and goddesses as both immanent as well as transcendent realities. This divine immanence means that deities' power and influence manifest in the natural world as both awe inspiring and beneficial, and simultaneously as fearsome and overwhelming. By fearsome we do not mean the kind of fear we likely would feel if we discovered there was a lion in the next room, but rather how we would feel if we discovered a ghost or spirit was present. It would be more an uncanny sense of awe and of being overwhelmed with wonder.

This experience of divinity as something mysterious that causes both "shuddering" and "fascination"–to use the apt expression of the eminent theologian and scholar of comparative religion Rudolf Otto, *"mysterium tremendum et fascinans"*–points to an experience of the "otherness" of the divine in ancient Egypt. There was a deep sense of the sacred that called forth for the Egyptian precisely such a sense of awe and wonder, reverence and humility. This vision of divinity's numinous quality is sorely lacking in our contemporary society, soaked as it is in consumerism and materialism. Even for many believers God is often seen as a sort of heavenly pal or buddy with little remaining of the majesty and splendor and "otherness" of divinity. Perhaps this is a corrective to the equally impoverished notion of God as stern Judge and wrathful punisher of sinners. Be that as it may, in either case in Western culture an experience of the majesty and awe inspiring beauty of deity is wanting.

At the same time as the ancient Egyptian experienced that sacred "otherness" of his gods and goddesses there was an equally compelling desire to bring these same deities into a beneficial relationship with and presence *in this world*. Spirituality, therefore, had everything to do *with this world*, and not with escape from the world. The cosmos was seen as essentially and profoundly good, not fallen, sinful, and corrupt. Religion and spirituality, therefore, celebrated life *in this world*. As part of that vision the temple with its central cult statues was established and maintained as a means of effecting a union of heaven and earth, bringing the gods into an ongoing relationship with humanity.

In Egypt the temple functioned as the god's or goddess's residence or house, not as a gathering place for a congregation. The material image of the deity, whether of wood, metal or stone, was seen as the true and actual dwelling place of a divine being. It was not seen as a symbol of something *absent*, but very much as a material *presence*, an incarnation of the deity. A similar idea of divinity's "real presence" was to reappear in the Roman Catholic and Eastern Orthodox Christian doctrine concerning the bread and wine of the Christian Eucharist or Holy Communion where Jesus is believed to be present under the appearance of bread and wine. Among Hindu worshippers the sense of divinity's true and real presence in sacred statues continues to the present day. In many pagan cultures spanning the continents sacred images were and continue to be seen and experienced as the material vehicle for an indwelling deity. In the ancient cultures of Mesopotamia, Assyria, Egypt, Greece, and Rome cult statues were revered as genuine repositories of a divine presence. In the first three instances we are fortunate to actually have the preserved texts for consecrating and enlivening cult statues. In modern day India again we find ritual texts for enlivening the sacred image dating from the Vedic era (1200 BCE) still in use.

For many of us who come out of a monotheist background it may be difficult to understand this "indwelling" of divinity in an object crafted by human hands. We may think of statues as no more than artistic reminders of a deity, or perhaps convenient focal points to help us concentrate or direct our thoughts and prayers. As monotheists typically we were taught that this material world is fallen and needs to be overcome through prayer and ascetical effort, or at least that "spirit" is qualitatively superior to matter. In extreme forms of this viewpoint matter becomes the enemy of spirit, or, in the very least, an obstacle to be somehow overcome.

Such religions are religions of salvation, that is, deliverance *from* materiality.

The great polytheist religions on the other hand recognize and celebrate divinity *in this world*. Matter is seen as a manifestation of divine power and presence–not as a hindrance to it. Matter, whether it is our earth, plant life, animals, or the very air we breathe–all are emanations of divinity, visible signs and assurances of divine presence. In fact, for the polytheist the natural world is the vehicle for countless "epiphanies" showing forth invisible but utterly real divine powers.

The gods reveal themselves through the created world itself for all nature, while not divine, nevertheless radiates a divine presence, a divine plan, and an awe-inspiring response in those who take time to see. To help understand emanation we can recall the manner in which radio and television waves penetrate and pass through material objects, including our own bodies, without diminishment or adverse effect. So, too, does divine presence emanate throughout the cosmos. All parts of creation are imbued and infused with a divine presence. This means that all creation is sacred and can be a pathway to deity. Modern man has lost this sense of divine presence, but it does not mean that deity is any less present. We have only to recover our inner vision. The teachings of the ancient Egyptian priesthood show us a way.

It was the persistent belief in ancient Egypt–as in classical Greece, Mesopotamia, and throughout cultures of the Middle East as well as around the entire world–that gods and goddesses are both transcendent realities and simultaneously immanent in the world. In addition, these polytheists believed that the deities could and would be present in visible form in images crafted by men. Each of these cultures developed sacred rituals aimed at transforming an image made by human hands into a worthy vessel for divinity. In fact, these ancient cultures invariably believed that the gods and goddesses *wanted* to be incarnated by means of human ingenuity and craftsmanship. The sacred image serves both as vessel for the god and revelation of that god.

Very much as the human spirit "inhabits" the physical body but is not identical to that body, so the sacred image is the earthly, material vessel for a deity. The animate force in the statue shares in a certain way with the divine essence but does not diminish that essence. In Egypt it was the *ka* that comprised the "vital essence" or "life force" of the individual. In the same way it is the *ka* of the deity which quickens the statue. It is also true that in some sense the *ka* was divisible without diminishment. Multiple cult statues of a god or goddess had nothing less than a whole *ka*. This insight is perhaps derived from everyday observation: just as human or animal life is passed along from one generation to the next, without diminishment of the life force of either the older or the new generation, so the life force of an individual (divine or human) can pass into sacred statues, whether for temple or tomb, without diminishment of any sort. In both cases, whether it was the tomb statue of an individual or a cult statue of a deity, the vital force or *ka* was the indwelling presence that inhabited the sacred image.

A very revealing text from Dynasty 25 (c. 700 BCE) provides insight into how the ancient Egyptian priesthood regarded sacred statues. It is referred to as the Memphite Theology, a theological tract about Ptah, the chief deity of the ancient city of Mennefer (Greek Memphis). Referring to Ptah as creator god it states:

> He bore the gods, he created the cities, he founded the nomes [regional districts], he placed the gods in their cult places, he established their offerings and equipped their sanctuaries; he made their bodies according to their wishes.

> So the gods entered their bodies, of all kinds of wood, all kinds of minerals, all kinds of clay, and of everything that grows upon him (the earth = creator god), in which they took form.

In commenting on this text noted Egyptologist Jan Assmann explains:

> . . . a clear distinction is drawn between the two "natures" of divine images: the god on the one hand, and on the

other, their "bodies" of more or less perishable earthly materials. The text unequivocally expresses what we must emphasize as the basic Egyptian concept regarding this point: *The statue is not the image of the deity's body, but the body itself.* [Italics are Assmann's.] It does not represent his form, but rather gives him form. The deity takes form in the statue, just as in a sacred animal or a natural phenomenon.[223]

A key statement in the Memphite Theology is found in the words, *"the gods entered their bodies."* This "entering" or "indwelling" of a god or goddess in an image crafted by human hands is further described and clarified in a statement within the Instruction for Merikare, an example of wisdom literature from the Middle Kingdom:

Generation after generation passes by among humankind, but the god who knows characters has hidden himself. There is none who can repel the blow of the "lord of the hand" (requital); he strikes without eyes seeing it.

Revere the god on his way (i.e., the statue on the processional route) who is made of precious stones and made (literally "born") of bronze. Like water that is replaced by other water, but there is no stream that allows itself to be hidden; it destroys the canal in which it was hidden.[224]

In this passage a distinction is made between the hidden god who acts as "lord of the hand," delivering justice to the guilty, and the god made of precious stones and bronze. Readers are directed to "revere the god on his way," that is, the local cult statue. But at the same time, as Assmann explains, "they must know that the god who is present in his cult statue, reigns everywhere in his hiddenness and can at any time burst forth from this "channeled" form in which he dwells like a river that overflows its dam."[225]

It is obvious that for the thoughtful Egyptian there was a real sense of divine presence both unseen and seen. The gods resided in their cult statues but were not restricted to them. Humanity's response is likewise twofold: first, to the unseen deity there is a moral and ethical response; then to the visible image of the god there is a cultic response. The two responses complement and complete one another.

Sacred Image and Cult

The temples of Egypt were known in antiquity for being filled "with unceasing cultic worship" (*Asclepius* 23). The Greek historian Herodotus refers to the Egyptian people as "the most pious" of all peoples (*Histories* II 37). The entire temple cult revolved around the central sacred image of the deity as well as other divine images housed in various chapels throughout the temple. As Jan Assmann so aptly expresses it, ". . . the basis on which everything rested, was neither holy scripture, nor shamanistic visions, nor ecstatic or mystic experiences of something wholly other, but rather the cult, the daily routine of . . . service rendered to the deities in the forms in which they were locally resident, their cult statues."[226] Each of those other forms of religious expression was present in some manner, but it was the daily cult that *par excellence* expressed the spiritual vision of the Egyptian people for over thirty-six centuries.

We may ask what purpose is served now in reviving and restoring these ancient rites surrounding the image of the deity? Have we not developed a more "spiritual" approach to divinity? Might we not loose ourselves in empty formalism? These are important and necessary questions. The purpose remains what it was for the ancient Egyptians: to bring heaven to earth–to bridge the gap between the unseen and the visible worlds, and in so doing to restore and re-sanctify time and matter. As for whether or not the cultic approach is more or less "spiritual" than some other path, we maintain that *all* true paths to deity are worthwhile. Unlike the monotheist religions that insist on the correctness of their one point of view, we as polytheists maintain that divinity is *not* to be boxed in as "one size fits–and *must* fit–all."

The ancient Egyptians, and today we Kemetic Reconstructionists, take an expansive view of the world, seeing it as a worthy goal to bring divinity into immanent contact through the service of sacred ritual. In our view, together with the ancient Egyptians, the gods actively desire to be embodied in the divine image crafted by human hands. For the ancient Egyptian, both priest and layman, there was a firm commitment to the embodiment of their gods. This great religious tradition regards embodiment as an essential and indispensible aspect of the divine nature, and, at the same time, it affirms the infinitude of the embodied gods. In fact our personal relationship with a deity is enhanced as a consequence of divine embodiment.

The sanctification of time and matter remains the primary purpose for restoring the ancient practice of divine embodiment together with the daily rituals marking the cyclical passage of time, the seasons of the year, life and afterlife. The presence of the divine in matter and, therefore, the intrinsic holiness of matter can be seen in ancient texts that directly address material objects: "O water, may you remove all evil as Ra who bathes in the Lake of Rushes"; and "Homage to you, o censer of the *Netjeru* (gods) who are in the following of Djehuty."[227]

This may be startling to our contemporary sensibility which sees matter as only an assemblage of molecules, devoid of spirit, devoid of the divine. In reviving and restoring the ancient metaphysics of emanation and the theology of divine enbodiment, we reclaim the original Egyptian vision of a cosmos imbued with divine energy, alive with the possibility of true communion with the gods and goddesses.

Each temple housed in its innermost "holies of holies" one central sacred, vivified statue. This most holy of spots was regarded mythologically as the original mound of creation from which the god or goddess began the process of creating the world. Today when we approach the embodied deity in sacred ritual we enter into that mythic "First Time," we ascend, as it were, the mound of creation. As we light the candle or oil lamp, we participate in lighting the world with divine light as we recite the ancient formula, "Come, come in peace, O glorious Eye of Heru (Horus)." The vivified statue, then, is a point of entry for deity to have a palpable presence in our world. Yes, of course, deity is present everywhere, emanates everywhere, being the ground of all that exists. But the vivified image is the one place where there is a divine transformation of a material object in which the specific vital force or *Ka* of the deity is present. And this is possible because the sacred image is made by human hands and then, through the collaborative effort of god and human, it becomes the vessel for deity. The world of gods and the world of humans share a life-giving point of contact. Matter, in the form of a statue or sacred image, becomes animated with divinity.

Does this mean that any image of a deity is de facto a divine embodiment? The answer is to be found in the rite employed to bring divine life into an image. In order for a statue or image to receive the divine essence or *Ka* of a deity, specific rites need to be enacted. In Egyptian spirituality these rites are known as Opening the Mouth (Egyptian *wp.t-r3*).

Background and Context for this Translation

The full title of the ritual is "Performing the Opening of the Mouth in the workshop for the statue of NN." In addition to being performed on statues, this ritual was used on mummies, anthropoid sarcophagi, ushabtis, heart scarabs, temple carvings, and figurines fashioned for magical purposes.[228] Evidence of its use dates as early as Dynasty IV (c. 2600 BCE) and continues all the way through Egyptian history to include the Graeco-Roman era.

Very much like the daily temple rituals, the Opening of the Mouth is made up of numerous and distinct sections or stages. On the walls of many tombs these separate stages are illustrated graphically and, hence, Egyptologists refer to them as "scenes" or "vignettes." The principle ritualists for this rite are the *sem*-priest and the *khery hebet*, literally, "the one who carries the book roll [papyrus scroll]." Conventional academic usage refers to the *khery hebet* (Egyptian *ḫrj-hb(t)*) as the "lector priest." The *khery hebet* was the ritual specialist responsible for assuring that all sacred rites were carried out in accordance with care and exactness. The *sem*-priest was responsible for conducting the Opening of the Mouth rites for deceased individuals as well as for all sacred images.

Due to circumstances of their preservation the extant texts for this ritual all come from the funerary rites and consequently need to be amended so as to remove those many elements that are specifically intended for enlivening the deceased. The three available scholarly translations of the texts–E. A. Wallis Budge (1909), Eberhard Otto (1960), and Jean-Claude Goyon (1972)–are all based on funerary versions of the ritual.[229] Since Otto's and Goyon's works are only available in German and French respectively, I have used Budge's English translation for purposes of endnoting so that the reader can refer to an easily available scholarly source. Budge's version, although the earliest and quite awkward in expression, is still basically reliable for presenting the sequence of ritual actions and a translation that generally captures the literal meaning of the hieroglyphs. A new comprehensive English language translation is long overdue. My purpose, however, is to present a text that can be recited aloud without unduely awkward or antiquated expressions, but a text that nevertheless remains fundamentally faithful to the Egyptian original. The text you are about to encounter contains no elements from other spiritual traditions whether ancient or modern.

A final question that needs to be addressed is whether the reader should actually perform an Opening of the Mouth ritual on an image of a god or goddess. It is the practice of the Temple of Ra to enact this rite only if the individual is prepared and willing to serve the god or goddess *on a daily basis*. It is not enough to conduct a ritual of service on an occasional basis–when the mood strikes, when some special need comes up, or on any schedule other than a daily basis. The daily ritual may be as brief as the one outlined in the previous chapter, but it is very important that each day the god/goddess who is embodied in the sacred image be worshipped and served. The image, after all, is the receptacle of a divine essence whose continued presence is made possible through the mediation of the priest or priestess, who literally is the "god's servant." If the reader is not prepared or is unable to dedicate some small portion each day to serve the incarnate deity, then the Opening of the Mouth should not be enacted. Under that circumstance the reader may simply use the unconsecrated image of the deity as a focal point for prayer and worship. To open the mouth of an image and then to neglect to serve it each day only invites the displeasure of the deity, not a blessing.

This ritual is a powerful means of creating a receptacle for divinity. It is not in accord with *ma'at* to neglect the embodied god. But to serve an embodied god brings untold blessings upon the god's servant. That has been the continuous experience of the Temple of Ra. The gods are not to be outdone in generosity. In the modern pagan and neopagan communities many style themselves priests or priestesses. But in Kemetic practice priesthood carries a special responsibility for daily service. This does not make a priest/ess somehow "better" than the devotee who honors the gods in a less formal manner. It is merely a distinction in the type of service. Priestly service should be undertaken in a spirit of joy and love for the particular deity, with a strong sense of being "called" to servanthood. If this inner sense of calling is absent, it is much better to simply remain a lay devotee. Both are important in the up-building of *ma'at*.

Understanding the Elements of the Ritual

The first ceremonial action consists in placing the statue on a mound of sand with its face toward the south. The mound of sand recalls the First Time, *Zep Tepi*, when creation first unfolded. The statue crafted by human hands is about to undergo a new creation as an embodied god. The southerly direction, coupled with the noon time or mid point of daylight, positions the image to receive maximum exposure to the life-giving rays of the sun-god. Some manuscripts actually name the place for this rite as the "workshop of the artisans." It is significant that the ceremony does *not* take place in a temple. By this requirement the ancient Egyptians firmly acknowledged the role that humans have in crafting a sacred image. This is in full accord with their belief that it is both gods and humans who are responsible for the up-building and maintenance of *ma'at*. Although we lack definitive evidence, it is not unlikely that such artisans were carefully chosen and likely underwent rituals to prepare them for the task of crafting a divine image. Be that as it may, we do know that their role was acknowledged and that at least in the funeral version of the rite they actively participated in the ritual itself.

The second through the seventh ceremonial actions consist in lustrations and censings whose purpose is to ritually purify the image. The significance of water and incense has been explained in the previous section on the general ritual. Each lustration and censing is repeated four times, signifying the four quarters of the universe, that is, totality. The gods referred to–Heru, Sutekh, Djehuty, and Geb–symbolize four aspects of the cosmos. Heru represents lawful social order; Sutekh embodies physical force and strength; Djehuty stands for intellect, and Geb as earth god is emblem of the material world. Through the creative power of the spoken word–an essential aspect of Egyptian *heka* or magic–the Liturgist proclaims and therefore brings into existence this fourfold state-of-being as the image's own–order, strength, intellect, and materiality.

The first lustration calls for water in four white vases. The second lustration calls for four red vases. The two colors recall the white and red crowns representing Upper (southern) and Lower (northern) Egypt respectively, that is, the terrestrial totality of the civilized land. In addition to representing the two crowns, the colored vases are identified with the Eyes of Heru, the ultimate symbol of that which has been restored and renewed.

The next rite (The Fifth Ceremonial Action) calls for a mixture of natron and incense to be presented before the image. The purificatory nature of both natron and incense provides one more sign of the great importance the Egyptians attached to ritual purity, that is, freedom from anything that might taint or compromise the utter holiness required for an image about to be enlivened with the *Ka* or vital force of a divine being. Our modern world has lost much of this sense of the sacred. It is our task, however, to emulate our ancient forebears and thereby restore to our own spirits that lost sense of the holy.

The Fifth Ceremonial Action concludes with the gesture of a two-fold touching of the mouth and eyes and one hand of the image. This will be repeated at the conclusion of the Sixth Ceremonial Action. Through touching with his/her hand the Liturgist imparts a life-energy to the image. Recall that in an emanationist theology the divine emanates or radiates in and through created beings. Therefore, through ritual touch divine energy is transmitted from Liturgist to image. This is the beginning of the divine transformation. Humans participate directly through this transformative act of touch.

The Sixth and Seventh Ceremonial Actions involve ritual utterances stating what has been accomplished, namely, the purification of the image in preparation for the actual opening of the mouth and the embodiment of the deity.

The second major section of the Opening of the Mouth ritual consists in seven distinct performative acts, namely, the Eighth through the Fourteenth Ceremonial Actions. These actions make up the specific events that cause the image to become a divine embodiment. All of them involve one or another ritual tool or implement: a staff, a leg of beef, a heart, a sculptor's carving tool known as an adze, a magical staff carved with a ram's head (the *Ur-Hekau* staff), and, finally, a fish-tail shaped blade of flint (the *Pesesh-kef*).

The staff is used to ceremonially "strike" or tap the statue, thereby dedicating it for sacred use. Many cultures throughout the ages make use of this sort of gesture to indicate that something or someone is set aside for a special purpose. Knights are made through the tapping of the sword on their shoulders. In the Roman church the bishop taps the face of the person being confirmed. In these and similar instances a ceremonial striking indicates a change in status for the person or object. In the Opening of the Mouth, after the image has been properly purified, it is then ritually "set apart" by means of the dedicatory "striking" because it is about to become the vessel of divinity.

With the Ninth Ceremonial Action the Liturgist puts on the panther skin. The word for panther is *ba*, which also means "manifest power." The ancient Egyptian penchant for word-links is here evident. The panther is a Setian animal and Sutekh (Set) is known for his aggressive but very effective acts. As Egyptologist David Lorton explains,

> The application of the concept *ba* "manifest power" to the *sem*-priest must again refer to his ability to act with ritual effectiveness. However, we must also note that there is a word (perhaps from the same root) *ba* that means "panther." Thus, when the ritualist says that the *sem*-priest will be "manifestly powerful" or will "manifest power," the statement (through the punning meaning "that you may be a panther") implies that he will specifically manifest the power of the animal whose skin he is wearing.[230]

The power of Sutekh in this instance is the power to effectively transform the subject from one state of existence to another. By donning the panther skin the Liturgist absorbs and therefore controls the wild force of that totemic animal as well as the transformative power/force of Sutekh. Once again we have multiple layers of meaning for an element of ritual.

A more problematic issue is the use of the foreleg of a bull and its heart. The obvious idea behind the presentation of a fresh foreleg of beef and heart is that the "life force" of the animal in some way "flows out" from the object into the statue. Is it then necessary for us to use an actual leg of beef and heart? The answer is in the negative. The ancient Egyptians were quite accustomed to using items fabricated by humans in place of something else. The tomb of Tutankhamun contained a manmade "leopard skin" for use in priestly rituals. Tombs were regularly equipped with miniature figures and models that served as viable substitutes for their material and human counterparts. By means of such symbolic imitation magical rituals were performed involving fabricated substitutes for persons and objects. Ancient Egypt in fact has a rich and continuous history of such usage.

The hieroglyph for the heart–resembling a flat-topped vase with handles on both sides–appears in many tombs depicting that portion of the Opening of the Mouth ceremony. It is the practice of the Temple of Ra to use a "foreleg of a bull" shaped to resemble the hieroglyph for that item. Likewise, we employ a fabricated heart-hieroglyph in place of an actual bull's heart. This practice falls within the parameters of the ancient tradition of the Egyptian priesthood. Whereas that society lived life much closer to the land, and, hence, animal slaughter was not unusual, it is not magically necessary today. The fabricated items are ritually dedicated for use as replacements for actual animal parts. In this way the Temple of Ra adheres to the spirit of the original rite.

The Foreleg of the Bull carries important symbolism. It represents the constellation called by the Egyptians Foreleg (or Thigh) of the Bull and also the Adze (*Meshkhetyu* in Egyptian), a sculptor's tool with an arched blade set at right angles to the handle. Its seven stars are known today as the Big Dipper. In Egyptian mythology this constellation was also regarded as "the Imperishable Ones," meaning Pole stars that never appear to set but visibly revolve counterclockwise during the entire night. The god Sutekh was regarded as ruler of this constellation. Mythologically it was this god's foreleg that appears as the seven stars. This is a northern constellation and meteor showers appear to come from it. This gave rise to the insight that meteoric iron was Sutekh's own special metal. Ancient Egypt only had iron of meteoric origin, and so its use in the cutting tip of the sculptor's adze became identified with the constellation and both then became symbols of immortality. Egyptologist Lanny Bell explains, "The symbolic blade of this tool was a small bit of meteoric iron–a magical metal, associated with the heavens, that had provided the 'spark' or 'lightning strike' that brought the first generation of beings into existence."[231]

Like many things in Egyptian mythology the foreleg and adze carry multiple meanings. Through Egyptian eyes the constellation looked like both the hieroglyph for foreleg and also the sculptor's adze. Both play key roles in the Opening of the Mouth. Both make reference to Sutekh, and in the ritual the Liturgist proclaims, "Sutekh himself has opened for you your mouth with the instrument of iron wherewith he opened the mouths of the *Netjeru.*"

Mythologically the Bull's Foreleg (*Khepesh* in Egyptian) belongs to Sutekh who, because of his role in slaying Ausir (Osiris), is regarded as Dread Initiator into new forms of existence. Through a violent act Sutekh slew Ausir. Then through the "violent act" committed by craftsmen carving, chiseling, and shaping raw material, be it stone, wood, or metal, into a god's image, followed by the symbolically aggressive or "violent" ritual action of opening the mouth and eyes, a material object is "reborn" as a god. Violence in this case makes possible the embodiment of deity.

The ancient Egyptians recognized and ritually acknowledged that certain aggressive or violent acts are necessary for the up-building of *ma'at*. Both Heru and Sutekh, in fact, were seen as aggressive powers and both play critical roles in the Opening of the Mouth.

The Foreleg of the Bull represents the cosmic friend as well as the cosmic foe. Both are subsumed into the god Sutekh. The text clearly states that the foreleg and heart belong to the "enemy," the Bull: "I have seized your enemies and I have brought them to you." But immediately the priest continues, "I have presented to you the leg as the Eye of Heru." The profound mystical connection of the Foreleg of the Bull with the healed and restored Eye of Heru affirms the reconciliation and union of opposites. In regard to Heru and Sutekh the ancient Egyptians envisioned a composite entity symbolically shown as a single body with two heads, that of Heru and Sutekh. The true union of these polarities is fundamental to understanding the original vision of Egypt.

This is seen by the way the Liturgist first speaks as one and then in quick succession as the other of the two gods. "Hail (*name of deity*)! I have come to embrace you. I am Heru. I have pressed for you your mouth with the Leg of the Bull." This is immediately followed with a second touching of the mouth with the Foreleg and the statement: "I am Sutekh, Your beloved. I have opened for you your mouth . . . with the Leg, the Eye of Heru." (Tenth Ceremonial Action)

Immediately following the presentation of the Foreleg the priest presents the heart saying, "Never again shall an attack be made against this *Netjer.*" The heart symbolizes the psychic center of an individual. In presenting the Bull's heart the priest ritually affirms the transformation of the Bull from deadly enemy to life-giving friend. That which was capable of destructive violence now becomes one of the means for divine transformation.

In the Eleventh Ceremonial Action the Liturgist presses the sculptor's adze to the mouth and eyes of the image. This tool is identified as being made of "the iron which comes forth from Sutekh, with the *Meshkhetyu* (adze) instrument of iron wherewith He opened the mouths of the *Netjeru.*" This undoubtedly echoes a now lost mythological story involving Sutekh's power of engendering divine life. We must remember that in the decadent final stages of Egyptian history all traces of the worship of Sutekh were methodically destroyed in as much as possible. Nevertheless, certain signs of his beneficial role such as we find in the Opening of the Mouth remained to the very end of the ancient civilization.

The Twelfth and Thirteenth Ceremonial Actions involve the magical ram-headed wand called *"Ur-Hekau,"* or Great-One of Words-of-(Magical) Power. This instrument is a wooden staff with an undulating serpent shape, having a ram's head surmounted with a uraeus. The ram's head represents Khnum, creator god from Elephantine (Egyptian *Abu*). The ram was renowned for its considerable procreative power. The uraeus atop the ram's head carries multiple associations. The word comes from the Greek word for cobra (ouraios) and is associated with the royal cobra goddess, Wadjet, as well as with manifestations of other protective deities including the Eye of Ra, Sekhmet. The *Ur-Hekau*, then, carries solar symbolism as well as the creative powers of Khnum. Recalling that the Opening of the Mouth ritual is to take place when the sun is at its height reinforces the significance of solar power–that is, the power of the creator Ra in animating and giving life to the image. Ra-Khnum in fact is one recognized hypostasis of the creator/life-giver in Egyptian myth. Such a mystical union or blending of gods is a common motif for the ancient Egyptians. It should also be noted that the pairing of Khnum with the uraeus represents the creative masculine principle with the protective feminine. Again, as with Heru and Sutekh, we have two polarities represented in the act of giving life to the image.

The Utterance to be recited while touching the image with the *Ur-Hekau* refers to several important deities as well as to the two crowns which are regularly pictured as uraeus serpents. The great mother-goddess Nut, and Shu, one of the oldest cosmic deities, the Lord of Air and Light, as well as Heru and Sutekh and "all the *Netjeru*" (deities) are envisioned as helping in this divine transformation. Magic in ancient Egypt is a communal undertaking. Even if it is undertaken by a single individual it is never a solitary event. The magician acts as a god among gods as he calls upon the divine powers to work with and through him. And such workings are always to be in accord with *ma'at*.

The Liturgist uses the *Ur-Hekau* to make passes four times over the neck and down the spine of the image. These passes effectively convey the "fluid of life" to the image. Here we see at work echoes of modern day Reiki energy work, chakra balancing, Quantum Touch, and other modalities of putative energy medicine. "The passes have been made; life fills this image . . . Your fluid of life is round about You, and the image of this *Netjer/Netjeret* shall never die."

The Fourteenth Ceremonial Action instructs the Liturgist to touch the jaws and the various orifices of the statue's head with the *Pesesh-kef* instrument, a blade made of flint and shaped like the bifurcated tail of a fish. The *Pesesh-kef* blade dates from the Predynastic period and served as a practical as well as a ritual implement. The inner surface of the bifurcated portion of the original blade was sharpened and sometimes even serrated. From the many examples of the *Pesesh-kef* this indicates that a cutting function was intended. The inner sharp portion of the two "tails" was used to cut the umbilical cord of newborn infants. Its adoption for ritual use in the Opening of the Mouth ceremony demonstrates clearly that the ancient Egyptians regarded the enlivening of a statue as a kind of birth: the deity went from the invisible spiritual world and was "born" into the material statue.

The word *kef* refers to flint. The word *Pesesh* means "that which divides" or the "divider,"[232] the idea being that this implement "divides" the newborn from its mother. By analogy the statue or mummy is "born" into a new life and the ritual use of this implement causes the subject to separate (divide) from its former existence and take on a new form of existence. In ritual the *Pesesh-kef* came to be used for several functions including "making firm (i.e., strengthening) the jaws" of the mummy or statue. The mouth, of course, is the symbolic means by which the "newborn" will receive food offerings. Therefore, the strengthening of the jaws was seen as essential for the survival of the subject. The *Pesesh-kef* is also used to "open" the eyelids, lips, and other facial orifices. By means of these magical acts the image is enabled to serve as an adequate vessel for deity.

The theme of birth is especially prominent in the Opening of the Mouth rite for the deceased human, but it appears much less frequently and in a different tonality in the Opening of the Mouth for statues of deities. The reason for this is that a deceased human enters his/her new life for the first time and quite literally is a newborn being initially in need of special care and sustenance. The gods, on the other hand, are beings of a higher nature and their taking up residence in a sacred image is qualitatively different. Their embodiment in a material statue is not a stressful first-time event as it is for the deceased human who returns to a new life after having undergone the traumatic pangs of death.[233] The gods come from their celestial realm and so their "birth" differs in an essential, fundamental way from that of a deceased human.

With the conclusion of the Fourteenth Ceremonial Action the Liturgist announces that the god's mouth is now opened. Deity is present in the sacred image. The Fifteenth Ceremonial Action has the Liturgist offering incense for the first time to the newborn god.

The Sixteenth to the Twenty-Second Ceremonial Actions consist in a series of symbolic offerings of four colored cloths, an ornamental necklace, and a scepter. Each item both represents a divine entity and conveys with it a special quality bestowed upon the newborn deity. To understand the multi-layered symbolism of these items we need to know the importance placed on certain geographic places in ancient Egypt. The white *nemes* cloth head covering represents the city of Nekhen, called "City of the Hawk" (Hierakonpolis) by the Greeks, the hawk being Heru (Horus), the royal god *par excellence*. Thus, this head covering symbolized royal–that is, effective–power for the wearer. As a very ancient and important predynastic town, Nekhen also was honored as the home of an important group of ancestors, "The *Ba*-Souls of Nekhen." The support and blessing of these ancient and revered "forefathers" was considered essential for later generations. The recitation clearly states, "The Nejeru array you with this." It is a gift of *all* the gods, the divine forbearers.

The light blue cloth (for us oddly referred to as a "white"cloth) represents the city of the royal protectress Nekhbet, the vulture goddess of Nekheb, a town across the Nile from Nekhen. By association with her town the protection of this goddess is assured. The text itself states that the cobra-headed goddess Renenutet bestows the light blue cloth upon the image. Renenutet's name means "The Provider of Nourishment." She is also recognized as a goddess of fate, being herself the consort of Shay (Fate). Each of these associations plays a role in the ancient Egyptian penchant for creating rich, multi-layered meanings for any ritual action.

In the Eighteenth Ceremonial Action a green (*wadj*) cloth, signifying renewal, is presented as the gift of another cobra-headed goddess Wadjet, patroness of Lower (Northern) Egypt. Wadjet is the complement to Nekhbet, divine patroness of Upper (Southern) Egypt. On pharaoh's crown the two images of cobra and vulture symbolize the entire "civilized" world (i.e., Egypt).

With the Nineteenth Ceremonial Action the fourth and last cloth is bestowed. This red cloth symbolizes the special blessing and protection of Sekhmet, the Eye of Ra. Notice that each colored cloth is the gift of deity, bestowing upon the wearer the power and protection of those deities. It is especially significant that three of the four cloths are gifts of goddesses. The divine feminine is here pictured as powerful, power-giving, protective, and nourishing.

As with every offering to deity each cloth is ultimately described as the "Eye of Heru." As I state in Part One of the present work,

> The Eye of Heru is that victorious life restored after its injury is healed, just as Heru's Eye is healed and made sound or whole again after having been injured in cosmic battle. Once blinded, it is now restored to wholeness. The Eye of Heru possesses the power of renewal, the creative power of the god. Both gods and humans are restored and

renewed by offerings once those offerings are transformed through the power of naming into the Eye of Heru. The priest "names" the offering or gift as the Eye of Heru and through this potent magical act of speech the offering is revealed as containing divine life itself, a divine life emanating from products of the earth or of human manufacture–food and drink, incense, flowers, precious oils, cloth, jewelry, artifacts of various kinds–the list is lengthy but not arbitrary. Every item used in offering has a mystical meaning and dimension. As water is seen to bring life, offerings identified with the Eye of Heru are seen to *renew* life. This vocabulary of mystical correspondences acts as a continuing revelation: divinity pushes through, as it were, the veil of material creation. It does not destroy the veil, but it casts a penetrating light that breaks through the denseness of the veil of materiality.[234]

The newly ensouled image is literally clothed in the protective and life-enhancing Eye of Heru for as the Liturgist states, "You are arrayed in the Eye of Heru" (from the Seventeenth Ceremonial Action). This is truly a liturgy of divine transfiguration: the material vessel has become the abode of divinity. "Therefore shall you be hymned on account of your beauty" (from the Nineteenth Ceremonial Action).

With the Twentieth Ceremonial Action the Liturgist presents a beaded necklace, calling upon the primeval creator Atum to embrace the newly enfleshed divine image with his own *Ka*, to unite himself with the image, and to protect that image from every evil. This reference to the most primeval of the gods underscores the fact that we are working this great creative act in *Zep Tepi*, the First Time, from which emanate all gods, all humans, and all creation. As a necklace encircles the wearer, so does the *Ka*-spirit of the First Creator, the great He-She, encircle the newly born god. This is truly a mystical insight into what happens through the ritual of Opening the Mouth.

In the Twenty-First Ceremonial Action four sacred oils are applied to the mouth and eyes of the sacred image. The oils selected should be appropriate to the deity embodied in the image. One of the oils should be oil of myrrh, which in pharaonic texts was called *madjet* oil. It and the other oils are applied with the little finger. First, *madjet* oil is applied to the mouth. Next, oil is applied to the eyes. Appropriate oils include olive oil, lotus, lily, and iris oils, as well as rose, cinnamon, pine, juniper berry, and sage oil. The interested reader is referred to Lise Manniche's book, *Sacred Luxuries: Fragrance, Aromatherapy, and Cosmetics in Ancient Egypt* (Ithaca, NY: Cornell University Press, 1999). A detailed list of recipes for sacred oils on the walls of the temple of Heru at Edfu includes nine different unguents. In six of those very complex mixtures frankincense appears as an ingredient (Manniche, 108). Therefore, it is fitting and in keeping with the spirit of the ancient tradition to use oil of frankincense as one of the four oils for anointing.

The precise duplication of the original recipes is problematic due to the current inability to locate or even identify some of the ingredients with any degree of certainty. Some words continue to elude precise botanical identification. Therefore, we are thrown back on our own devices to create effective magical oils for ritual. It is the practice of the Temple of Ra to use only the highest quality essential oils. Whatever oils are used, they should first be purified with a lustration of water, sprinkled with natron, and passed through smoking incense. A simple dedicatory recitation should accompany these ritual acts. Once dedicated, they should be used exclusively for sacred rites.

The Twenty-Second Ceremonial Action consists in the presentation of a scepter. In case the image of the deity does not already come with a removable scepter, one of your own making may easily be substituted. It should be of a size that would be appropriate for the height of the image. The scepter represents power and authority. Again the recitation refers to both Heru and Sutekh, the two polarities in balance.

The Twenty-Third and Twenty-Fourth Ceremonial Actions are both offerings of incense, first to all the deities invoked during the preceding rite, and then to the newly enfleshed deity. The frequent and repeated use of incense underscores the importance of these aromatic substances in worship. The resin used in incense comes from living botanicals, both plants and trees. Frankincense exudes from a certain variety of tree in the form of large translucent tears. Myrrh also is a gum-resin from a tree. Mythologically some were regarded as exudations of the Eye of Ra, or the eye of Ausir (Osiris), the Eye of Heru, or even the eye of Djehuty. Such identifications of incense with the eye of a god ultimately spring from the paradigm of the Eye of Heru which was healed, restored, and made perfect. As a "perfect" offering, incense then is capable of cleansing, restoring, and perfecting the recipient whether human or divine. It is important for the modern day Kemetic ritualist to be aware that every item offered–water, wine, bread, incense, various foods, fabrics, etc.–holds more than one symbolic significance. As a diamond has many facets showing a rainbow of colors so items offered to deity hold multiple associations. These associations are neither arbitrary nor random. By means of study, reflection, *and* use in worship the hidden meanings will be revealed.

The Twenty-Fifth Ceremonial Action is a final offering of incense, this time to Amun-Ra. Recall that the ceremony takes place outside in the sunlight which bathes the image in divine light. As we move to the conclusion of the Opening of the Mouth rite, this recitation reminds us that this has been a divine action.The Liturgist proclaims, "I am Djehuty. I am Your (Ra's) *Sahu* (energy body). . . . I have fashioned this god/goddess. I have fashioned him/her. I have made his/her divine transformations. He/she breathes Ma'at. . . ." Repeatedly throughout this ceremony we hear words indicating that these vivifying actions are the actions of a god or goddess. This is consistent with all acts of Egyptian *heka*-magic. The power and energy is always of divine origin. Humans participate as conduits for the gods' divine power.

The Twenty-Sixth and final action belonging to the Opening of the Mouth rite proper is the procession to the Naos or shrine house and the placing of the image into that shrine. The lightless interior of the Naos recalls the time before creation. The vivified image rests in readiness for the light of the next day's dawn, a dawn of new creation. The image now becomes the object of a daily cult which again and again will recall and renew the First

Time of creation. Once again a divine being has entered the material plane, revealing that plane to be sacred and sanctified, bright with promise, bright with divine energy. For the ancient Egyptians and for those following the Kemetic path, we agree with the Roman Neoplatonist philosopher Plotinus, born and educated in Egypt, who refers to "ancient sages, who sought to secure the presence of divine beings by the erection of shrines and statues . . . . [because] they perceived that, though this Soul [the Soul of the World] is everywhere tractable, its presence will be secured all the more readily when an appropriate receptacle is elaborated, a place especially capable of receiving some portion or phase of it . . . ."[235] Although Plotinus used the categories of the Neoplatonic School, he gave expression to an insight common to the ancient world: the living presence of deity is made possible through the creative efforts of human hands. We believe that today more than ever the world has need of this divine, material presence.

After the doors are closed, the ritual concludes with the "removing the foot" rite and recitation. The newly animated image rests within its sacred shrine from which it will emerge the next day to be the subject for a cycle of service at the hands of the priests and priestesses. The indwelling divine presence of the deity becomes a living testimony to the sacredness of this world. The three-dimensional physical image has become the "body" for a divine being. By means of it humans can have a special and unique form of personal contact with the god. Unlike the three monotheistic religions, for the ancient Egyptians and other polytheists the physical world is not experienced as a collection of empty shells, devoid of spirit. Rather, the whole world is filled with an interior, spiritual dimension. And this dimension is capable of hosting divinity. The two worlds–physical and spiritual–can flow and interpenetrate, thereby creating the sanctification of both time and space.

It is the experience of members in the Temple of Ra that the gods and goddesses will and do respond to anyone who with a good heart seeks to serve them on a daily basis.We have found again and again that the gods are not to be outdone in generosity.

The Opening of the Mouth Ceremony–
Vivifying the Image of a *Netjer/Netjeret*

Refer to conclusion of ritual for list of items needed.

THE FIRST CEREMONIAL ACTION

As near as possible to the middle hour of daylight when the sun is at its zenith the priests prepare a mound of pure sand upon which the statue is to be placed. This is to take place out of doors so the sunlight radiates down upon the image. The statue should be placed so it is facing south.[236]

THE SECOND CEREMONIAL ACTION

The Liturgist takes in his/her hand a censer of burning incense and walks around the statue four times, and, addressing the image, says:

"You are pure. You are pure, O *(name of deity)*.
You are pure. You are pure, O *(name of deity)*.
You are pure. You are pure, O *(name of deity)*.
You are pure. You are pure, O *(name of deity)*.**"[237]

THE THIRD CEREMONIAL ACTION

The Liturgist either sprinkles or pours water over the statue to make it a pure dwelling place for the deity. The water should come from four separate <u>white</u> vases. The Liturgist walks around the statue four times, each time emptying one of the vases over it, and reciting one of the following formulae:

(First perambulation and sprinkling or pouring)

"You are pure. You are pure. Your purifications are the purifications of Heru, and the purifications of Heru are your purifications.

(Second perambulation and sprinkling or pouring)

"You are pure. You are pure. Your purifications are the purifications of Sutekh, and the purifications of Sutekh are your purifications.

(Third perambulation and sprinkling or pouring)

"You are pure. You are pure. Your purifications are the purifications of Djehuty, and the purifications of Djehuty are your purifications.

(Fourth perambulation and sprinkling or pouring)

"You are pure. You are pure. Your purifications are the purifications of Geb, and the purifications of Geb are your purifications.

(Standing in front of the statue, recite)

"You have received your head, and your bones have been provided to you before Geb. Your body has been constituted whole and complete. Your body shall be firmly established, and it shall neither fall into ruin nor be destroyed on this earth."[238]

THE FOURTH CEREMONIAL ACTION

The Liturgist once again sprinkles or pours water over the statue. The water should come from four separate red vases. The Liturgist walks around the statue four times, each time emptying one of the vases over it, and reciting one of the following formulae:

(First perambulation and sprinkling or pouring)

"You are pure. You are pure. Your purifications are the purifications of Heru, and the purifications of Heru are your purifications.

(Second perambulation and sprinkling or pouring)

"**You are pure. You are pure. Your purifications are the purifications of Sutekh, and the purifications of Sutekh are your purifications.**

(Third perambulation and sprinkling or pouring)

"**You are pure. You are pure. Your purifications are the purifications of Djehuty, and the purifications of Djehuty are your purifications.**

(Fourth perambulation and sprinkling or pouring)

"**You are pure. You are pure. Your purifications are the purifications of Geb, and the purifications of Geb are your purifications.**

(Standing in front of the statue, recite)

"**You are pure. You are pure, O *(name of god/goddess)*. That which is in the two Eyes of Heru has been presented to you, and the two *tesher* (red) vases of Djehuty, and they purify youso that there may not exist in you any destruction that may pertain to you.**"[239]

THE FIFTH CEREMONIAL ACTION

The Liturgist places five grains of natron mixed with incense in a bowl and then walks around the statue four times as he/she recites the following Utterance. The bowl is to be cupped in two hands and with each Utterance the bowl should be raised up and lowered in the direction of the statue.

"**You are censed with natron. You are censed with natron.**"

(First perambulation and offering of the five grains)

"Your censings with natron are the censings of Heru, and the censings with natron of Heru are your censings."

(Second perambulation and offering of the five grains)

"Your censings with natron are the censings of Sutekh, and the censings with natron of Sutekh are your censings."

(Third perambulation and offering of the five grains)

"Your censings with natron are the censings of Djehuty, and the censings with natron of Djehuty are your censings."

(Fourth perambulation and offering of the five grains)

"Your censings with natron are the censings of Geb, and the censings with natron of Geb are your censings."

(Standing in front of the statue recite:)

"You are established among your brethren, the *Netjeru*. Your mouth is the mouth of a milking calf on the day that it was born."

The Liturgist now touches the mouth of the statue twice, and the eyes twice, and one hand twice.[240]

THE SIXTH CEREMONIAL ACTION

"Your *Ka* is purified. You are censed, you are censed, you are censed. Your head is censed for you, and your mouth is censed for you. Your bones have been purified for you, and no corruption shall come upon you.

"O (*name of god/goddess*), I have given to you the Eye of Heru, and your face is filled therewith. You are enveloped in incense of the North. You are enveloped in incense of the South."[241]

Once again the Liturgist <u>touches</u> the mouth of the statue twice, and the eyes twice, and one hand twice.

THE SEVENTH CEREMONIAL ACTION

The Liturgist now takes <u>a censer of burning incense</u> (myrrh for purification) and presents it to the statue saying:

"O (*name of deity*), I have presented to you the Eye of Heru, and the odor thereof comes to you. The scent of the Eye of Heru is for you. The scent of Nekhbet, which proceeds from the city of Nekheb, it washes you clean, it adorns you, and it makes its seat on your two hands.

You are pure, you are pure, O (*name of deity*)." (*4 times*)[242]

The ceremonies of sprinkling and censing are now complete, and the statue is ritually pure.

THE EIGHTH CEREMONIAL ACTION

The Liturgist picks up a staff and ceremonially "strikes" or taps (i.e., dedicates) the statue with the staff in his right hand, and touches its mouth with the little finger of his left hand as he/she says:

"Hail, (*name of deity*), I have come to embrace you. I am Heru. I have pressed for you your mouth."[243]

THE NINTH CEREMONIAL ACTION

Putting aside the staff, the Liturgist puts on the panther skin, picks up the leg of beef–either actual or fabricated–and presents it to the statue, saying:

"I have seized your enemies and I have brought them to you. I have presented to you the Leg as the Eye of Heru."

The Liturgist then presents the heart–either actual or fabricated in the shape of the heart hieroglyph.

"I have brought to you the heart which was in him (the enemy; that is, the bull). **Never again shall an attack be made against this *Netjer*."**[244]

THE TENTH CEREMONIAL ACTION

The Liturgist touches the mouth of the statue with the leg of beef and says:

"Hail (*name of deity*)! I have come to embrace you. I am Heru. I have pressed for you your mouth with this Leg of the bull."

For a second time the Liturgist touches the mouth of the statue with the leg of beef and says:

"I am Sutekh, your beloved. I have opened for you your mouth. Your mouth has been made firm. Hail (*name of deity*)! I have opened for you your mouth with the Leg, the Eye of Heru."[245]

THE ELEVENTH CEREMONIAL ACTION

The Liturgist picks up the ritual adze and touches it to the mouth and eyes of the statue, saying:

"Hail (*name of deity*)! Your mouth has been made firm. I have opened for you your mouth. I have opened for you your two eyes. Hail, (*name of deity*)! I have opened for you your mouth with the iron which comes forth from Sutekh, with the *Meshkhetyu* (adze) instrument of iron wherewith He opened the mouths of the *Netjeru*."[246]

THE TWELFTH CEREMONIAL ACTION

The Liturgist picks up the ram-headed instrument called *Ur-Hekau,* i.e., "the Great One of Words of Power." With the instrument the Liturgist touches the mouth and eyelids four times and says:

"Your mouth has been made firm for you. The *Netjeret* Nut has lifted up your head. The *Netjer* Heru has taken possession of His crown and His words of power. Behold, Sutekh has taken possession of His crown and His words of power. Behold, the *Nejeret* Nut has appeared with you. All the *Netjeru* bring words of power; they recite them for you; they make you to live by them. You become a lord of two-fold might.

"Their fluid of life surrounds you. You are protected, and you shall not die. You shall make your transformations among the *Ka*-spirits of all the *Netjeru*. You are endowed with strength like all the *Netjeru* and their *Ka*-spirits."

"You rise as King/Queen of the South."
"You rise as King/Queen of the North."

"And behold, this statue of (*name of deity*), is as Shu, the son of Temu, and as he lives, even so shall you live. Shu has provided you with all things. Shu has exalted you to the height of heaven. Shu has made you to be a wonder. Shu has endowed you with strength."[247]

THE THIRTEENTH CEREMONIAL ACTION

The Liturgist passes the ram-headed *Ur-Hekau* instrument four times over the neck and down the spine of the statue.

"The passes have been made; life fills this image of (*name of deity*). Your fluid of life is round about you, and the image of this *Netjer/Netjeret* shall never die."[248]

THE FOURTEENTH CEREMONIAL ACTION

Holding the *Pesesh-kef* blade and touching it to the jaw of the statue which he holds in his other hand, the Liturgist says:

"O (*name of deity*), your two jawbones which were separated have been established for You."[249]

(touching the mouth): **"O (*name of deity*), the two *Netjeru* Heru and Sutekh have opened for you your mouth."** *(2 times)*

(touching the eyes): **"O (*name of deity*), the two *Netjeru* Heru and Sutekh have opened for you your eyes."** *(2 times)*

(touching the nostrils): **O (*name of deity*), the two *Netjeru* Heru and Sutekh have opened for you your nostrils."** *(2 times)*

(touching the ears): **"O (*name of deity*), the two *Netjeru* Heru and Sutekh have opened for you your ears."** *(2 times)*

"Sutekh himself has opened for you your mouth with the instrument of iron wherewith he opened the mouths of the *Netjeru*.

"I have given to you your mouth. Your mouth is opened for you and it is fully formed. Your two eyes have been opened for you, and you see with them.

"A passage has been made into your ears, and you hear with them. Your nostrils take in your own scent and it is the scent of the Great One of Words of Power. You live! You live!"²⁵⁰

"O statue of (*name of deity*), I have opened for you your mouth with the instrument of Sutekh, with the *Meshkhetyu* (adze) of iron wherewith were opened the mouths of the *Netjeru*.

"Heru has opened the mouth of the statue of (*name of deity*), even as he opened the mouth of his father Ausir (Osiris) with the *Meshkhetyu* (adze), with the iron which came forth from Sutekh, with the iron *Meshkhetyu* (adze) wherewith Sutekh opened the mouth of the *Netjeru* has he opened the mouth of the statue of (*name of deity*).

"(*Name of deity*) walks; he/she has obtained the power of speech.
His/her body is with the Great Company of the *Netjeru*.

"Hail, (*name of deity*)! Heru has opened for you your mouth.

"Sutekh has opened for you your mouth with the *Meshkhetyu* (adze) instrument of iron wherewith were opened the mouth of every god and goddess, and the mouth of Atum (Temu), Lord of Iunu (Heliopolis), and the mouth of Ptah of the South Wall (Memphis), Lord of the Life of the Two Lands, and the mouths of the great *Netjeru*."²⁵¹

THE FIFTEENTH CEREMONIAL ACTION

Frankincense is placed on the charcoal and the statue is censed.

"Pure, pure is your *Ka*. Pure is the *Ka* of (*name of deity*). Your head is shrouded in the sweet-smelling incense. The dew of the god/goddess is upon your members. The two great *Netjeru*, Heru and Sutekh, who preside over the Land, purify you. Heru has shrouded you with his Eye.

"Hail, (*name of deity*)! You are shrouded with the Eye of Heru. You are censed with the Eye of Heru. You are filled with the Eye of Heru as is the god. The odor thereof is for you. Behold, the odor of the Eye of Heru is for you!"[252]

THE SIXTEENTH CEREMONIAL ACTION

Taking a white cloth ribbon, the Liturgist offers it to the statue and then places it around the shoulders and neck of the statue and says:

"The *Nemes* comes; the White Cloth comes. The White Cloth comes. The Eye of Heru comes. The *Netjeru* array you with this; You are arrayed with this. You are adorned with this in its name of 'White One of Nekhen.'"[253]

THE SEVENTEENTH CEREMONIAL ACTION

Then the Liturgist presents a blue cloth ribbon, placing it around the shoulders and neck of the image, and says:

"Receive, receive, receive your beauties. Receive your two eyes. Receive this bandlet, the Eye of Heru, the White One, which comes forth from the city of Nekhebet. You have risen like the Sun. It fills you with strength in its name of *Menkhet*. It unifies you in its name of *Atemu*. It makes you great in its name of *Aat*. It fills your face with gladness in its name of *Qemayt*.

"You are arrayed in the Eye of Heru, and the *Netjeret* Rennut has arrayed you in your *Menkhet* bandlet. The Eye of Heru has been presented to you. It gives strength to the *Netjeru*, and the *Netjeru* give you strength, even as the Eye of Heru gives them strength."[254]

THE EIGHTEENTH CEREMONIAL ACTION

The Liturgist presents a <u>green</u> cloth ribbon and places it around the shoulders and neck of the image and says:

"The *Netjeret* Wadjet, Lady of the City of Flame, the Perfect One, who cannot be repulsed in heaven or on earth, has risen like the Sun, and she will make green (i.e., to flourish) (*name of deity*). She will make him/her perfect with Her *Mankhet* bandlet; she will make him/her flourish with the power which dwells in her *Wadj* bandlet. You shall renew your youth even as she renews her youth.

"Hail (*name of deity*)! The Eye of Heru has been presented to you, and that which is in you has been made strong!"[255]

THE NINETEENTH CEREMONIAL ACTION

The Liturgist presents the <u>red</u> cloth ribbon and places it around the shoulders and neck of the image and says:

"The Eye of Heru has risen! The Lady of the Two Lands, the Eye of Ra, Mistress in the city of Double Flame, the Mighty One, Lady of the Storm, the Mistress who made the word to go forth whereby the Ennead of the *Netjeru* came into being, and she shall make (*name of deity*) to flourish; she shall go before him/her. She shall rise in front of him/her, appearing upon his/her brow. She causes the fear of him/her to go forth as the Mighty One of twofold strength. She will rise up in front of him/her, and he/she will be protected and made stronger than the *Netjeru*.

"Hail, (*name of deity*)! You have been made alive; you have been made new, and your youth shall be renewed like that of Ra every day. Therefore shall you be hymned on account of your beauty by those of the Two Lands, and by mortals, and your arm shall not be resisted throughout the Earth. The Eye of Heru has been presented to you, and you have your sight through it."[256]

THE TWENTIETH CEREMONIAL ACTION

The Liturgist presents the beaded necklace and says:

"Homage to you, O Atum. Homage to you, O Khepera, who are exalted upon your High Place, who shine as the God of the Obelisk in the Chamber of the Obelisk which is in Iunu (Heliopolis). You spat, and Shu came into being. You emitted water, and Tefnut came into being. You embraced them with the arms of your *Ka*, and your *Ka* is in them. O Atum, embrace (*name of deity*) with the arms of your *Ka*, and let him/her live with his/her *Ka* forever. O Atum, unite yourself to (*name of deity*), protect him/her, and let not any evil whatsoever come upon him/her, even as you did unite yourself to Shu and Tefnut."[257]

THE TWENTY-FIRST CEREMONIAL ACTION

The statue is now to be anointed with oils.The Liturgist should use four oils appropriate to the deity, or oils symbolic of the four cardinal points. Use the little finger to apply each oil. The following should be said while applying each oil to the eyes of the image:

"Hail, (*name of deity*)! I have filled your face with oil of (*name of oil*), and I have bound thereto for you the Eye of Heru, and your face is strong. I have come and I have anointed your two eyes with oils of perfume of all kinds.

"Hail, (*name of deity*), who has been born this day. You have been made a being with knowledge among those who have no knowledge. You have been made strong by Geb, who was the first of the Company of the *Netjeru* to be born."[258]

317

THE TWENTY-SECOND CEREMONIAL ACTION

The Liturgist should wipe any excess oil off his/her finger. If the statue comes with a scepter, it should now be placed in the hand of the image or simply placed in front of the statue while the following is said:

"Join yourself. Join yourself to this scepter, the 'Smiter of Rebels, Divine Power which rules the Two Lands.' Your *Ka* is provided with divine power. The twofold strength of Heru is with you. The twofold strength of Sutekh is with you, and you do rule this earth, O *(name of deity)*."[259]

THE TWENTY-THIRD CEREMONIAL ACTION

The Liturgist shall offer incense to the *Netjeru* invoked during the ritual and say:

"Offerings of incense are made to all the *Netjeru*. All you *Netjeru* whose names have been invoked this day, come and cause Ma'at to approach. Destroy all defects which are in this image of *(name of deity)*. Establish his/her heart in his/her body. Open his/her mouth. Make a passage in his/her ears. Open his/her nostrils. Make his/her flesh and bone to grow with Ma'at."[260]

THE TWENTY-FOURTH CEREMONIAL ACTION

The Liturgist walks around the statue while carrying the incense burner and says:

"Hail, *(name of deity)*! I have opened your mouth for you. I have equipped your mouth to receive offerings and to speak. Ra has opened your mouth and He has opened your two eyes. The mouth of *(name)* has been opened. His/Her heart is in his/her body forever!"[261]

THE TWENTY-FIFTH CEREMONIAL ACTION

A final offering of incense is made to Amun-Ra. The Liturgist recites the following:

"Hail, Ra, who live in Ma'at. Hail, Ra, who feed upon Ma'at. Hail, Ra, who rejoice in Ma'at. Hail, Ra, who are perfect in Ma'at. Hail, Ra, who are united to Ma'at, to whose brow Ma'at is united. Hail, Ra, who make destinies to flourish, who are perfect in plans, who possess Ma'at in Your very being.

"I have come to you. I am Djehuty. I am your *Sahu* (energy body). I have provided myself with your magical powers. I know the knowledge which is in you. I have taken possession of your strength and of your skill in handicraft. I have taken possession of the utterances of your mouth. I have come and I have brought Ma'at to you, wherein you live, wherein you rejoice, whereby you are perfect. Your heart rejoices when you see those who are in your shrine.

"I have given the *Wedjat* Eye to Heru, the *Wedjat* to its Lord. I have given the Testicles to Sutekh, the Testicles to their Lord. There are offerings for Heru and Sutekh in my hands.

"I have fashioned this god/goddess. I have fashioned him/her; I have made his/her divine transformations. He/she breathes Ma'at. His/her mouth is opened, and I have placed him/her in front of Ma'at. His/her name is established forever."[262]

THE TWENTY-SIXTH CEREMONIAL ACTION

At this point the Liturgist may present offerings as per the ordinary rite or proceed directly to placing the newly vivified image into its shrine house.

The Liturgist opens the two doors of the shrine and says:

"The doors of heaven are opened. The doors of the house of the *Netjer/Netjeret* are thrown back wide. The House is open for its Lord/Mistress. Let me come forth as he/she shall come forth. Let me enter in as he/she shall enter in. May the *Netjer/ Netjeret* enter therein! I am Djehuty. Let the door be thrust open for the *Netjer/Netjeret*."[263]

The sacred image is placed within the shrine house. The Liturgist says;

"You have life, like a *Netjer*, at the head of the *Netjeru* for ever.

"The beauties of this *Netjer/Netjeret* are exalted. Splendor is with you, O (*name of deity*), and majesty is with you."[264]

The double doors to the shrine house are now closed.

Afterwards all present back out of the Temple Chamber with heads slightly bowed while the Liturgist performs the **"removing the foot."**

With the **broom** the Liturgist, as the last person to exit, ritually sweeps the area beginning at the altar. (This is known as **"removing the foot."**) While performing this action the Liturgist recites the following:

"The distress that causes confusion has been driven away, and all the *Netjeru* are in harmony. I have given Heru his Eye; I have placed the *Wedjat*-Eye in the correct position. I have given Sutekh his Testicles, so that the two Lords are content through the work of my hands."

"I know the sky, I know the earth;
I know Heru, I know Sutekh.
Heru is appeased with his Eyes,
Sutekh is appeased with his Testicles.

I am Djehuty, who reconciles the *Netjeru,*
who makes offerings in their correct form."

The double doors are solemnly closed as the following is said:

"Djehuty has come.
He has filled the Eye of Heru.
He has restored the Testicles of Sutekh.
No evil shall enter this Temple.
Ptah has closed the door,
Djehuty has set it fast.
The door is closed; the door is set fast with the bolt."

All bow, touching the palms of their hands to their knees.

APPENDIX J

Items Needed for the Opening of the Mouth

- eight small vases for water (four red vases; the other four may be white or clear glass)
- a bowl with five small balls of natron
- myrrh incense
- frankincense
- panther skin vestment—A cloth print fabric is a perfectly acceptable substitute since even in the tomb of Tutankhamen such a faux fur garment was found!
- leg of beef
- heart–either actual or fabricated to resemble the hieroglyph for heart
- sculptor's adze
- *Ur-Hekau* wand
- *Pesesh-kef* blade of flint
- four colored cloth ribbons (white, blue, green, red)–each 14 inches in length
- one beaded necklace, sized appropriately for the image to be vivified
- four oils for anointing–use oils appropriate to the deity or oils of the four cardinal points
- a scepter
- incense appropriate for the *Netjeru* in your shrine/temple
- Naos shrine for the vivified image: Customarily one of two different designs for the *Kar*-shrine (Naos) was used: one design was favored in Upper Egypt and the other typical for Lower Egypt. In any case, the shrine should be constructed with two doors opening outward. It can be of a very simple design or patterned after one of the ancient models. It should be used for no other purpose.

Works Cited

Alliot, M. *Le Culte d'Horus à Edfou au temps des Ptolémées*. Cairo: Institut français d'Archéologie orientale, 1954.

Assmann, Jan. "Egyptian Mortuary Liturgies." *Studies in Egyptology Presented to Miriam Lichtheim*. Vol. I. Ed. Sarah Israelit-Groll. Jerusalem: Magnes Press, Hebrew University, 1990.

------. *Egyptian Solar Religion in the New Kingdom: Re, Amun, and the Crisis of Polytheism*. Trans. from the German by Anthony Alcock. London and New York: Kegan Paul International, 1995.

------. *The Mind of Egypt*. Trans. Andrew Jenkins. New York: Henry Holt, 2002.

Bell, Lanny. "The New Kingdom 'Divine' Temple: The Example of Luxor." *Temples of Ancient Egypt*. Ed. Byron E. Shafer. Ithaca, New York: Cornell University Press, 1997.

Blackman, Aylward M. "The Significance of Incense and Libations in Funerary and Temple Ritual," by Aylward M. Blackman. Originally published in *ZAS* 50 (1912), 69-75 [*ZAS=Zeitschrift fur Agyptische Sprache und Altertumskunde*]; reprinted in *Gods, Priests and Men: Studies in the Religion of Pharaonic Egypt by Aylward M. Blackman*. Collected and edited by Alan B. Lloyd (Columbia University Press, 1999).

Bleeker, C. J. *Egyptian Festivals: Enactments of Religious Renewal*. Leiden: E.J. Brill, 1967.

Boylan, Patrick. *Thoth: The Hermes of Egypt*. London: Oxford, Oxford University Press, 1922.

Budge, E. A. Wallis. *The Book of Opening the Mouth:The Egyptian Texts with English Translations*. First published in London,

1909. Reissued in 1972 by Benjamin Blom, New York. Reissued in 1980 by Arno Press, New York.

------. *The Gods of the Egyptians: Studies in Egyptian Mythology.* Vol I. London, 1904.

------. *The Liturgy of Funerary Offerings.* Orig. 1909; Dover reprint, 1994.

Cauville, Sylvie. *Dendura I: Traduction.* Leuven, Belgium: Uitgeveru Peeters, 1998.

Clagett, Marshall. *Ancient Egyptian Science: A Source Book.* Vol. 1. (Containing a translation of the Great Litany, with commentary.) Philadelphia, 1989.

David, A. Rosalie. *Religious Ritual at Abydos.* Warminster, England: Aris and Phillips, Ltd., 1973.

Demarée, Robert Johannes, *The 3h ikr n Rc-stelae: On Ancestor Worship in Ancient Egypt,* Leiden: Nederlands Instituut, 1983.

Dickey, M. W. *Magic and Magicians in the Graeco-Roman World.* London, 1970.

Dunand, Francoise, and Christiane Zivie-Coche. *Gods and Men in Egypt.* Trans. David Lorton. Ithaca, New York: Cornell University Press, 2004.

Eliade, Mircea. *Myth and Reality.* Trans. William R. Trask. New York: Harper and Row, 1963.

Faulkner, Robert O. *The Egyptian Book of the Dead: The Book of Going Forth by Day.* Second Revised Edition. With additional translations by Ogden Goelet, Jr. San Francisco: Chronicle Books, 1998.

––––––. *The Ancient Egyptian Pyramid Texts.* Warminster, England: Aris and Phillips, Ltd., 1969.

Fairman, Herbert W. "A Scene of the Offering of Truth in the Temple of Edfu," *MDAIK* 16 (1958): 86-92. [*MDAIK* = *Mitteilungen des Deutschen Archaologischen Instituts, Abteilung Kairo*]

Faulkner, Robert O. *The Ancient Egyptian Pyramid Texts.* Warminster, England: Oxford University Press, 1969.

––––––. "The Bremner-Rhind Papyrus," *Journal of Egyptian Archaeology.* Volumes XXII (December 1936) through Volume XXIV (June 1938).

––––––. *The Ancient Egyptian Coffin Texts.* Warminster, England: Oxford University Press, 1994 and 1996.

Fowden, Garth. *The Egyptian Hermes: A Historical Approach to the Late Pagan Mind.* Princeton University Press, 1986.

Frankfurter, David, "Narrating Power: The Theory and Practice of the Magical *Historiola* in Ritual Spells," in *Ancient Magic and Ritual Power,* ed. Marvin Meyer and Paul Mirecki. Leiden: Brill, 1995.

Gardiner, Alan H. (ed.) *Hieratic Papyri in the British Museum.* 3rd Series. Volume I Text. (Containing the Ritual of Amenophis I) London: British Museum, 1935.

Goyon, Jean-Claude. *Rituels funéraires de l'ancienne Égypte: Le Rituel de l'Embaumement, Le Rituel de l'Ouverture de la Bouche, les Livres des Respirations.* Paris: du Cerf, 1972.

Haikal, Fayza Mohamed Hussein. *Two Hieratic Funerary Papyri of Nesmin.* Part One: Introduction, Transcriptions and Plates. Part Two: Translation and Commentary. Bruxelles: Foundation Egyptologique Reine Elisabeth, 1972.

Hornung, Erik. *The Ancient Egyptian Books of the Afterlife.* Trans. David Lorton. Ithaca and London: Cornell University Press, 1999.

------. *Conceptions of God in Ancient Egypt.* Trans. John Baines. Ithaca, New York: Cornell University Press, 1982.

Iverson, Erik. *The Myth of Egypt and its Hieroglyphs in European Tradition.* 2nd Ed. Princeton, 1993.

Kristensen, W. Brede. *Life Out of Death: Studies in the Religions of Egypt and Ancient Greece.* Trans. H. J. Franken and G. R. H. Wright. Louvain, Belgium: Peeters Press, 1992.

Lefébure, G. *Les Hypogées Royaux de Thèbes.* Paris, 1886.

Lindsay, Jack. *The Origins of Alchemy in Graeco-Roman Egypt.* London, 1970.

Lorton, David. "The Invocation Hymn at the Temple of Hibis," *SAK* 21 (1994): 159-217. [*SAK* = *Studien zur Altagyptischen Kultur*]

------. "The Theology of Cult Statues in Ancient Egypt." *Born in Heaven, Made on Earth: The Making of the Cult Image in the Ancient Near East.* Ed. Michael B. Dick. Winona Lake, Indiana: Eisenbrauns, 1999.

Luck, Georg. Ed. and trans. "The Precepts of Hermes Trismegistus." *Arcana Mundi: Magic and the Occult in the Greek and Roman Worlds. A Collection of Ancient Texts.* 2nd ed. Baltimore: The Johns Hopkins University Press, 1985 and 2006.

Manniche, Lise. *An Ancient Egyptian Herbal.* Austin: University of Texas Press, 1989.

------. *Sacred Luxuries: Fragrance, Aromatherapy, and Cosmetics in Ancient Egypt.* Ithaca, NY: Cornell University Press, 1999.

Moret, Alexandre. *Le Rituel du Culte Divin Journalier.* Paris: Annales du Musee Guimet, Bibliotheque d'Etudes 14, Ernest Leroux, Editeur, 1902.

Morgan, Mogg. *Tankhem: Seth and Egyptian Magick.* 2nd Rev. Ed. Oxford, UK: Mandrake of Oxford, 2003.

Naydler, Jeremy. *Temple of the Cosmos: The Ancient Egyptian Experience of the Sacred.* Rochester, Vermont: Inner Traditions, 1996.

Nelson, Harold H. "Certain Reliefs at Karnak and Medinet Habu and the Ritual of Amenophis I," JNES 8 (1949): 201-232 and 310-345. [*JNES=Journal of Near Eastern Studies*]

------. "The Rite of 'Bringing the Foot' as Portrayed in Temple Reliefs," *JEA* 35 (1976): 82-86. [*JEA=Journal of Egyptian Archaeology*]

Otto, Eberhard. *Das Ägypyische Mundöffnungsritual.* 2 vols. Wiesbaden: Harrassowitz, 1960.

Piankoff, Alexandre. *The Litany of Re. Texts Translated with Commentary.* Bollingen Series XL-4. New York: Pantheon Books, 1964.

Pinch, Geraldine. *Egyptian Mythology: A Guide to the Gods, Goddesses, and Traditions of Ancient Egypt.* Oxford University Press, 2002.

Poo, Mu-Chou. *Wine and Wine Offering in the Religion of Ancient Egypt.* London and New York: Kegan Paul International, 1995.

Quirke, Stephen. *The Cult of Ra: Sun-Worship in Ancient Egypt.* New York: Thames and Hudson, 2001.

Ritner, Robert Kriech. *The Mechanics of Ancient Egyptian Magical Practice.* The Oriental Institute of the University of Chicago, 1993; third printing 1997.

------. "Religion VS. Magic. The Evidence of the Magical Statue Bases." *The Intellectual Heritage of Egypt.* Ed. Ulrich Luft. Budapest, 1992.

Roberts, Alison. *My Heart, My Mother: Death and Rebirth in Ancient Egypt.* Rottingdean, England: North Gate Publishers, 2000.

Roth, Ann Macy. "Fingers, Stars, and the 'Opening of the Mouth': The Nature and Function of the *NTRWJ*-Blades." *Journal of Egyptian Archaeology.* Vol. 79 (1993), 57-79.

------. "The *PSS-KF* and the 'Opening of the Mouth' Ceremony: A Ritual of Birth and Rebirth." *Journal of Egyptian Archaeology.* Vol. 78 (1992), 113-147.

Sauneron, Serge. *The Priests of Ancient Egypt.* Trans. David Lorton. New Ed. New York: Cornell University Press, 2000.

Simpson, William Kelly. *The Literature of Ancient Egypt.* 3rd Ed. New Haven, Conn.: Yale University Press, 2003.

Smith, Mark. *Catalogue of Demotic Papyri in the British Museum, Vol. III: The Mortuary Texts of Papyrus BM 10507.* London: British Museum, 1987.

Sørensen, Jørgen Podemann. "The Argument in Ancient Egyptian Magical Formulae," *Acta Orientalia*, Issue 45 (1984).

te Velde, Herman. *Seth, God of Confusion: A Study of His Role in Egyptian Mythology and Religion.* Leiden, Netherlands: E. J. Brill, 1977.

Van der Leeuw, G. *Religion in Essence and Manifestation.* Trans. J. E. Turner. London: George Allen and Unwin, 1964. Reprinted, Princeton University Press, 1986.

Wasserman, James. *The Egyptian Book of the Dead,* translations by Raymond O. Faulkner. San Francisco: Chronicle Books, 1994, 1998.

Wisner, Kerry. *Ancient Egyptian Ritual Magic.* Nashua, New Hampshire: Hwt-Hrw Publications, 2002. This book is available in electronic format only as a PDF file. This requires Adobe Acrobat Reader. http://www.hwt-hrw.com/akhetcatalog.php (accessed Oct. 10, 2009).

———. *Eye of the Sun: The Sacred Legacy of Ancient Egypt.* Nashua, New Hampshire: Hwt-Hrw Publications, 2000 and 2002. http://www.hwt-hrw.com/akhetcatalog.php (accessed Oct. 10, 2009).

———. *Song of Hathor: Ancient Egyptian Ritual for Today.* Nashua, New Hampshire: Hwt-Hrw Publications, 2002. http://www.hwt-hrw.com/akhetcatalog.php (accessed Oct. 10, 2009).

Notes

1   W. Brede Kristensen, *Life Out of Death: Studies in the Religions of Egypt and of Ancient Greece*, trans. H.J. Franken and G.R.H. Wright from the Second Dutch Edition of 1949 (Louvain, Belgium: Peeters Press, 1992), 3.

2   Quoted by Alison Roberts, *My Heart My Mother: Death and Rebirth in Ancient Egypt* (Rottingdean, East Sussex, England: Northgate Publishers, 2005), 221.

3   Kristensen., 18-19.

4   Louis V. Zabkar, *A Study of the Ba Concept in Ancient Egyptian Texts* (Chicago, Illinois: The Oriental Institute of the University of Chicago, Studies in Ancient Oriental Civilization 34, 1968), 49-50.

5   Jan Assmann, *Egyptian Solar Religion in the New Kingdom* (London & New York: Kegan Paul International, 1995), 35.

6   Serge Sauneron, *The Priests of Ancient Egypt*, new edition, trans. David Lorton (Ithaca, New York: Cornell University Press, 2000), 124.

7   Ibid.

8   Aylward M. Blackman, *Gods, Priests, and Men: Studies in the Religion of Pharaonic Egypt*, compiled and edited by Alan B. Lloyd (London & New York: Kegan Paul International, 1998, orig. publ. in 1912), 168. Originally the text appeared as an article entitled "Worship (Egyptian)" in James Hastings' *Encyclopedia of Religion and Ethics* (New York: Scribner's, 1917-1925) Volume 12 (1921)776-82.

9   Ibid.

10 Adapted from Fairman, 91.

11 Adapted from Moret, 9, and Budge, 197.

12 Adapted from Moret, 16, and Budge, 198.

13 Adapted from Moret, 19, and Budge, 198.

14 Adapted from Moret, 78, and Budge, 207.

15 Adapted from Assmann, 15, and Budge, 197.

16 Adapted from Lorton, 159.

[17] Adapted from Moret, 21, and Budge, 199.
[18] Adapted from Budge, 201.
[19] Adapted from Moret, 55, and Budge, 202.
[20] Adapted from Moret, 57-59, and Budge, 202-203.
[21] Adapted from Moret, 59-60, and Budge, 203.
[22] Adapted from Moret, 81-82, and Budge, 208.
[23] Adapted from Moret, 63, and Budge, 204.
[24] Adapted from Budge, 212.
[25] Adapted from Moret, 9, and Budge, 197.
[26] Adapted from Moret, 138-147, and Budge, 221.
[27] Adapted from Moret, 71, and Budge, 206.
[28] Adapted from David, 99.
[29] Adapted from Moret, 171, Budge, 227, and Gardiner, 82.
[30] Adapted from Moret, 172-174, and Budge, 228.
[31] Adapted from Budge, 228.
[32] Adapted from Wisner, Lesson Seven, 9.
[33] Adapted from Moret, 179-180, and Budge, 229.
[34] Adapted from Moret, 182, and Budge, 230.
[35] Adapted from Moret, 184, and Budge, 230.
[36] Adapted from Moret, 185-187, and Budge, 231.
[37] Adapted from Moret, 187-188, and Budge, 232.
[38] Adapted from Moret, 194-195, and Budge, 232-234.
[39] Adapted from Gardiner, 84.
[40] Adapted from Gardiner, 84. Refer to Nelson's *JNES* article, 329-331, regarding the rubrical act accompanying the recitation.
[41] Adapted from Gardiner, 85.
[42] Adapted from Gardiner, 87.
[43] Adapted from Nelson, *JNES* article, 211 (also see 209).
[44] Adapted from Assmann, 148.
[45] Adapted from Assmann, 198.
[46] Adapted from Gardiner, 91, and Nelson, *JNES* article, 325-327.
[47] Adapted from Moret, 201.
[48] Adapted from Moret, 202-203.
[49] Adapted from Gardiner, 90-91.
[50] Adapted from te Velde, 50, and Gardiner, 83. Refer to Nelson's *JEA* article regarding the ritual action intended to accompany

the recitation.

[51] Adapted from te Velde, 50, and Gardiner, 83.

[52] Adapted from David, 104.

[53] Adapted from Nelson, *JNES* article, 315-317.

[54] Stephen Quirke, *The Cult of Ra: Sun-Worship in Ancient Egypt* (New York: Thames and Hudson, 2001), 30.

[55] Alexandre Piankoff, *The Litany of Re*, Texts Translated with Commentary, Bollingen Series XL-4 (New York: Pantheon Books, 1964.), 16; and Erik Hornung, *The Ancient Egyptian Books of the Afterlife*, trans. David Lorton (Ithaca and London: Cornell University Press, 1999), 137.

[56] Quirke, 67.

[57] Piankoff, 10.

[58] Ibid., 23, Note 16.

[59] Quirke, 31.

[60] Erik Hornung, *Conceptions of God in Ancient Egypt.* Trans. John Baines. (Ithaca, New York: Cornell University Press, 1982), 86.

[61] Ibid., 90.

[62] Piankoff, 19.

[63] Hornung, *Conceptions of God in Ancient Egypt*, 93.

[64] Ibid., 95.

[65] Piankoff, 22.

[66] Ibid., 30.

[67] Ibid., 31.

[68] Adapted from David, 57. This text appears in Seti's great temple at Abydos.

[69] Ibid., 98.

[70] Adapted from Assmann, 14. This is a classic solar sunset hymn.

[71] Adapted from Gardiner, 90 (from the Ritual of Amenophis I).

[72] Adapted from Nelson, 319. This libation spell appears in the temples of Edfu, Dendera, and Philae as well as in the Ritual of Amenophis I (See Note 103 on page 319 in Nelson).

[73] Adapted from David, 58.

[74] Adapted from Gardiner, 91.

[75] Ibid., 91-92.

[76] Adapted from Piankoff, 22 ff., and Clagett, 511-529. The version of the Great Litany in the present work reflects elements from both Piankoff's as well as Clagett's translation. An effort was made to create a text that is appropriate for oral recitation as well as true to both the original content and meaning.

[77] Adapted from David, 57-58.

[78] Adapted from Gardiner, 90-91.

[79] Adapted from te Velde, 50, and Gardiner, 83. Refer to Nelson's *JEA* article regarding the ritual action accompanying this recitation.

[80] Adapted from te Velde, 50, and Gardiner, 83.

[81] Adapted from David, 104, and te Velde, 50.

[82] Adapted from Nelson, *JNES* article, 315-317, and Note 96 (315).

[83] Jan Assmann, *The Mind of Egypt,* trans. Andrew Jenkins (New York: Henry Holt and Company, 2002), 364.

[84] Fayza Mohamed Hussein Haikal, *Two Hieratic Funerary Papyri of Nesmin,* Part One (Bruxelles: Fondation Egyptologique Reine Elisabeth, 1970), 13.

[85] Ibid., 7.

[86] Jan Assmann, *The Search for God in Ancient Egypt,* trans. David Lorton (Ithaca and London: Cornell University Press, 2001), 49.

[87] Ibid., 50.

[88] Ibid., 51.

[89] The interested reader is referred to the following three sources:

Frankfurter, David, "The Magic of Writing and the Writing of Magic: The Power of the Word in Egyptian and Greek   Traditions," *Helios* 21 (1994), 189-221.

------, "Narrating Power: The Theory and Practice of the Magical *Historiola* in Ritual Spells," in *Ancient Magic and Ritual Power,* edited by Marvin Meyer and Paul Mirecki (Leiden: Brill, 1995), 457-476.

Sørensen, Jørgen Podemann, "The Argument in Ancient Egyptian Magical Formulae," *Acta Orientalia*, Issue 45 (1984), 5-19.

90 Van der Leeuw, G., *Religion in Essence and Manifestation*, trans. J.E. Turner (London: George Allen and Unwin, 1964; repr. ed. Princeton Univ. Press, 1986), 424.

91 Adapted from Papyrus BM 10209 (I, 3-5), trans. Haikal, Vol. II, 16.

92 Adapted from the Book of the Dead, Chapter 137A, trans. Faulkner, 119.

93 Adapted from Pap. BM 10209, (I, 5-12), 16-17.

94 Adapted from Pap. BM 10209, (I, 13-17), 17.

95 Adapted from Pap. BM 10209, (I, 19), 17.

96 Adapted from Pap. BM 10209, (I, 20-22), 17.

97 Adapted from Pyramid Text, Utterance 223, in *The Ancient Egyptian Pyramid Texts*, trans. Faulkner, 51-52.

98 From *Das schöne Fest vom Wüstentale, Festbräuche einer Totenstadt*, by S. Schott, (1953) 95. Quoted in C. J. Bleeker's *Egyptian Festivals: Enactments of Religious Renewal*, 137.

99 Adapted from Pap. BM 10209, (I, 23-28), 17.

100 Adapted from Pap. BM 10209, (I, 29-40), 17-18.

101 Adapted from Pap. BM 10209, (I, 40-II, 6), 18.

102 Adapted from Pap. BM 10209, (II, 6-10), 18.

103 Adapted from Pap. BM 10209, (II, 10-17), 18-19.

104 Adapted from Pap. BM 10209, (II, 17-40), 19.

105 Adapted from Pap. BM 10209, (III, 1-2), 20.

106 Adapted from Pap. BM 10209, (III, 3-22), 20.

107 Adapted from Pap. BM 10209, (III, 23-27), 20-21.

108 Adapted from Pap. BM 10209, (IV, 1-10), 21.

109 Adapted from Pap. BM 10209, (IV, 11-20), 21.

110 Adapted from Pap. BM 10209, (V, 1-7), 21-22.

111 Adapted from the Ritual of Amenophis, in *Hieratic Papyri in the British Museum*, ed. Alan H. Gardiner (London, 1935), 97.

112 Adapted from Gardiner, 90-91.

113 Adapted from te Velde, 50, and Gardiner, 83. Refer to

Nelson's *JEA* article regarding the ritual action intended to accompany the recitation.

[114] Adapted from te Velde, 50, and Gardiner, 83.

[115] Adapted from David, 104, and te Velde, 50.

[116] Adapted from Nelson, *JNES* article, 315-317. Also see Note 96 in the same article.

[117] Schott, op. cit. 82, quoted in Bleeker, 138.

[118] Mark Smith, *Catalogue of Demotic Papyri in the British Museum, Vol. III: The Mortuary Texts of Papyrus BM 10507* (London: British Museum, 1987), 20.

[119] Jan Assmann, "Egyptian Mortuary Liturgies," in *Studies in Egyptology Presented to Miriam Lichtheim*, Vol. I, edited by Sarah Israelit-Groll (Jerusalem: The Magnes Press, Hebrew University, 1990), 9.

[120] Smith, op. cit., 20.

[121] Assmann, op. cit., 9.

[122] Ibid., 10.

[123] Ibid., 11.

[124] Ibid., 35-6.

[125] Adapted from Pyramid Text 223, *The Ancient Egyptian Pyramid Texts*, trans. Raymond O. Faulkner, (Warminster, England: Oxford University Press, 1969), 51-52.

[126] Trans. Jan Assmann, "Egyptian Mortuary Liturgies," *Studies in Egyptology Presented to Miriam Lichtheim*, Vol. I. Ed. Sarah Israelit-Groll (Jerusalem: The Magnes Press, The Hebrew University, 1990), 9.

[127] The Second Utterance, and each subsequent utterance extending to and including the Twenty-fourth Utterance (Section One), are adapted from the English translation of Raymond O. Faulkner, *The Ancient Egyptian Pyramid Texts*. The concluding utterances (i.e., the Twenty-fourth [Section Two] through the Twenty-fifth) are adapted from Faulkner's *The Ancient Egyptian Coffin Texts*, Volumes II and III ((Warminster, England: Oxford University Press, 1994 and 1996).

[128] Adapted from the Ritual of Amenophis, in *Hieratic Papyri in the British Museum*, Alan H. Gardner, ed.; 3rd Series,

Volume I, Text (London: British Museum, 1935), 90-91.

129 Adapted from "Certain Reliefs at Karnak and Medinet Habu and the Ritual of Amenophis I," Harold H. Nelson, *JNES* 8 (1949): 315-317. [*JNES=Journal of Near Eastern Studies*]

130 Serge Sauneron, trans. by David Lorton, *The Priests of Ancient Egypt*, New Edition (Ithaca, NY: Cornell University Press, 2000), 28.

131 Dimitri Meeks and Christine Favard-Meeks, *Daily Life of the Egyptian Gods*, trans. by G. M. Goshgarian (Ithaca, NY: Cornell University Press, 1996), 20.

132 Erik Hornung, *Conceptions of God in Ancient Egypt*, trans. by John Baines (Ithaca, NY: Cornell University Press, 1982), 177.

133 Stephen Quirke, *Ancient Egyptian Religion* (New York: Dover Publications, Inc., 1992), 36.

134 William Kelly Simpson, ed., *The Literature of Ancient Egypt*, Third Ed. (New Haven, Conn.: Yale University Press, 2003), 164-5.

135 Robert O. Faulkner, "The Bremner-Rhind Papyrus–III," *Journal of Egyptian Archaeology* 23 (1937b), 166.

136 ------, "The Bremner-Rhind Papyrus–IV," *Journal of Egyptian Archaeology* 24 (1938), 42, lines 10-11.

137 Jørgen Podemann Sørensen, "The Argument in Ancient Egyptian Magical Formulae," *Acta Orientalia*, Issue 45 (1984), 7-8.

138 Robert O. Faulkner, "The Bremner-Rhind Papyrus–IV," *Journal of Egyptian Archaeology* 24 (1938), 42, lines 11-12.

139 Richard J. Reidy, from the Seventh Ceremony: The Chapter of Looking Upon the God, *The Morning Ritual in the Temple of Amun-Ra*. Also see Alexandre Moret, *Le Rituel du Culte Divin Journalier* (Paris: Annales du Musée Guimet, 1902), 55.

140 Robert Kriech Ritner, *The Mechanics of Ancient Egyptian Magical Practice* (Chicago: The Oriental Institute of the University of Chicago, 1993), 221.

141 Mogg Morgan, *Tankhem: Seth and Egyptian Magick.* vol. 1,

2nd rev. ed. (Oxford, UK: Mandrake of Oxford, 2003), 62.

[142] Kerry E. Wisner, *Eye of the Sun: The Sacred Legacy of Ancient Egypt* (Nashua, New Hampshire: Akhet Hwt-Hrw, 2000).

------, *Song of Hathor:Ancient Egyptian Ritual for Today* (Nashua, New Hampshire: Akhet Hwt-Hrw, 2002).
------, *Pillar of Ra: Ancient Egyptian Festivals for Today* (Nashua, New Hampshire: Akhet Hwt-Hrw, 2004). Currently all three books are provided in electronic format only, using Adobe Acrobat Reader software to download the PDF file. Visit http://www.hwt-hrw.com for details.

[143] See Geraldine Pinch's *Magic in Ancient Egypt* (Austin: Univesity of Texas, 1995), 130.

[144] The reader is referred to Erik Iverson's *The Myth of Egypt and its Hieroglyphs in European Tradition* (2nd ed.; Princeton 1993), 38-56, and Jan Assmann's *Weisheit und Mysterium. Das Bild der Griechen von Agypten* (Munich 2000), 31-73.

[145] See Jack Lindsay, *The Origins of Alchemy in Graeco-Roman Egypt* (London 1970) 90-100; and M.W. Dickey, *Magic and Magicians in the Graeco-Roman World* (London, New York 2001) 119-123, 195. Also on this subject see C. J. Bleeker, *Egyptian Festivals: Enactments of Religious Renewal* (Leiden: E. J. Brill, 1967), 13.

[146] *Ascl.* 24: "An ignoras, o Asclepi, quod Aegyptus imago sit caeli aut, quod est verius, translatio aut descensio omnium, quae gubernantur atque exercentur in caelo? et si dicendum est verius, terra nostra mundi totius est templum." Quoted in Garth Fowden's *The Egyptian Hermes: A Historical Approach to the Late Pagan Mind* (Princeton, New Jersey 1993 paperback ed.), 13.

[147] Adapted from Jan Assmann, *Egyptian Solar Religion in the New Kingdom*, trans. from the German by Anthony Alcock (London and New York: Kegan Paul International, 1995),

198.

[148] For more on Egyptian resistence to assimilating Greek and Roman religious categories see Garth Fowden's *The Egyptian Hermes: A Historical Approach to the Late Pagan Mind* (Princeton University Press, 1986), 15-20.

[149] From "The Teaching for King Merikare" in *The Literature of Ancient Egypt*, edited by William Kelly Simpson, 3rd ed. (New Haven: Yale University Press, 2003), 164-65.

[150] Geraldine Pinch, *Magic in Ancient Egypt* (Austin: University of Texas Press, 1995), 24.

[151] Mircea Eliade, *Myth and Reality*, trans. William R. Trask (New York: Harper and Row, 1963), 25, cf. 21-38.

[152] G. Van der Leeuw, *Religion in Essence and Manifestation*, trans. J. E. Turner (London: George Allen and Unwin, 1964); repr. ed. Princeton University Press, 1986), 424.

[153] Utterances 253, 323, 325, 479, and 564 in *The Ancient Egyptian Pyramid Texts*, translated into English by R. O. Faulkner (Warminster, England: Aris and Phillips, 1969).

[154] Based on Kerry Wisner's *Eye of the Sun*, 16.

[155] For further information on divine identifications of parts of the body found in funerary and magical texts please see Adhemar Massart, "A propos des 'listes' dans les textes Egyptiens funeraires et magiques," *Analecta Biblica* (Rome) 12 (1959), 227-246. For another example of such an itemized identification of the subject's limbs with those of deities, see Robert K. Ritner's article, "Religion VS. Magic. The Evidence of the Magical Statue Bases," in *The Intellectual Heritage of Egypt: Studies Presented to Laszlo Kakosy by Friends and Colleagues on the Occasion of His 60th Birthday*, edited by Ulrich Luft (Budapest, 1992), 495-501. An exhaustive list of the Egyptian identification texts, together with a brief but informative analysis is found in W. R. Dawson's "Notes on Egyptian Magic," *Aegyptus* 11:1 (1931), 23-28., see especially Section II: Protection of Parts of the Body by the Gods.

[156] From Alexandre Piankoff, *The Litany of Re. Texts Translated with Commentary*. Bollingen Series XL-4 (New

York: Panteon Books, 1964), 39.

[157] From two versions of Chapter 42, The Book of Going Forth by Day, with minor additions.

[158] Inscription from the Temple of Seti I at Abydos (North Wall, Scene B). The reader is referred to A. M. Calverley and M. F. Broome, *The Temple of King Sethos I at Abydos*. 4 Vols. 1933-1958 (London and Chicago: Egypt Exploration Society).

[159] Adapted from David Lorton, "The Invocation Hymn at the Temple of Hibis," *SAK* 21 (1994): 159. [*SAK* = *Studien zur Altagyptischen Kultur*]

[160] Taken from, Section 44 "Chapitre de mettre ses deux bras sur le dieu," 167-69 in Alexandre Moret, *Le Rituel du Culte Divin Journalier* (Paris: Annales du Musee Guimet, Bibliotheque d'Etudes 14, Ernest Leroux, Editeur, 1902); also see the Thirty-second Ceremony, 226-27 in E. A. Wallis Budge, *The Book of Opening the Mouth: The Egyptian Texts with English Translations*. London, 1909. Reissued in 1980 by Arno Press, New York. The second half of this book contains a translation of the Morning Temple Liturgy.

[161] Taken from the Ritual of Amenophis I, in *Hieratic Papyri in the British Museum*, Vol. I. TEXT, edited by Alan H. Gardiner (London: British Museum, 1935), 81.

[162] Ibid., 84.

[163] Taken from E. A. Wallis Budge, Chapter I: The Doctrine of Offerings, in *The Liturgy of Funerary Offerings* (originally published in 1909; reprinted by Dover Publications, New York, 1994), 24-28. The transliteration guide is updated and not that found in Budge. A century of research since Budge has greatly improved our understanding of how ancient Egyptian was spoken.

[164] For more about divine constellations see Jan Assmann, *The Search for God in Ancient Egypt*, trans. David Lorton (Ithaca and London: Cornell University Press, 2001), 98-102.

[165] Ibid., 49.

[166] Barbara Watterson, *The House of Horus at Edfu: Ritual*

in an Ancient Egyptian Temple (Stroud, Gloucestershire, England: Tempus Publ. Ltd., 1998), 82. For the use of water in purification rites also see Serge Sauneron, *The Priests of Ancient Egypt*, trans. David Lorton, new ed. (Cornell University Press, 2000), 36, 77, 78, 88.

167   W. Brede Kristensen. *Life Out of Death: Studies in the Religions of Egypt and Ancient Greece*, trans. H. J. Franken and G. R. H. Wright from the Second Dutch Edition, Haarlem, 1949 (Louvain, Belgium: Peeters Press, 1992), 93.

168   Norman Lockyer, *The Dawn of Astronomy* (1894: reprint Cambridge, MA: MIT Press, 1964).

169   "The Precepts of Hermes Trismegistus," in *Arcana Mundi: Magic and the Occult in the Greek and Roman Worlds. A Collection of Ancient Texts*. 2nd ed., trans. and ed. by Georg Luck (Baltimore: The Johns Hopkins University Press, 1985 and 2006), 445.

170   Alexandre Moret. *Le Rituel du Culte Divin Journalier*. (Paris: Annales du Musee Guimet, Bibliotheque d'Etudes 14, Ernest Leroux, Editeur, 1902), 78.

171   Quoted in "The Significance of Incense and Libations in Funerary and Temple Ritual," by Aylward M Blackman. Originally published in *ZAS* 50 (1912), 69-75 [*ZAS=Zeitschrift fur Agyptische Sprache und Altertumskunde*]; reprinted in *Gods, Priests and Men: Studies in the Religion of Pharaonic Egypt by Aylward M. Blackman*, collected and edited by Alan B. Lloyd (Columbia University Press, 1999).

172   Robert Kriech Ritner. *The Mechanics of Ancient Egyptian Magical Practice*. (The Oriental Institute of the University of Chicago, 1993, third printing 1997), 155-6.

173   Moret, op. cit., 201.

174   Mu-Chou Poo. *Wine and Wine Offering in the Religion of Ancient Egypt*. (London and New York: Kegan Paul International, 1995), 169.

175   Ibid., 25.

176   Ibid., 109.

177   Kristensen, op. cit., 39-40.

178 Stephen Quirke. *The Cult of Ra: Sun-Worship in Ancient Egypt*. (New York: Thames and Hudson, 2001), 32.

179 Quoted in Harold H. Nelson's "Certain Reliefs at Karnak and Medinet Habu and the Ritual of Amenophis I," Part 2, *Journal of Near Eastern Studies* (8) 1949, 327-28.

180 For further information on the *"peret er kheru"* formula see Alexandre Moret, *Le Rituel du Culte Divin Journalier* (Paris: Annales du Musee Guimet, Bibliotheque d'Etudes 14, Ernest Leroux, Editeur, 1902), 156-57, as well as E. A. Wallis Budge, *The Liturgy of Funerary Offerings* (originally published in 1909; Dover reprint, 1994), 25-28.

181 Jan Assmann. *The Search for God in Ancient Egypt*, trans. David Lorton (Ithaca and London: Cornell University Press, 2001), paperback ed., 78-79.

182 All references to these ceremonies are taken from Part I of the present work. See The Morning Ritual in the Temple of Amun-Ra.

183 Quoted by Alison Roberts in *My Heart My Mother: Death and Rebirth in Ancient Egypt* (Rottingdean, East Essex, England: North Gate Publishers, 2005), 221.

184 Moret, op. cit., 63.

185 Jeremy Naydler, *Temple of the Cosmos: The Ancient Egyptian Experience of the Sacred* (Rochester, Vermont: Inner Traditions, 1996), 185-86.

186 James Wasserman, *The Egyptian Book of the Dead*, translations by Raymond O. Faulkner (San Francisco: Chronicle Books, 1994, 1998), see plate 15 (no pagination).

187 Jorgen Podemann Sorensen, "The Argument in Ancient Egyptian Magical Formulae," *Acta Orientalia*, Issue 45 (1984), 17.

188 From an Utterance in the Ritual of Amenophis I, Chester Beatty Papyrus No. IX, in *Hieratic Papyri in the British Museum*, Alan H. Gardiner, editor. *Vol. I. Text.* (London: British Museum, 1935), 86.

189 Patrick Boylan, *Thoth the Hermes of Egypt: A Study of Some Aspects of Theological Thought in Ancient Egypt* (London: Oxford University Press, 1922), 134-35.

190 Harold H. Nelson, "The Rite of 'Bringing the Foot' as Portrayed in Temple Reliefs," *Journal of Egyptian Archaeology* 35 (1976), 82.

191 Rainer Hannig, *Ägyptisches Wörterbuch II (Mittleres Reich und Zweite Zwischenzeit)*, vol. 1, 1581. Also see Erman-Grapow, in the *Wörterbuch der Ägyptischen Sprache*, Bd II, 506, which gives the following: "*hdn* also and even 'eine Pflanze (aus Nubien eingeführt)' i.e., plant imported from Nubia: 1) in medical context; 2) im Ritual als Stoff zu dem Wedel mit dem die Zeremonie des [*ini.t rd*] *die Fußspuren entfernen* (= removing the footsteps) vollzogen wird," i.e., for the ritual as material for the brush with which the ceremony of *ini.t rd* is carried out.

192 Raven Grimassi, *Wiccan Magick: Inner Teachings of the Craft* (St. Paul, Minnesota: Llewellyn, 1998), 42; also see Scott Cunningham, *Wicca: A Guide for the Solitary Practitioner* (St. Paul, Minnesota: Llewellyn, 1998), 26-27.

193 Francoise Dunand and Christiane Zivie-Coche, *Gods and Men in Egypt*, trans. David Lorton (Ithaca, NY: Cornell University Press, 2004), 90.

194 E. A. Wallis Budge. *The Book of Opening the Mouth: The Egyptian Texts with English Translations*. London, 1909. Reissued in 1980 by Arno Press, New York. The second half of this book contains a translation of the Morning Temple Liturgy. See page 201 for the Sixth Ceremony: The Chapter of Opening the Doors of the Naos.

195 Geraldine Pinch, *Egyptian Mythology: A Guide to the Gods, Goddesses, and Traditions of Ancient Egypt* (Oxford University Press, 2002), 62-63.

196 H. W. Fairman, "A Scene of the Offering of Truth in the Temple of Edfu," *MDAIK* 16 (1958), 90. [*MDAIK=Mitteilungen des Deutschen Archaologischen Instituts, Abteilung Kairo*]

197 Ibid., 89.

198 Adapted from Herbert W. Fairman, "A Scene of the Offering of Truth in the Temple of Edfu," *MDAIK* 16 (1958), 91. [*MDAIK = Mitteilungen des Deutschen Archaologischen*

Instituts, Abteilung Kairo]

[199] Adapted from Alexandre Moret, *Le Rituel du Culte Divin Journalier* (Paris: Annales du Musee Guimet, Bibliotheque d'Etudes 14, Ernest Leroux, Editeur, 1902), 21, and E. A. Wallis Budge (*The Book of Opening the Mouth: The Egyptian Texts with English Translations* (London, 1909. Reissued in 1980 by Arno Press, New York), 199. The first volume of Budge's book includes "The Ritual of the Divine Cult," 197-246. This complements Moret's text.

[200] Adapted from Alexandre Moret, 49-50, and E. A. Wallis Budge, 201-202.

[201] Adapted from Pyramid Text Utterance 323.

[202] Adapted from Pyramid Text Utterance 35, and Budge, 22-23.

[203] Adapted from Sylvie Cauville, *Dendera I: Traduction* (Leuven, Belgium: Uitgeveru Peeters, 1998), 63-65.

[204] Ibid., Tableau I, 107.

[205] These two original Utterances for natron and water are employed by members in the Temple of Ra. The purpose is to purify and consecrate a space for sacred ritual. In ancient Egypt the daily rite would be performed in a permanently consecrated temple. In the current age groups and individuals often must use non-consecrated areas for the occasional ritual. These two Utterances reflect classic Egyptian magical formulations: the god or goddess performs the action. The priest/ess serves as the human enabler for the divine action. The directional sequence–south, north, west, east–is repeatedly attested in the ancient documents. There is no "circle casting" as appears in some Western magical traditions.

[206] Adapted from Moret, 9. Also see Budge, 197.

[207] Adapted from Pyramid Text Utterance 269.

[208] Adapted from Cauville, 37 and 97.

[209] Adapted from E. A. Wallis Budge, *The Gods of the Egyptians: Studies in Egyptian Mythology*. Vol. 1 (N.Y.: Dover Publications; reprint of original work first published in 1904), 518-20. Budge identifies this prayer as coming

from a late dynastic version of the Book of the Dead (Chapter clxiv). In the case of the "name of power" *zfy pr m Hs Hr hApu Dt.f* (pronounced "seh-fee per em Hes' Her h'poo jet-ef"), E. A. Wallis Budge provides the original hieroglyphs for this epithet, however, subsequent advances in linguistics show that his pronunciation is outdated. Therefore, I have replaced his pronunciation with an updated transliteration of the hieroglyphs.

210   Adapted from Budge, *The Liturgy of Funerary Offerings* (London: Kegan Paul, 1909; reprinted by Dover Publications, 1994), 48, 95-96, and 152-53.

211   Adapted from Budge, *The Book of Opening the Mouth*, op. cit., 203.

212   Adapted from Moret, 138-47. Also see Budge, *The Book of Opening the Mouth*, op. cit., 221-25.

213   Adapted from Budge, *The Liturgy of Funerary Offerings*, op. cit., 51-52 and 96-97.

214   Adapted from A. Rosalie David, *Religious Ritual at Abydos* (Warminster, England: Aris and Phillips Ltd., 1973), Scene 30, 103.

215   Adapted from Mu-Chou Poo, *Wine and Wine Offerings in Ancient Egypt* (London: Kegan Paul International, 1995), 92, 93, 99, and 105 (from inscriptions found at Dendera and Edfu).

216   Adapted from Alan H. Gardiner, *Hieratic Papyri in the British Museum* 3rd Series. Volume I Text (London: British Museum, 1935), 84.

217   Adapted from Budge, *The Book of Opening the Mouth*, op. cit., 25-28.

218   Adapted from Moret, 63. Also see Budge, *The Book of Opening the Mouth*, op. cit., 204.

219   Adapted from M. Alliot, *Le Culte d'Horus à Edfou au temps des Ptolémées* (Cairo: Institut Français d'Archéologie Orientale, 1954), 491ff. For an English translation see Lucie Lamy, *Egyptian Mysteries: New Light on Ancient Knowledge* (New York: Thames and Hudson Inc., 1981; reprinted 1997), 82.

[220] Adapted from Herman te Velde, *Seth, God of Confusion: A Study of His Role in Egyptian Mythology and Religion* (Leiden, Netherlands: E. J. Brill, 1977), 50. Also adapted from Alan H. Gardiner, *Hieratic Papyri in the British Museum* 3rd Series. Volume I Text. (London: British Museum, 1935), 83. For the ritual action accompanying this Utterance see Harold H. Nelson, "The Rite of 'Bringing the Foot' as Portrayed in Temple Reliefs," *Journal of Egyptian Archaeology* 35 (1976): 82-86.

[221] Adapted from Rosalie A. David, op. cit., 104, and Herman te Velde, 50.

[222] Adapted from Harold H. Nelson, op. cit., 315-17. Also see note 96 in the same article.

[223] Jan Assmann, *The Search for God in Ancient Egypt* (Ithaca and London: Cornell University Press, 2001), 46.

[224] Ibid., 46-47.

[225] Ibid., 47.

[226] Ibid., 40.

[227] Alexandre Moret, *Le Rituel du Culte Divin Journalier* (Paris: Annales du Musee Guimet, Bibliotheque d'Etudes 14, Ernest Leroux, Editeur, 1902), 19; also see E. A. Wallis Budge, *The Book of Opening the Mouth: The Egyptian Texts with English Translations* (First published in London, 1909; reissued in 1980 by Arno Press, New York), 198.

[228] David Lorton, "The Theology of Cult Statues in Ancient Egypt," in *Born in Heaven, Made on Earth: The Making of the Cult Image in the Ancient Near East*, edited by Michael B. Dick (Winona Lake, Indiana: Eisenbrauns, 1999), 148.

[229] E. A. Wallis Budge, *The Book of Opening the Mouth: The Egyptian Texts with English Translations* (London: Kegan Paul, Trench, Trübner, 1909); Eberhard Otto, *Das Ägypyische Mundöffnungsritual* 2 vols. Ägyptologische Abhandlungen 3 (Wiesbaden: Harrassowitz, 1960); Jean-Claude Goyon, *Rituels funéraires de l'ancienne Égypte: Le Ritual de l'ouverture de la bouche, les Livres des repirations* (Paris: du Cerf, 1972).

NOTICE: The reader is advised that although Budge's work may be used by the non-scholar for a tolerably useful but awkward English-language translation of the ritual, his rendering of Egyptian pronunciation is totally outdated and should not be relied upon at all.

230 Lorton, op. cit., 159.
231 Lanny Bell, "The New Kingdom 'Divine' Temple: The Example of Luxor," in *Temples of Ancient Egypt*, edited by Byron E. Shafer (Ithaca, New York: Cornell University Press, 1997), 176.
232 Ann Macy Roth, "The *PSS-KF* and the 'Opening of the Mouth' Ceremony: A Ritual of Birth and Rebirth," *Journal of Egyptian Archaeology*, Vol. 78 (1992), 113-147; see specifically 116.
233 For a detailed exploration of the theme of birth the reader is referred to the previous article by Ann Macy Roth as well as her article, "Fingers, Stars, and the 'Opening of the Mouth': The Nature and Function of the *NTRWJ*-Blades," *Journal of Egyptian Archaeology*, Vol. 79 (1993), 57-79. In this article the author presents archaeological, textual, and iconographic evidence in support of the centrality of the theme of birth in the Opening of the Mouth ritual.
234 See Part One of the present book.
235 Plotinus, *Enneads*, trans. Stephen MacKenna (London: Faber, 1956), 4.3.11.

NOTICE: In order to help the interested reader locate an English-language translation for each ritual Utterance in the Opening of the Mouth ceremony, I have provided the following Notes to the only edition currently available in English. This is the work of E. A. Wallis Budge, *The Book of Opening the Mouth: The Egyptian Texts with English Translations* (London: Kegan Paul, Trench, Trübner, 1909). Reprints of Budge's work were issued in 1972 by Benjamin Blom, Inc., and again in 1980 by Arno Press. The pagination in the Blom reprint is quite faulty, with certain pages entirely omitted. The reader is advised to consult the reprint from Arno Press (New York, 1980).

The translation and commentary (German language) that is regarded among scholars as being the finest and most thorough is that of Eberhard Otto, *Das Ägypyische Mundöffnungsritual* 2 vols. Ägyptologische Abhandlungen 3 (Wiesbaden: Harrassowitz, 1960). I have also extensively used and found very helpful the French translation of Jean-Claude Goyon, *Rituels funéraires de l'ancienne Égypte: Le Ritual de l'ouverture de la bouche, les Livres des repirations* (Paris: du Cerf, 1972).

[236]   Budge, 9-11.
[237]   Ibid., 13.
[238]   Ibid., 14-17.
[239]   Ibid., 18-19.
[240]   Ibid., 22-23.
[241]   Ibid., 24-25.
[242]   Ibid., 25-26.
[243]   Ibid., 39-41.
[244]   Ibid., 48-50; 89.
[245]   Ibid., 67.
[246]   Ibid., 68-69.
[247]   Ibid., 70-72.
[248]   Ibid., 72.
[249]   Ibid., 83.
[250]   Ibid., 111.
[251]   Ibid., 91-92.
[252]   Ibid., 93-94.
[253]   Ibid., 95.
[254]   Ibid., 97-98.
[255]   Ibid., 99-100.
[256]   Ibid., 100-101.
[257]   Ibid., 102.
[258]   Ibid., 105-107.
[259]   Ibid., 108-109.
[260]   Ibid., 115-119.

[261] Ibid., 119-120.
[262] Ibid., 140-142.
[263] Ibid., 145-146.
[264] Ibid., 147.